OPTING **OUT**

OPTING **OUT**

Losing the Potential of
America's Young Black Elite

Maya A. Beasley

THE UNIVERSITY OF CHICAGO PRESS

CHICAGO & LONDON

MAYA A. BEASLEY is assistant professor in the
Department of Sociology and a member of the
advisory board of the Institute for African Studies at
the University of Connecticut.

The University of Chicago Press, Chicago 60637
The University of Chicago Press, Ltd., London
© 2011 by The University of Chicago
All rights reserved. Published 2011.
Printed in the United States of America

20 19 18 17 16 15 14 13 12 11   1 2 3 4 5

ISBN-13: 978-0-226-04013-4 (cloth)

ISBN-13: 978-0-226-04014-1 (paper)

ISBN-10: 0-226-04013-5 (cloth)

ISBN-10: 0-226-04014-3 (paper)

Library of Congress Cataloging-in-Publication Data

Beasley, Maya A.
  Opting out : losing the potential of America's young
black elite / Maya A. Beasley.
      p. cm.
  Includes bibliographical references and index.
  ISBN-13: 978-0-226-04013-4 (cloth : alk. paper)
  ISBN-10: 0-226-04013-5 (cloth : alk. paper)
  ISBN-13: 978-0-226-04014-1 (pbk. : alk. paper)
  ISBN-10: 0-226-04014-3 (pbk. : alk. paper) 1. African
Americans—Employment. 2. African Americans—
Education (Higher) 3. Discrimination in employment.
4. Income distribution—United States. I. Title.
  HD8081.A65B43 2011
  331.6'396073—dc22
                    2011016216

♾ This paper meets the requirements of ANSI/NISO
Z39.48-1992 (Permanence of Paper).

CONTENTS

LIST OF ILLUSTRATIONS

ACKNOWLEDGMENTS

The inspiration for this book comes from my time in Palo Alto toward the end of the dot-com boom. As a graduate student living on a small stipend, I was keenly aware of the immense wealth flowing through Silicon Valley and the opportunities being taken up by young professionals. As a woman of color, however, I was also acutely aware of the dearth of African Americans that were a part of this phenomenon. I had known many intelligent, creative black students during my college years at Harvard, and as a graduate student at Stanford I encountered a diverse undergraduate student body. I wondered how it was that Harvard and Stanford had relatively large black undergraduate populations, yet so few of the professionals I observed off campus were black.

I am therefore especially appreciative of the faculty and staff at Stanford University who encouraged me to pursue this question. Doug McAdam, Susan Olzak, and Monica McDermott provided me with excellent guidance and support in my initial examination of this issue. I am also grateful for the help I received from Claude Steele and everyone else at the Center for Comparative Studies in Race and Ethnicity. I will forever appreciate the assistance and exposure to interdisciplinary work they provided me, which was critical to writing this book. I am also indebted to Provost John Etchemendy for taking an interest in this research and providing essential financial support.

My editor Elizabeth Branch Dyson deserves special acknowledgment. She saw me through the publication process with patience and wisdom. I will always be grateful for her sincere interest in this project and the excellent advice she provided me from beginning to end. I could not have asked for an editor more intelligent, insightful, or genuinely nice.

I have also been fortunate to have received editorial advice and moral support from a variety of people. I am particularly grateful to Kyra Greene for all the assistance and encouragement she provided from the conception of this project onward. At a time when others questioned my interest in studying this group of students, she offered encouragement and insight. I am also grateful for her many, many readings of my manuscript; her honesty about the substance of my writing was invaluable. Simon Weffer and Yang Su also provided significant feedback for which I am extremely appreciative.

I am also indebted to my parents, Roy Beasley and Judith Fieldstone, for the lifetime of support and encouragement they have given me. I am especially thankful for all the time my father spent discussing, editing, and helping me to see the value of this work. The older I get, the more I recognize how fortunate I am to have parents I both love and admire.

Last, but not least, I am grateful to all of the students who participated in this research. They spoke openly about their aspirations, experiences, and thought processes, and I greatly enjoyed interviewing each one of them. Their candor and willingness to discuss sensitive issues were crucial to making this book possible.

1

INTRODUCTION

The Negro race, like all races, is going to be saved by its exceptional men.
W. E. B. DUBOIS, "The Talented Tenth"

On July 2, President Johnson signed into law the 1964 Civil Rights Act prohibiting discrimination in public facilities, education, and employment. This act, coupled with the initiative of a number of colleges and universities across the country, produced a significant rise in black college attendance. By 2000, nearly 18 percent of African Americans aged 25 to 54 had received at least a bachelor's degree compared with only 7 percent in 1969 (US Census Bureau 1973, 2001). While college education is inarguably a key factor in the upward mobility of African Americans, blacks with college degrees still face considerable hurdles. Indeed, over this same period of time, the difference in average earnings of black and white college graduates dropped by only one percentage point (US Census Bureau 1973, 2001).[1] Thirty-five years after racial discrimination was legally banned, the question remains: what continues to hold African Americans back, if not the law?

The persistence of inequality among well-educated African Americans is at odds with claims that members of this population are the privileged beneficiaries of civil rights legislation. Certainly, relative to their low-income counterparts, the black middle class has been in a better position to profit from the efforts of the civil rights movement. That is, affirmative action and the Civil Rights Act largely served well-educated African Americans who were able to take advantage of the growing corporate and government sectors in the 1960s and 1970s, while lower-class, less-educated African

1

Americans suffered severely from the decline of the manufacturing industry (Wilson 1978). Yet as previous research can attest, legislation has proved incapable of leveling the playing field for well-educated African Americans, and the black middle class is considerably poorer and less advantaged than its white counterpart (Landry 1987; Oliver and Shapiro 1997; Pattillo-McCoy 2000; Collins 1997).

Despite the stark contrasts in the educational and occupational achievements between well-educated whites and African Americans, the majority of contemporary research on black inequality has concerned African Americans living in poverty. This may reflect the compelling findings and rich data sources available to those focused on the urban underclass, or it may indicate a strong ascription to the Rawlsian principle of helping the most disadvantaged in society. Nonetheless, to focus primarily on only one segment of the population is to overlook the severe problems and consequences of other economic sectors within the black population. While poverty, with all its associated handicaps, is inarguably a significant contributor to the continuing economic and status disparities between African Americans and whites, the greatest differences remain at higher levels of income and education.

For example, whites with only a high school degree earn 15 percent more than African Americans, but whites with a bachelor's, master's, professional, or doctor's degree earn 21, 35, 52, and 50 percent more, respectively, than African Americans (fig. 1; US Census Bureau 2001). These figures clearly demonstrate the significance of inequality between the growing population of college-educated African Americans and whites. Yet, because of the political implications of the success of well-educated African Americans, neither liberals nor conservatives have been willing to address candidly the causes of lower black advancement. Those on the left tend to emphasize only the positive attributes of high-achieving African Americans while sweeping aside the serious problems facing this population. The benefits African Americans bring to the educational and occupational experiences of students and colleagues of other races, for example, is seen as proof of the importance of maintaining public policies benefiting this group.

The problem is that the lower rate of upward mobility of African American college graduates and the conspicuous underrepresentation of African Americans in corporate and scientific occupations are often eclipsed by the very studies and testimony intended to improve both mobility and representation and are not accorded the serious scrutiny they deserve from those with sympathetic motivations.

Instead, this same topic has been exploited and used by conservatives as

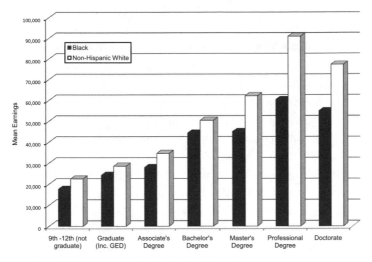

Fig. 1. Difference in earnings by level of education, ages 25 to 44

proof of African American inferiority and can be traced to one basic theme
that cites the lower achievements of college-educated African Americans
as confirmation that racial preferences have placed underqualified blacks
at prestigious institutions while displacing their more deserving white
counterparts. This argument first appeared in the 1960s and has reemerged
whenever the opportunity to test the validity of affirmative action in court
presents itself. Conservative analyst Dinesh D'Souza (1991) has repeatedly
asserted that "the abolition of race based affirmative action would allow
minorities to compete in a free and fair academic environment and would
not be subject to the undue pressures of intellectual mismatch" (p. 253). His
position, however, discounts the very real possibility that the experiences of
black students in universities and the embedded nature of racial inequality
in the structure of society have significant and direct effects on the academic and occupational successes of this group far larger than any measure
of "ability" can explain.

Shifting the Focus to Occupations

To provide an honest account of the disparate fates of individuals from different racial groups, it is essential to find suitable measures. This book takes
the stance that a considerable portion of the inequality in income between
well-educated African Americans and whites is due to the different occupa-

tional fields where these two groups predominate. While part of the occupational schism results from enduring institutional racism, it cannot explain the virtual absence of African Americans from certain career fields, among them science, academia, technology, financial management, and engineering. It also fails to account for the concentration of African Americans in other fields, for example, education, social work, and government administration, as well as racialized specialties—jobs directed at, disproportionately used by, or concerned with African Americans (Collins 1997)—within mainstream occupations and organizations.[2]

Across the board, the disparities in the mean earnings of African Americans and whites within professional occupations are actually relatively small. African Americans who are engineers earn approximately 6 percent less than their white counterparts, similar to the 11 percent difference in black and white primary and secondary school teachers. Even in fields where there is considerable variance in pay, such as law and medicine (in which African Americans are paid 20 and 30 percent less than whites, respectively), much of the difference is accounted for by variations in pay among specialties (US Census Bureau 2002). That is, the disparity in earnings of black and white lawyers reflects closely the differences in the average earnings of government and public interest law and private practice (Chambliss 2000).

The greatest differences in annual earnings are actually found between the jobs in which African Americans are most numerous and those in which they are least represented. Thus, the 1 percent of African Americans in professional and managerial occupations who are lawyers and judges earn an average of $63,000 more than the 17 percent of African Americans who work as teachers and over $48,000 more than the 9 percent in health professions (US Census Bureau 2000). In contrast, whites are spread evenly among pay grades, making the $14,000 difference in pay between natural scientists or mathematicians and health professionals, who compose 6 and 7 percent of white professionals, respectively, far less of an impact on the white population.

Limited diversity is a significant shortcoming of the occupations chosen by African Americans. According to data from the 2000 census (US Census Bureau 2008), the most prevalent white-collar occupations among African Americans and whites are appreciably different. While the top twenty careers for both groups include elementary, middle-school, and secondary-school teachers as well as registered nurses, the range of occupations among these two groups is quite different. The top twenty white-collar occupations of whites include financial managers, general and operations managers, lawyers, designers, physicians and surgeons as well as chief executives. In contrast, the top twenty white-collar occupations of blacks shows a very clear trend of service-oriented, racialized jobs including counselors, education administrators, preschool and kindergarten teachers, community and social service specialists, other teachers and instructors, and human resources managers. Hence, chief executives are the fifth most common white-collar occupation among whites, but only the thirty-fifth among blacks. Lawyers rank tenth among whites, but twenty-seventh among blacks; physicians nineteenth among whites, but thirty-first among blacks. And, while there are six different engineering specialties listed among the top fifty white occupations, there are only three listed for blacks and they are considerably lower on the list. Effectively, education and social service work dominate among African Americans, while whites hold a far greater diversity of positions.

The occupational trends among those who graduated from the top institutions in the country—persons who should be the leaders within their generations—are much the same. The types of careers aspired to and eventually occupied by African Americans and whites from highly selective institutions are assuredly dissimilar. Bowen and Bok's seminal work on the experiences and life outcomes of college students at elite universities (1998) shows that African American and white students occupy career sectors in very different proportions. For example, while 76 percent of the white male graduates they tracked were working in the private sector, only 67 percent of black men and 48 percent of black women did so. Instead, African American graduates were disproportionately working in government or nonprofit sectors—34 percent of black men and 52 percent of black women relative to 24 percent of white men and 39 percent of white women.

The problem does not lie with the individuals in these positions or with the positions themselves. Service-oriented occupations and those closely related to minority communities are extremely valuable. The point is that a lack of diversity among careers carries with it two inherent flaws similar to those of undiversified financial portfolios: it does not minimize risk, nor does it maximize the potential for returns. Among economists, one of the dominant investment paradigms is portfolio theory, first introduced in an article published in 1952 and developed in subsequent decades into what is known as modern portfolio theory (MPT) by Harry Markowitz, winner of the Nobel Prize in 1991. MPT provides an insightful framework which advocates that financial investors diversify their holdings across a wide variety of unrelated assets so as to maximize their potential returns and hedge their losses. That is, we can reduce the risk inherent in any one investment and maximize the likelihood that one of our investments will pay off if our portfolio is diversified (Markowitz 1952).

Black communities would also be well advised to diversify their most important assets, their young people's careers, across a wide variety of occupational opportunities. Whereas a diverse portfolio minimizes financial losses and maximizes financial gains for individual investors, so too can encouraging their youth to pursue diverse careers provide black communities with a diverse occupational portfolio that will minimize social, political, and economic losses and maximize social, political, and economic gains.[3] And just as individual investors are advised to shift their investments from less promising to more promising asset categories from time to time, so too should black communities shift their children's career aspirations. Racialized occupations are still important today, but other career tracks are likely to yield comparable, if not substantially greater, returns both to the individual students as well as to black communities as a whole.

Revisiting Racial Inequality

This book seeks to understand what the statistics already show. There has not been a substantial increase in occupational diversity among well-educated African Americans despite the civil rights movement. African Americans have undoubtedly made progress, but a high degree of occupational segregation among black and white professionals remains. Unfortunately, there is a misperception of the advancements derived from civil rights legislation, which, when examined closely, was never directed at the black middle class in so far as it relates to jobs. I thoroughly document the limited impact of this legislation and its consequent failure to enhance African American upward mobility. This misperception has survived because the legislation that passed in the 1960s and 1970s was groundbreaking and ostensibly solid. As the 1970s began, there was genuine progress for African Americans, both in educational achievements and in blue-collar occupations. However, the way the legislation was written, in conjunction with judicial activism (which devalued it) and inadequate enforcement, meant that any progress that might initially have accrued was lost.

While there is certainly more occupational diversity among black professionals than there was in the 1960s, there is a tendency to see any progress as great progress. This is not only a distortion of facts, but it skirts the root of the problem. The persistent lack of black Americans within certain fields can be considered the source of significant economic and status disparities between African Americans and whites. Collins (1997) regards the opening of black consumer markets within white corporate America and the expansion of social services following the civil rights movement as two of the primary culprits for the systematic movement of African Americans into racialized career paths. Likewise, David Thomas's research on minority executives (Thomas and Gabarro 1999) places responsibility on early career experiences and movement into specialized niches. Whereas Collins and Thomas trace the experiences of African Americans who began their careers shortly after the civil rights movement, implicating the lack of mentors available to African Americans and the pull of blacks to racialized tracks once within an organization or during the hiring process, I contend that for the generations now entering the workforce, the tendency toward homogenous, racialized fields starts well before that first job or career search.

This analysis offers a new perspective on racial inequality by exploring the occupational aspirations of African American and white college students rather than their ultimate career achievements or earnings. Focusing on the preference of career fields rather than differences in average income paints a considerably different picture of the mechanisms underlying racial inequality in America than is commonly perceived. One of the central arguments of this book is that some African Americans choose racialized careers or avoid higher-status, higher-paying fields for which they are educationally eligible. In effect, some black students are opting out of the very careers in which they are least represented and most needed.

I differ, however, with those who contend that the aspirations of African Americans are the result of deficiencies in culture and ability or merely the byproduct of poor educational backgrounds. Whereas white student aspirations are based primarily on parental expectations and social class backgrounds and motivated in ranked order of the highest paying jobs, the occupational aspirations of African Americans are the result of a complex series of structural, institutional, and psychological forces operating both within and on the black population. In particular, concerns about racism and a desire to help other African Americans weigh heavily in decisions and interests which, because of a deficit of social capital relevant to upward mobility among African Americans, are often not fully informed. Therefore, I view well-educated African Americans as a distinct population—one that differs from less-educated African Americans and well-educated populations of other races—and one deserving of careful consideration.

A Generation of Difference

Although the dynamics I have identified may resonate with some people, they do not account for why some African Americans today appear inclined to recoil in the face of conspicuous increases in opportunity when previous generations persevered in spite of a considerably more overt racism and a more limited opportunity structure. In chapter 2 I begin to explore this issue by examining the historical relationships between black higher education, structural opportunities, and occupational attainment. In so doing, I present a case that historical trends have several significant implications for the decisions made by contemporary young adults.

First, as Collins (1997) has documented in her research on black corporate executives, the opportunity structure that moved college-educated African Americans into racialized career paths thirty to forty years ago has resulted in considerably different profiles of black and white professionals today. So, as African American youth move through life—despite verbal reinforcements about advances in opportunity—the opportunity structure they see, the one they learn of, and, often, the one they expect as they are making their career decisions, reflects the career paths of older generations. Moreover, as young African Americans see the limitations placed on their elders, they may look for what may appear to be more opportune ways to achieve, rather than risk languishing in the white opportunity structure.

Second, the movement of African Americans into racialized careers and specialties from the 1960s onward has fortified the significance of careers with direct or visible social implications. Through the years, as African Americans have received social services, it has come primarily through the hands of other black people, making certain careers easily identifiable as beneficial to the black community and therefore more in tune with the high value placed on social responsibility by African Americans.

Third, the relative newness of the black middle class, coupled with the impact of persistent residential segregation has resulted in a considerable disparity in the degree and forms of social capital held by African Americans and whites entering college. Although there have been professional and middle-class African Americans for over a century, the critical mass needed to refer to the people in these positions collectively as a class did not arise until the 1970s (Landry 1987). In 1960, for example, only 13 percent of black workers held middle-class jobs, while, during that same year, 44 percent of all white workers occupied middle-class positions. This effectively makes the parents of some of the students I consider in this book the first generation in the black middle class and the first generation with a critical mass to have access to higher education, the majority of professions, and ownership of wealth.

The stories of the students profiled in this study therefore unravel against a contextual backdrop of history. As a friend once pointed out, history is not as far away as we may think. For African Americans, history is, in fact, intricately interwoven in the opportunity structure, value systems, and social networks that are partially responsible for their career choices.

The Study

The data on African American professionals is unassailable, yet the question remains: why have they not achieved greater diversity within occupations? My work gives some insight into the thoughts and behaviors of young African Americans which, in aggregate, lead to a continuing pattern of occupational homogeneity. The point is to understand what the statistics already show.

To explore potential disparities in black and white career preferences, I conducted a series of in-depth interviews with African American and white college juniors at Stanford University and the University of California at Berkeley, one a prestigious private research university and the other a highly selective public research university. I chose these elite schools in order to focus on students whose academic abilities and professional qualifications would be least likely to negatively impact their occupational aspirations. Prestigious schools such as these attract students with higher average SAT scores and GPAs and have lower admission rates as well as higher average graduation rates among students of all races than those at less selective institutions.[4] Moreover, students who graduate from these schools have a pedigree that, on its own, puts them at the top of the pile for job placement, career mobility, and graduate school admission. Black and white graduates from highly selective institutions earn appreciably more than graduates from less selective schools (Bowen and Bok 1998). As Bowen and Bok point out, "while graduation from a selective college hardly guarantees a successful career, it may open doors, help black matriculants overcome any negative stereotypes that may still be held by some employers, and create opportunities not otherwise available" (1998, p. 130). And while there are a small number of prestigious historically black colleges and universities, over 75 percent of black undergraduates are awarded degrees by predominantly white institutions. Hence, any investigation of African American professionals, especially those whose degrees are from prestigious schools, should begin with the majority white institutions where they are most numerous.

I interviewed students in their junior year because their career aspirations at this point are salient and well formed. By conducting the interviews prior to the job-search process, which begins in the senior year, I minimized the need to consider the frustration many seniors may have encountered during their job searches in the current market and other variables beyond their control. To locate potential interview subjects, I went through several channels at each university. At Stanford I gained access to the registrar's official roster of African American and white students in the junior class and sent out email solicitations to the students on the list. At Berkeley, I sent emails to all students in the junior class through the Office of Student Life. I also posted solicitations for participants on electronic kiosks and by way of electronic messages sent from the office of African American student development at each school. Emails were also disseminated through several academic departments (science, math, and engineering as well as social sciences and humanities) targeting their majors, dormitories, and a small number of African American student organizations.

The interviews were structured so that each student was asked a series of open-ended questions based on several broad themes including family background, academic interests, aspirations, racial antagonism, racial identities, school experiences, and activities. Interviewees were given the opportunity to discuss any other topics they felt were relevant.[5] This design allowed me to delve into new topics that arose during the interviews and to follow up on compelling responses (Neuman 2006). The interviews lasted about two to three hours; all were transcribed verbatim and then coded for analysis.[6] And although the focus of this book is on African Americans, I frequently discuss interview responses from white students for the sake of comparison.

Over the course of the 2002/3 academic year I performed 60 in-depth, one-on-one interviews between the two schools, 30 from each: 20 African American women, 10 African American men, 17 white women and 13 white men.[7] This sample offers both a contrast in the occupational aspirations of African American and white students, as well as enough intragroup variation to discern potential sources of these differences.[8] Most important, it is evident that black students often chose occupations in which African Americans are highly concentrated and/or they chose racialized occupations.[9] In contrast, their white counterparts listed a wider range of occupations that lack racial relevance.

Ten of the black students interviewed indicated a preference for a racialized specialty within a broader career field, such as nonprofit work for African Americans, black product marketing, civil rights law, and the like, and twelve students indicated interest in fields in which African Americans are more strongly represented, including nonprofit management and social work, where African Americans comprise 20 and 13 percent of the workforce, respectively (see fig. 2; US Census Bureau 2003). Only 13 of the African Americans interviewed selected occupations that were not racial-

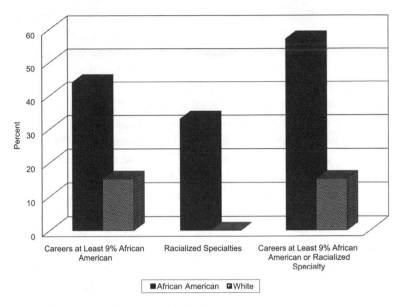

Fig. 1. Occupational aspirations by race

ized specialties and/or at least 9 percent black, such as strategic consulting, foreign service, computer programming, and investment banking.[10] The figures for white students are considerably different. Only four white students indicated an interest in fields that were at least 9 percent African American and none reported interest in racialized occupations.

It is evident that the aspirations of the African American and white students in this study corresponded to what is effectively the status quo. Many black students aspired to careers in which they have greater numbers and/or to racialized occupations whereas white students showed a more diverse range of occupational interests, free of racialized substance.

The Organization of This Book

This book draws on the words and stories of the students themselves to provide a rich picture of their experiences and choices. It is my hope that a broad audience of academics, policymakers, and educational professionals, as well as young African Americans trying to understand their own situations, will learn, as I did, that what may appear on the surface to be irrational choices, are instead further proof of the embedded nature of the color line in both how society is structured and how we perceive society.

Chapter 2 sets the context of this study by examining the opportunity structure and history of the generations of African Americans who are today the parents and grandparents of the students I studied. It also introduces one of the book's central questions: why are some African Americans willing to pursue careers that, based on the experiences of previous generations, seem riskier, while others seek safer, more traditional routes?

Chapter 3 provides an overview of the students' backgrounds. Although past research would lead us to suspect that the difference in occupational aspirations of African Americans and whites is due to socioeconomic factors or cultural deficiencies, it is clear that what drives African American aspirations may be significantly different from and more complex than what drives whites. The black students in this study did not come from a culture of deprivation, nor did the majority come from desperately poor families. Although on average the African Americans were raised in less affluent homes than the white students were, the majority of black students were from middle-class backgrounds. Likewise, the African American students reported their parents as having equally high if not higher expectations for their children than the parents of white students did. What differed to the deficit of black students was the degree of concrete support and advice black parents were able to provide. Despite good intentions and extraordinarily high expectations, the relative impotence of black parents—low and middle class alike—to provide their children with the social and cultural capital necessary to explore and pursue their interests annulled some of the strong positive effects of their standards and support. The African American and white students who participated in this study therefore entered college with notably different familiarity or awareness of professional options.

Chapter 4 profiles the two universities from which these samples are derived and describes the impact of differences between the two institutions and their student bodies, the most significant being the strength and popularity of segregated social networks on campus. While at the time of our interviews African Americans comprised approximately 12 percent of the 7,000 undergraduates at Stanford University, they composed only 3 percent of the 24,000 undergraduates at the University of California at Berkeley. The greater proportion of African American students at Stanford, coupled with the institutional nature of its Black Community, a highly segregated African American social circle, seemed to influence the black students' ability and desire to maintain segregated social networks at college.

Chapter 5 addresses an important question pertaining to subjective understandings of structural opportunities: whether perceptions of racial antagonism deter African Americans from certain careers in which they are severely underrepresented. While previous research (Allen 1992) implicates perceived discrimination by faculty, peers, and administrators in the negative academic performance of black college students, this book exposes a potentially greater problem: African American students disassociate from and overlook certain careers based on the anticipation of discrimination and prejudice.

Along this vein, chapter 6 demonstrates the prevalence of stereotype threat in day-to-day classroom situations and examines its impact on students' goals and behaviors. Contrary to claims that the race and gender of faculty are of little consequence to occupational outcomes (Cole and Barber 2003), this chapter exposes the ways in which the perceptions, if not the actual experiences of African American students in classrooms depend largely on the racial composition of the class and teaching staff.

In chapter 7, I illustrate the salience of race not only for the types of values embraced by students but also for the role those values play in career choice. While the majority of black students sought to avoid "selling out" their black community, how they felt best equipped to do so corresponded directly with their career interests. The African American students who believed role modeling or infusing money into black communities were valuable goals tended to express interest in a wide range of careers. Other black students, however, believed that only careers directly targeting black populations were beneficial to the advancement of African Americans and aspired to careers in nonprofit work or services targeting black populations. Thus, not only were some of the black students in this study avoiding careers in which African Americans are underrepresented, but they were simultaneously pursuing careers in which they felt they would make the greatest difference.

For those African Americans who did not believe mainstream careers were antithetical to black advancement and who were able to subdue their apprehensions about such occupations, there remained one significant hurdle which I address in chapter 8: a lack of social capital relevant to a diversity of careers. One of the greatest legacies of segregation is that it has left African Americans generations behind their white counterparts in terms of the social networks important to succeed in and choose from among all the opportunities that are today open to them. By having segregated social groups prior to and during college, black students may have stifled the flow of information imperative to making educated career decisions and having more career options.

Conclusion

A cursory reading of this book might lead some critics to interpret its find-ings as an exercise in blaming-the-victim. This would be a mistake because it would ignore the inescapable reality that many African American col-lege students are currently making career decisions that are partly based on their anticipations of racial hostility and on their commitments to social responsibility. As I noted at the beginning of this chapter, it is a statistical fact that the greatest differences in earnings appear between the most edu-cated black and white members of our community. Qualified black teachers and nonprofit organizers are extraordinary assets whose value should not be underestimated. However, just as diversification and risk are essential to building strong stock portfolios, diversity in the career options pursued by the brightest African American students is crucial in terms of greater wealth and power for the African American community as a whole, albeit at somewhat greater risk. Doubtless if more African Americans pursued careers that led them to the highest positions in our corporate and govern-ment infrastructures, they would be able to use their influence to reduce the discriminatory practices inflicted on other African Americans and could provide greater opportunities for them. As DuBois (1903) asked, "Can the masses of the Negro people be in any possible way more quickly raised than by the effort and example of this aristocracy of talent and character?"

This book explores the reasoning behind the career choices of a small sample of today's "talented tenth" in the hope that its insights will enable other members of the African American community's best and brightest to make decisions that provide them with the most satisfying careers and also have the largest positive impact on the African American community as a whole. Given the small size of my sample, my findings must be regarded as suggestive and tentative. However, as per the extensive references in the chapters that follow, some of my findings may be unexpected, but most are consistent with results reported elsewhere in the literature.

2

THE SIGNIFICANCE OF HISTORY

The history of African Americans, and of the black elite in particular, is central to the beliefs and actions of the participants in this study. The air in which they were raised, the opportunities they saw, and the outlooks of those close to them play a significant role in the ways in which black students make choices. This chapter situates these students amidst a climate of growing pessimism brought about by disappointments in the efficacy and sustainability of civil rights legislation of the 1960s and early 1970s. This history has affected these students' families, their communities, and the students themselves, limiting their social networks and heightening their concerns about racial antagonism. Their sense of efficacy is based on models that, although compassionate, are outdated. A natural question arises from this research: why are the African American participants in this study, ones who face relatively fewer and less arduous challenges than their predecessors, reluctant to confront these problems directly?

A Modest Start

At midcentury, when these students' grandparents were beginning to start their families, only 10 percent of all black workers held middle-class jobs; for them that meant working as teachers, ministers, social workers, and occasionally doctors and lawyers in black communities. By contrast, 40 percent of white workers filled middle-class occupations. While much of the distinction between the black and white middle classes was due to direct employment discrimination and residential segregation, it was buttressed by the unavailability of professional and graduate-level education for African Americans. In the North, a few schools welcomed African Americans in small numbers whereas in the South—home to the bulk of the black population—graduate training was restricted primarily to degrees in education. Due in large part to lack of financial support, by 1945 only Howard University was able to offer a full array of professional schools (Landry 1987). In fact, until 1968, 80 percent of all African Americans with a bachelor's degree had attended historically black colleges and universities (Gurin and Epps 2002).

To challenge their exclusion from white colleges and universities, a number of African Americans took to the courts. Although there were victories, several states, such as Maryland and Oklahoma, opened segregated black professional schools to forestall integration (Sniderman and Piazza 2002).[1] It was not until the late 1960s and early 1970s, when these students' parents were growing up, that African American higher education became a norm. Yet, even in the late 1970s, African Americans were concentrated in two-year institutions, unlikely to transfer into four-year colleges or universities. Moreover, within community colleges, blacks were frequently funneled into vocational tracks controlled by state and local industrial interests (Brint and Karabel 1989).

Nevertheless, the increase in African American college graduates ushered in a new black middle class (Landry 1987), and the seeds of this new middle class were primarily responsible for launching the large-scale protests of the 1960s. "It was a middle-class movement" that eventually "broadened to include equal access to jobs and the ballot box" (Landry 1987, p. 72).

In response to this burgeoning movement, President Kennedy issued Executive Order 10925 in 1961 mandating federal contractors to "take affirmative action" by guaranteeing against discrimination based on race, color, creed, or national origin. Just three years later, Congress passed the 1964 Civil Rights Act, which expanded the order to include the private sector as well, making discrimination on the basis of race illegal in access to voting, public accommodations, education, and employment. Shortly thereafter, Johnson issued his famous speech on affirmative action at Howard University's 1965 Commencement. He asserted,

> You do not take a person who, for years, has been hobbled by chains and liberate him, bring him to the starting line of a race and then say, 'you are free to compete with all the others' and still justly believe that you have been completely fair . . . It is not enough just to open the gates of opportunity. All

our citizens must have the ability to walk through those gates . . . We seek . . . not just equality as a right and a theory, but equality as a fact and as a result.

Following that, Johnson issued Executive Order 11246 in 1967, which established the Philadelphia Plan requiring federal contractors to employ minorities as a prerequisite for federal contracts.[2] The Office of Federal Contract Compliance Programs (OFCCP) was charged with monitoring minority and female hiring goals. Noncompliant companies could have their contracts terminated or be prohibited from bidding on federal contracts in the future.[3] Civil rights legislation was therefore gaining an increasing foothold as the parents of our students were in their youth and their grandparents were well into their careers.

While the enactment of civil rights legislation may have had an initial placebo effect of discouraging discrimination, the enforcement of equal employment opportunity began in earnest in 1972, when the Equal Employment Opportunity Act was passed, providing the Equal Employment Opportunity Commission (EEOC) with the power to initiate lawsuits against private sector firms with more than fifty employees, or twenty-five if federal contracts were involved. The 1970s proved to be a busy time for the EEOC, which investigated and successfully achieved settlements with several major American companies, including General Motors, Sears Roebuck, Ford, General Electric, United Airlines, Bechtel, and several major steel producers, railroads, and unions (Equal Employment Opportunity Commission 2004).[4]

Concurrent with equal employment legislation were policies regarding black businesses. In 1969, the Small Business Administration (SBA) began operating a program under section 8(a) of the Small Business Act addressing minority businesses' lack of key resources to compete successfully for contracts against larger, more established firms with the goal of helping these firms become self-sufficient competitors.[5] Similarly, the Federal Works Employment Act was passed in 1977, setting aside 10 percent of federal construction grants for minority-owned firms (United States Commission on Civil Rights 2005).[6] Comparable legislation was passed in the 1980s and early 1990s pertaining to defense and transportation contract goals, and throughout the country this legislation was replicated by state and local governments.

Among other things, two exemplars of black success emerged from these civil rights victories: black officials (elected and appointed) and social welfare work. As the civil rights movement came to a close, it was clear that additional manpower was needed to work in the offices created by public and private organizations. In private organizations, African Americans were increasingly employed in community relations fields, while in the public sphere, demand for services and rights enforcement meant newly created positions. For example, the onset of Small Business Administration protection, as well as the creation of the OFCCP and EEOC required a multitude of new workers; this call was primarily facilitated by the rising number of well-educated African Americans and former civil rights workers. Likewise, heightened import placed on elections (especially given the success in electing Kennedy), equated to an increasing reliance on public officials and offices. Between 1970 and 1974, the number of black elected officials more than doubled (from 1,469 to 2,991; US Bureau of Census 2008).

In essence, the success of the civil rights movement coupled with increasing labor force demands for middle-class African Americans endowed black citizens with a sense of efficacy and a paradigm to reproduce, one in which the focus was at the group rather than the individual level and the slant would be racialized, not mainstream.

Rising and Ebbing Tides of Optimism

The civil rights movement and its byproducts (e.g., racialized job openings), coupled with improving economic conditions in the United States, increased the percent of black middle-class workers to 27 in 1970 from only 10 percent in the 1950s. African Americans now had a middle-class unencumbered by de jure discrimination and found an increasing number of occupations open to them. The emergence of this new black middle class—in both size and character—marked, as Landry (1987, p. 3) explains,

> A major turning point in the life of black people in the United States. New opportunities at this level of the class structure gave renewed hope to the aspirations of working-class black parents. No longer were the doors of many colleges and universities closed to them . . . Now there was the chance that their sons and daughters could also aspire to become accountants, lawyers, engineers, scientists and architects.

There was indeed considerable reason for people to be hopeful. Not only had major legislation been passed barring discrimination in housing, employment, and education, but American colleges and universities were taking calculated measures to enforce affirmative action. Between 1964 and

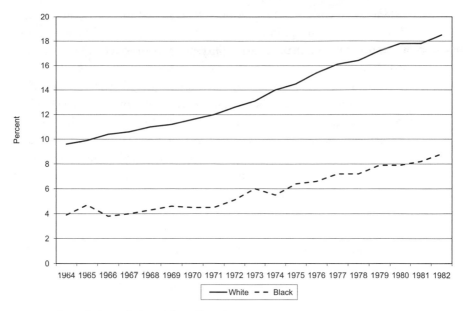

Fig. 3. Percent of population with a college degree

1982, the percent of African Americans and white Americans with at least a college degree increased significantly. Although in 1964 only 3.9 percent of African Americans had attended a four-year college or university, the number doubled to 8.8 percent by the early 1980s (US Census Bureau 2008), and increasing numbers of black students were attending predominantly white colleges and universities (fig. 3).

This type of effort would, in some cases, have a positive impact on the ability of black parents to attend college. Yet while 8 percent represents a clear improvement, it in no way meant that the black middle class was on par with its white counterpart. By 1982, when most students' parents would have graduated college if they had attended, the percent of the black population qualified for professional, upper-middle-class jobs had risen by less than 5 percent since 1964. The rate of whites attending college had also increased, however, and had more dramatic effects on their middle class. Between 1964 and 1982, the percent of whites who had attended a four-year college or university had grown from 9.6 to 18.5 percent. Thus, the proportion of whites who had attended college was over twice that of blacks and nearly a quarter of the white population had degrees.

Compounding the persistent competition with whites, the black middle class was brought to a standstill in terms of growth in the 1970s by recession and increasing inflation (Landry 1987). Yet it was the 1980s, when our students were coming into the world, that proved to be a decade of civil rights setbacks and significant black economic regression. Economic depression, coupled with political hostility, not only slowed black progress but made it futile. Workplace integration occurred only to the extent that there was pressure to desegregate, and, as research shows, "racial desegregation is more pronounced when the federal government more aggressively advocates U.S. equal employment opportunity (EEO) laws. Conversely, when the federal government reduces its enforcement activity and symbolic appeals, employment integration declines or stops altogether" (Stainback, Robinson, and Tomaskovic-Devey 2005, p. 1201).[7] Hence, although the recession caused white income to become increasingly polarized as well, the diminution of the top was substantially greater among African Americans.[8]

Our students were therefore born amidst a declining black upper and middle class, as their parents entered the working world and encountered increasing obstacles rather than opportunities. These parents had not created the civil rights movement, but some had participated and most had watched, anticipating far more progress than what actually developed. Just as their children were born, as they, in some cases, were beginning their professional careers, the rug was pulled out from under their feet. Their capacity to move out of segregated neighborhoods was limited by declining income, while upward mobility was hindered severely by the frequent shepherding of blacks toward unprofitable vocational training rather than liberal arts educations (Brint and Karabel 1989) and by organizations no longer threatened by civil rights enforcement or with an interest in the black population. Thus students in this sample were raised in, or close to, highly segregated communities in which poverty was increasing, joblessness was rampant, and black professionals were marginalized or absent. Those whose families had made it to more affluent neighborhoods would be token minorities, often seeking out other persons of color from predominantly black communities or social groups within their schools, not surrounded by black students whose parents were professionals.

The End of Progress: The Reagan-Bush Era and Beyond

The Reagan-Bush administration, the first in the post–civil rights era to openly and systematically thwart civil rights (Kennedy 1986), exacted dramatic changes in the laws against and enforcement of civil rights. This is vividly demonstrated by the administration's fiscal and legislative records, appointments, and strongly voiced opposition to affirmative action programs. Even before Reagan took office, his view of civil rights was apparent; he characterized the Civil Rights Act of 1964 as "a bad piece of legislation" and disapproved of the 1965 Voting Rights Act, in part because it "humiliated the South" (Dugger 1983). Reagan blamed his negative legacy on civil rights leaders themselves, who he claimed had errantly distorted his record.[9]

Reagan's record, however, speaks for itself. His entrance into office is marked by a significant cut in funding for employment-related civil rights enforcement, followed by a lengthy period of stagnation (see fig. 4). Between 1981 (President Carter's last year) and 1982 (President Reagan's first), funding for EEOC and OFCCP, the two agencies charged with the greatest proportion of antidiscrimination enforcement for employment, dropped from $332 to $318 million and from $118 to $91 in million in 2005 dollars, respectively. The EEOC, the agency responsible for interpreting federal employment discrimination laws; monitoring programs that protect federal and private employees from discrimination; filing suits on behalf of those aggrieved of discrimination in the workplace; and funding state and local fair employment practices agencies, suffered the greatest loss in funding over the 1980s. The initial drop in funding from 1981 to 1982 was succeeded by twelve years of stagnation, when the Reagan and Bush administrations consistently requested funding below that of the Carter administration.[10] Funding only returned to pre-Reagan levels in 1993. Ironically the number of complaints received by the EEOC increased by almost 60 percent during the Reagan-Bush administrations (United States Commission on Civil Rights 1995).[11]

The funding situation of the OFCCP, whose duties are an integral part of contract compliance enforcement, was much the same.[12] As with the EEOC, the OFCCP received its greatest budgetary hit when Reagan took office; unlike the EEOC, however, its funding never returned to pre-Reagan levels. The only civil rights–related agency that was not damaged financially during the 1980s was the Department of Justice's Civil Rights Division (CRD), the office with the smallest budget and the one with the least involvement in employment-related civil rights enforcement. The CRD deals not only with employment, but also with education, disability rights, voting rights, and housing, among others. Thus its impact on employment-related civil rights enforcement activities was minimal from the start. Black parents of all classes would find it increasingly difficult to avoid discrimination in the workplace as heightened antagonism was met with declining penalties and recognition. As I discuss in chapter 5, their experiences with this

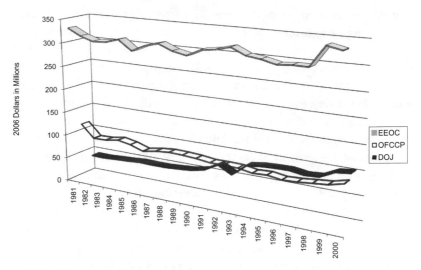

Fig. 4. Congressional appropriations, 1981–2000

unmonitored, unpenalized racism helped to form their children's fears about their own future workforce experiences and drew them farther away from occupational integration.

Reagan's anti–civil rights legacy was built atop not only its lack of funding but on his legislative and judicial activities as well. In 1988, his last year in office, Reagan vetoed a major piece of civil rights legislation directly related to black employment: The Civil Rights Restoration Act. This act reestablished the broad scope of coverage of the Civil Rights Act of 1964 and Title IX lost in a 1984 Supreme Court ruling and specified that institutions receiving federal funding were prohibited from discriminating even in programs or activities not directly benefiting from such funding.[13] Congress eventually overrode President Reagan's veto.

Much of the damage, however, had been done throughout his terms by the increasingly conservative Supreme Court appointed by Reagan himself. The most significant of these appointments, Justices Rehnquist and Scalia, in addition to Bush's own appointment of Clarence Thomas, influenced the court's subsequent rulings during the Bush-Quayle administration. In 1989, the Supreme Court made four decisions that all but erased the strides of antidiscrimination employment legislation of Title VII of the Civil Rights Act of 1964. First, in *The City of Richmond v. Croson,* the court held that past societal discrimination alone could not serve as the basis for minority set-asides. Instead, affirmative action would be subject to "strict scrutiny" and was unconstitutional unless discrimination could be proven to be "widespread throughout a particular industry" and the remedy "narrowly tailored" to counteract that threat (LaNoue 1994). In *Patterson v. McLean Credit Union,* the court ruled that the Civil Rights Act of 1866, which prohibits discrimination in the making and enforcement of contracts, does not apply to post-formation discrimination such as racial harassment, failure to promote, demotions, or dismissal. The *Wards Cove Packing Co. v. Antonio* decision limited the ability of individuals to prove disparate impact discrimination, as when employment practices unintentionally but disparately impact women and minorities. The court ruled that in order to prevail, plaintiffs must identify the employer's specific policies that had a discriminatory effect, not the effect itself. Moreover, if defendants could prove that such policies were actually "business necessities," the status quo could stand. And finally, in *Price Waterhouse v. Hopkins,* the court limited the ability of individuals to demonstrate discrimination, holding that even if an employee were able to establish that discrimination was a factor in an employment decision, the employer could avoid liability by demonstrating that it would have made the same decision absent the discrimination.

In response to the Supreme Court's recent decisions, the Democratic dominated Congress introduced the Civil Rights Restoration Act in 1990. Although it took nearly two years, the Congress compromised and President Bush capitulated, signing what became the Civil Rights Act of 1991 (Hagen and Hagen 1995). Superficially, the purpose of this act was to restore "the civil rights protections that were dramatically limited by those [Supreme Court] decisions; and strengthen existing protections and remedies available under federal civil rights laws to provide more effective deterrence and adequate compensation for victims of discrimination" (Civil Rights Act of 1991–Pub. L. 102-166). Under the 1991 act, employers could not escape liability simply by indicating a nondiscriminatory reason for rejecting an employee as had been articulated in the decision of *Price Waterhouse v. Hopkins.* Instead, employers had to prove the veracity of this nondiscriminatory reason.

The 1991 act also dealt with issues of disparate impact and directly overruled the treatment of a "business necessity" as it was used in the *Wards Cove* decision by requiring the employer, not the employee, to show evidence of the necessity of that practice. It also reversed the *Patterson v. McLean* ruling by specifying that claims alleging discrimination in performance, modification, benefits, and privileges (such as harassment) were covered by the Civil Rights Act of 1866 section 1981 (Civil Rights Act of 1991–Pub. L. 102-166).

In addition, the 1991 act amended several statutes enforced by the EEOC. Prior to this legislation, jury trials were permissible only in cases brought under the Equal Pay Act of 1963 and the Age Discrimination in Employment

Act of 1967. Thus, jury trials were allowed only in discrimination cases involving women or those over 55. The 1991 act, however, extended this right to parties covered by Title VII of the 1964 Civil Rights Act and the Americans with Disabilities Act, making it accessible to minorities of any age or condition. On the face of it, black parents would now be able to sue their employers without the burden of proof, utilize jury trials to do so, and receive punitive damages.

There were, however, considerable loopholes in this new act. First, there was a significant caveat involved in the disparate impact regulations. While cursorily it appeared to return the burden of proof to the employer, it also required a complaining party to identify and corroborate which specific practices contributed to the disparate impact if the court found that information "reasonably available" from the employer could do so (Civil Rights Act of 1991–Pub. L. 102-166). The 1991 act also limited damages recoverable by a complaining party in an intentional discrimination (disparate treatment) case. Although it made jury trials available to minorities, it placed caps on the amount awarded for punitive damages, pecuniary losses, and pain and suffering. The maximum award for combined damages was set at $300,000 for employers with over 500 employees (considered the largest employers). Moreover, a complainant could recover punitive damages only if he or she was able to demonstrate that the respondent engaged in a discriminatory practice or practices "with malice or with reckless indifference" to the federally protected rights of an aggrieved individual (Civil Rights Act of 1991–Pub. L. 102-166). Thus, not only did the responsibility remain on the employee, but he or she would now have to contend with the interpretive liberty of the courts.

Years of Inaction: The Clinton Administration

Despite being considerably more sympathetic toward civil rights in the abstract, the Clinton administration did little to counteract the effects of the 1980s. While the Clinton years did witness an increase in civil rights enforcement, the emphasis of this activity was not on employment. In particular, the EEOC's funding remained within the range it had been in from the 1980s until 1999, and the OFCCP budget diminished further. The only office that received a substantial increase in funding was the DOJ's Civil Rights Division, which, as I have explained, was responsible for civil rights enforcement pertaining to a variety of areas beyond employment (see fig. 4). Instead, the 1990s were marked by inactivity on the part of the executive and legislative branches and marred by judicial affronts to affirmative action in higher education and federal procurement. As our students got older, became increasingly cognizant of their parents' work situations, and grasped the perceptions of the larger American population, they would find a heightened resentment among whites who increasingly defined affirmative action as "reverse discrimination" and progressively limited opportunities for their parents and other black professionals.

In June 1995, the Supreme Court called, yet again, for "strict scrutiny" in measuring the existence of discrimination prior to the implementation of affirmative action programs (*Adarand Constructors v. Pena*). Accordingly, minorities could only be awarded preferences to correct specific instances of discrimination relevant to an agency or industry. In a White House memorandum issued the same day as the court's decision, Clinton called for the elimination of any program that "(a) creates a quota; (b) creates preferences for unqualified individuals; (c) creates reverse discrimination; or (d) continues even after its equal opportunity purposes have been achieved" (Clinton 1995). Following the lead of the Department of Transportation, the agency directly involved in the *Adarand* case, federal agencies began modifying their small disadvantaged business contracting programs. The result was increased inclusion of firms that were white and/or male (US Commission on Civil Rights 2005).

Following the Supreme Court's lead, strict scrutiny was applied once again the following year in a court ruling on university admissions. On March 18, 1996, the United States Court of Appeals for the Fifth Circuit suspended the University of Texas Law School's practice of affirmative action, ruling that the 1978 *Bakke* decision was invalid (*Hopwood v. Texas*). The court rejected the legitimacy of diversity as a goal, asserting that "achieving a diverse student body was not a compelling interest." Instead, it held the law school's admissions policy to the test of strict scrutiny, which it failed. Although the University of Texas appealed, the Supreme Court refused to hear the case. Accordingly, race could no longer be used in admissions in Texas, Louisiana, or Mississippi (the states under the jurisdiction of the Fifth Circuit). One year later, the California Legislature enacted Proposition 209, a state ban on all forms of affirmative action. This was echoed by Washington's Initiative 200 in 1998 and Jeb Bush's One Florida initiative for college admissions in 2000. In all three cases, universities in each state were mandated to avoid the use of race in college admissions. This would be the first time our students would be directly affected by a major public policy or court decision relevant to their future professional lives.

Three years later, during our students' junior year in college, the United

States Supreme Court heard its first major university affirmative action case since *Bakke*. In two separate decisions, the court upheld the University of Michigan Law School's policy, ruling that race can be one among many factors considered by colleges in admissions because it furthers "a compelling interest in obtaining the educational benefits that flow from a diverse student body." It further ruled that the formulaic approach of the University of Michigan's undergraduate college, which utilized a complex point system, had to be modified. Both proponents and opponents considered these 2003 decisions partial wins but vowed to proceed in their fights for and against affirmative action. In all cases, however, the impact on black enrollment and admissions was profound.

In California, for example, the defeat of affirmative action had sharp repercussions. Despite the university's adoption of a variety of measures designed to maintain access for underrepresented minorities, African Americans were largely shuffled from more prestigious campuses, such as Los Angeles and Berkeley, to significantly less selective and less rigorous institutions, such as Riverside and Santa Cruz. In 1997, the last year in which race could be considered in admissions decisions and two years prior to our students entering college, African Americans were admitted at a rate of 51 percent to the flagship campus Berkeley, one of the two schools at which our participants were enrolled. In 2003, five years into the colorblind admissions process, blacks were admitted at a rate of only 21 percent (University of California Office of the President 2004). In contrast, the overall resident freshman enrollment of African Americans to the University of California system had stabilized and begun to increase by 2003, from 917 to 983 (University of California Office of the President 2006). This accounts, in part, for the relatively small presence of African Americans at Berkeley for the time of this study. Similarly, the admission of African Americans to the University of Texas at Austin went from 66 percent in 1997 (the year prior to the *Hopwood* decision going into effect) to 33 percent in 2003 and to 38 percent in 2007 (University of Texas 2007).

The Inefficacy of Affirmative Action and Civil Rights Legislation for Professionals

Despite Reagan and Bush's obvious disregard for black economic progress, and Clinton's idleness, the lack of funding for civil rights enforcement and hostile court rulings concerning employment in the 1980s and 1990s had little direct effect on the direction of black professional development. Al-

though antidiscrimination and affirmative action legislation did have a significant positive effect on black and female employment integration overall,
it was of limited consequence to white women and African Americans at the
professional level. Thus, while the lives of some black parents and grandparents were initially positively influenced by legislation and enforcement and
later negatively impacted by the lack thereof, others never benefited at all.

Contract Compliance

On the issue of contract compliance and antidiscrimination, data show
that firms with government contracts made considerable strides in all levels of white female employment, as well as African American employment
in managerial positions, skilled white-collar occupations, and blue-collar
crafts. It did not, however, positively affect black professionals. Moreover,
OFCCP review of those firms did not substantially impact black professionals or white female professionals or managers (Leonard 1984). Thus, cuts in
antidiscrimination enforcement in the 1980s and 1990s had serious negative
repercussions for African American and white female blue collar and low
level white-collar workers but little impact on already unaffected black and
white female professionals.[14]

Hence, while the families of lower-middle- and working-class African
Americans were severely negatively impacted by the Reagan, Bush, and Clinton cuts in antidiscrimination enforcement, professional families were not
impacted as greatly since this enforcement had never had much impact to
begin with. Moreover, although our white students' mothers benefited only
slightly more than African Americans did, the gains made by white males
offset the stagnation of white female advancement among white families.
Unlike white men, black professionals were not moving into increasingly
prestigious job titles or occupations, nor were black communities benefiting from the same prosperity as were white communities. The black middle
class saw few of the benefits of affirmative action that conservatives argue
gave them an advantage over their white male counterparts.

The irrelevance of civil rights legislation to black professionals bled over
to the judiciary as well. Indeed, most if not all of the major cases concerning affirmative action and discrimination have involved lower white-collar
and blue-collar workers. It is virtually impossible for African American
professionals claiming discrimination to prevail in a court of law. In disparate impact claims, the law states that the plaintiff must "demonstrate that
a respondent uses a particular employment practice that causes a disparate
impact on the basis of race, color, religion, sex, or national origin." In order

to do this, the plaintiff needs statistically significant evidence of a racial imbalance. This is an especially difficult task given the relatively low number of African Americans and other minorities among professionals within the general population. In most cases, the actual number of minorities in similar positions within an organization will be so small that statistical evidence is at best unconvincing to the court. If a complainant is successful in providing evidence of a disparity in the workforce, he or she is then challenged to identify the specific practice(s) accountable for the disparate impact. The subjective nature of hiring, particularly at the professional level, makes it tricky to distinguish the reasons for the unfavorable outcome in a given case, further weakening any claims of discrimination (Flagg 1995).

Disparate treatment claims present a different set of obstacles. In these cases, once the plaintiff has established a prima facie case of discrimination,[15] the defendant must provide a nondiscriminatory reason for its action against the plaintiff. The trouble is that,

> This is only a burden of production, and not of proof; the burden of persuasion remains at all times with the plaintiff. If such an explanation is advanced by the defendant, the plaintiff must prove that the proffered reason was not the real reason for the challenged action. The plaintiff must demonstrate not only that the articulated reason is not credible, but that it is a pretext for discrimination. That is, the plaintiff must not only disprove the employer's legitimate, nondiscriminatory explanation, but also must show that race was the real reason for the adverse action. [Flagg 1995, p. 2016]

As with disparate impact, the relative subjectivity of professional employment makes the task of proving discrimination difficult. As one judge in a disparate treatment case (*Walton v. Cowin Equipment Co., Inc.*, 774 F.Supp. 1343 N.D. Ala.1991) expounded,

> It would indeed be a rare case in which a black employee (or a female employee in an Equal Pay Act case) is able to present a precise and exact comparison, or an equation, between her job responsibilities and those of a higher paid nonprotected employee. The workplace is very rarely that simple an environment. It is susceptible to discriminatory conduct of a very subtle nature.

It is no surprise that in a sample of 237 major federal and state court rulings on cases concerning discrimination between 1970 and 2007, African American plaintiffs prevailed in only 35.[16] Moreover, in more recent years, negative decisions by the courts have been accompanied by stereotyped descriptions of the plaintiff as uppity. For example, in 2000, a district court in the Midwest granted summary judgment to the defendant in a disparate treatment suit. The judge asserted that the plaintiff had not established a prima facie case against her employer and that her dismissal was the result of her "disruptive" and "insubordinate" behavior. Similarly, in 2007, an African American attorney, a graduate of Harvard Law School and editor of the *Harvard Law Review,* filed a complaint of disparate treatment against her former employer, a major corporate law firm. In its judgment for the defendant, the court noted that the plaintiff had "engaged in repeated baseless efforts" and characterized her as "a confrontational, stubborn, and insubordinate employee."

As my interviews indicate, black students found their parents increasingly pessimistic about fighting the discrimination they faced at work since not only was antidiscrimination law not enforced, but when African American professionals did go to court, they faced a virtually hopeless battle. As a result, some frustrated parents warned their children to steer clear of professions predominated by whites, thereby curbing their children's perception of their options considerably.

Set-Aside Programs

The impact of set-aside programs for black professionals has been equally bleak. The purpose of preferential procurement was to help nascent minority-owned firms become self-sufficient and secure a place in the market—one dominated by better-financed companies owned by whites that enjoy favorable tax and regulatory positions. This goal, however, was met with many obstacles (Herring and Collins 1995). First, the 8(a) program, which specifically applies to racial minorities, is targeted only at economically disadvantaged firms. In particular, 8(a) business owners were and remain required to have a net worth of $250,000 or less, a limit which firmly establishes that 8(a) firms be owned by less financially stable African Americans. This limit is closely related to the competitiveness or lack thereof of minority business enterprises eligible for government assistance. While findings indicate that larger, more established firms (both minority and majority) have greater access to government and corporate contracts, a greater portion of minority-owned firms are smaller (as measured by total sales revenue) and younger (Bates 2001). The eligibility restrictions reinforce this dynamic by ensuring that the limited assistance available goes to the smallest, least competitive black firms.

This approach has evidently met with limited success: most firms leave the 8(a) program not because they surpass the financial eligibility criterion as a result of the program's assistance but because they exceed the nine-year participation limit. In 2003, for example, only one of the 857 exiting firms did so because of financial success (US Commission on Civil Rights 2005). The downside of these restrictions is compounded by the minimal impact these programs have on participants. Specifically, the awards given to 8(a) programs have often been restricted to a small fraction of those eligible. In 1998, only 209 of the existing 6,000 firms that applied under 8(a), or 3.5 percent, were awarded 50 percent of the dollar total of 8(a) contracts, while over 3,000 8(a) firms received no contracts (Herring and Collins 1995). Thus, the benefit of 8(a) status has been dramatically limited to a small subsample of eligible firms.

The advantages provided to minority and female business enterprises are further diminished when we examine the very real problem of fraud. Since the 1980s, the appearance of minority and female front companies has claimed news headlines. Increasingly, small minority firms have acted as fronts for larger white male businesses to take advantage of the preferences provided to 8(a) and other small disadvantaged businesses. In 1987, for example, the Wedtech Corporation, a majority-controlled defense company, posed as a minority-owned firm in order to gain government set-asides. Among the problems eventually brought to light in criminal proceedings were that the founder of the company, John Mariotta, a Puerto Rican, had taken a white partner who owned a majority of the firm's stock, thus making it ineligible for preferential procurement. Wedtech, however, is only one among many white-controlled companies using minorities as front men to qualify for government set-asides (Perlman 1989).

Fronting is particularly commonplace within prime and subcontractor relationships. Specifically, most federal contracts contain a subcontractor compensation clause giving prime contractors financial incentive to subcontract to small disadvantaged businesses (ones owned by minorities, women, veterans, etc.). Prime contractors frequently use subcontractors with questionable small disadvantaged business status or hire real ones who do not do the work and are paid only to act as fronts (Powers 2006). Such was the case in 1991 when F. A. Taylor & Son were awarded an $850,000 contract for roofing repairs at BWI Airport in Baltimore, Maryland, by qualifying for minority participation through the award of $85,000 to a black-owned subcontractor, Roofex, Inc. As it turned out, however, Roofex did no work; instead it accepted "fronting fees" from Taylor in exchange for falsified payrolls and invoices (Witkin 1995). This type of scam directly limits the benefits of small disadvantaged business programs because it redistributes money to contractors who are already advantaged and it is apparently on the rise. Between 2001 and 2005, Department of Transportation officials noted that fraud had risen from 16.7 to 22.4 percent of their open investigations (Powers 2006).

Declining Black Optimism

Given the tremendous odds against them, it is understandable that African American optimism has dimmed since the waning days of the civil rights movement. In December 1963, the Gallup poll asked the following question: "Do you think that relations between blacks and whites will always be a problem for the United States, or that a solution will eventually be worked out?" At that time, 26 percent of African Americans responded that they believed it "would always be a problem." Thirty years later when the question was next asked, 55 percent of blacks answered in the affirmative; by 2001, it had climbed to 66 percent (Gallup 2005). This pessimistic trend is echoed by African American responses to a similar question by Gallup concerning racial inequality in occupations: "In general, do you think that blacks have as good a chance as white people in your community to get any kind of job for which they are qualified, or don't you think they have as good a chance?" In 1963, 24 percent of black respondents answered that blacks "have as good a chance," and by 1978, the percentage rose to 35. Despite the brief progress of the 1970s, positive responses remained chiefly in the range of 30 to 40 percent over the next thirty years.

What is interesting about these figures is not only that African Americans' sense of inequality did not significantly decrease over time, but also how different such impressions are from those of white respondents. In 1963, for example, 46 percent of whites (compared with 24 percent of African Americans) believed blacks had as good a chance as whites to get a job, and in 1978, this figure had nearly doubled to 78 percent (over twice that of African Americans). By 1993, when only 30 percent of African Americans responded affirmatively, 70 percent of whites did so (Gallup 2005). Thus, while African Americans were left with the realities of what little had changed since the close of the civil rights movement, whites remained firm in their belief that legislation had done just what it was supposed to do, level the playing field.

Although African Americans may well have seen the legislation of the 1960s and early 1970s as the start of something big, they were confronted quickly with the reality that civil rights legislation is only as good as the government and people who stand behind it. Since the 1970s, funding of anti-discrimination enforcement has been slashed, ineffective policies have been implemented and then summarily dismissed, courts have denounced efforts to take affirmative measures to aid African Americans, and some white people have conveniently rewritten history to relieve their feelings of guilt by indicting the general laziness of black people as the cause of their lack of progress or by citing an overwhelming but erroneous degree of progress.

It is easy to see why African Americans have become increasingly pessimistic over time when we look at the data (fig. 5). Whereas whites in the top 20th and 5th percentiles steadily increased their mean income over 30 years, their black counterparts experienced frequent periods of economic stagnation with little overall change (US Census Bureau 2006). Between 1970 and 2000, white income in both categories has consistently been between 1.5 and 1.9 times that of African Americans.

Contrary to what some scholars suggest, the black middle and upper classes have not fared particularly well relative to their white peers. The sizeable difference in earnings of African Americans and whites in the top three quintiles remained relatively stable over time and in some years has risen from the late 1970s through the mid 1990s (fig. 6).[17]

A closer look reveals that the ratio of white to black income among the top 20 and top 5 percent of households actually increased from the late 1980s

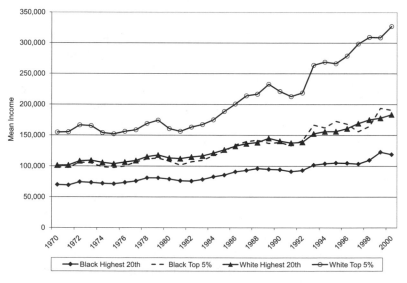

Fig. 5. Mean income of top quintile and top 5 percent of black and white households

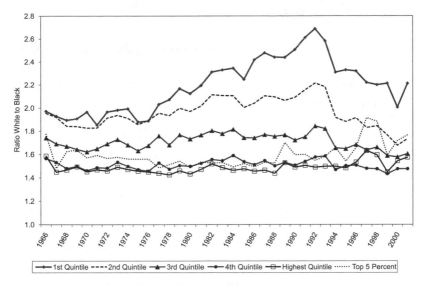

Fig. 6. Ratio of white to black family income by quintile

onward, the very period in which the students in our study were growing up (US Census Bureau 2006). One need only consider the difference in average earnings of the white and black parents in this sample: $120,000 and $70,000, respectively. Racial antagonism aside, as a feature of disadvantage, an average gap of $50,000 is significant enough to have provided for considerably different experiences for our students. While middle-class black families were in some instances able to move to predominantly white, more affluent suburbs, most were forced to remain within economically and racially segregated areas with limited work opportunities and high rates of joblessness. They would grow up not only aware of pervasive racism but also with few social resources to expose them to the opportunities awaiting them.

And whom might our youth look to as role models in this time of black immobility? Since 1980, the percent of African American professionals has remained stagnant at around 11 percent and teachers have consistently accounted for 30 to 37 percent of this population (US Census Bureau 1983, 1996, 2001). Meanwhile the percent of managers has steadily risen, but reached only as high as 11 percent of the black population, reflecting in large part, an increase in public and educational administrators. In essence, racial progress has remained at a veritable standstill since the late 1970s and early 1980s. The students in this study grew up amidst economic and social stagnation along with an increasing air of pessimism among African Americans.

Youth of Today, Professionals of Tomorrow

Given the resilience of racism and the economic inequality that stems from it, why then do African American youth not stand ready in the face of racist obstacles to launch a new civil rights movement as did the black middle class of the 1960s? The answer is complex, but it leads me to consider alternative means of change which I address in the concluding chapter. To directly address this question, however, it is essential to understand what induces mobilization. The widely accepted political process model of mobilization identifies four factors that shape insurgency: expanding political opportunities, organizational strength, shared understandings of the topic of grievance, and outside response to the movement itself (McAdam 1982). As is apparent throughout this book, the first three critical factors are largely missing for the current generation of college graduates and new workers.

Consider first the issue of political opportunity, which McAdam (1982, p. 41) defines as "any event or broad social process that serves to undermine the calculations and assumptions on which the political establishment is structured." The broader American political arena has been (until the Second Iraq War) generally stable: the Cold War ended in the 1980s; the economy stabilized and prospered in the 1990s; and the United States counted itself a vital link to the destabilization of the communist regime in East Germany. Although political opportunity can also stem from increased political strength, at the time of my interviews there had been few visible signals that the political establishment was or had been shifting in any way directly beneficial to African Americans. Since the mid 1970s, federal and state governments have systematically passed legislation wiping out many of the benefits gained from civil rights legislation, while the judiciary has sided with conservatives opposed to affirmative action in enterprise and education. Although businesses and professional organizations may well be open to a larger minority workforce, what is palpable among young African Americans and their elders is just the opposite.

If we were to pretend, however, that a tangible political opportunity had existed, African Americans would require the organizational capacity to exploit it. Yet one of the key components of organizational strength—leadership—disappeared at the close of the civil rights movement. In particular, many of the old guard activists of the movement took up jobs within government agencies in the early 1970s and were replaced by a small but growing number of elected officials (Piven and Cloward 1979; Nelson 2003). Absent leadership, it is difficult to imagine how young African Americans could be expected to organize on any scale, large or small, regardless of the opportunity to do so. This problem, however, is eclipsed by the reality that there is no consensus within the black community of how to prioritize and organize against the complex obstacles facing African Americans. While the majority of African Americans may well define black subjugation as an injustice they believe should be rectified, the changes in the nature of racism make it considerably more difficult to identify the roots of inequality.

The social, economic, political, and demographic shifts that took place in the 1960s and early 1970s are the source of change in the nature of racism, which went from open hostility to stealth degradation (Bonilla-Silva 2004). Racism is no longer flagrant, especially as it is experienced by middle- and upper-class African Americans. Instead, it is concealed behind the artifice of race-neutral structures and beliefs and fueled by antiblack sentiments, individualistic values, and group interests (Bobo 1998). It is expressed both in resentment toward preferential treatment, which is perceived as a competitive threat for resources, as well as denial of the existence of racism itself. This new racism is characterized by:

> (1) the increasingly covert nature of racial discourse and practices; (2) the avoidance of racial terminology and the ever growing claim by whites that they experience "reverse racism"; (3) the elaboration of a racial agenda over political matters that eschews direct racial references; (4) the invisibility of most mechanisms to reproduce racial inequality; and, finally, (5) the rearticulation of a number of racial practices characteristic of the Jim Crow period of race relations. [Bonilla-Silva and Lewis 1999, p. 56]

African American youth therefore must muddle through a far less conspicuous set of obstacles than did previous generations. They must consider that they will face more antagonism in mainstream, predominantly white careers than they would in racialized, largely minority occupations. This results not only in an indiscernible target, but also a growing sense of inefficacy and decreasing potential for mobilization. As others point out, "Social movements emerge from years of planning and debate among the aggrieved. Individuals feel that not only is their situation unjust, it is also something that can be alleviated through struggle and sacrifice" (Sniderman and Piazza 2005, pp. 22–23).

Yet, what lessons, if any, have African Americans learned about the efficacy of their efforts? Since the end of the civil rights movement, it has become increasingly clear that black inequality goes far deeper than civil liberties. While African Americans today are arguably better off than they were forty years ago, progress has not been as great as might have been anticipated. As people experience conditions in which they objectively have little command, they learn that they have minimal efficacy (Marino and Thornton 2004). Not surprisingly, research frequently indicates that regardless of socioeconomic factors, racial minorities feel less control than their white counterparts (Jackson and Stewart 2003).

Barack Obama's campaign for the office of president in 2008 is as close to a black movement for change as has been seen since the civil rights movement. Despite previously limited optimism concerning race relations and inequality among blacks, the campaign galvanized African Americans' desire for change. And while this well-organized campaign, headed by an inarguably charismatic leader, did, in fact, get black people, especially young black people, to push back and feel a sense of efficacy that had withered since the 1970s, its role as a movement was short lived. Not only did many of the organizational ties fall apart when the campaign was over, but reality eventually set in. The Gallup Organization's public opinion poll provides clear evidence of the brief sense of opportunity African Americans felt about the Obama campaign and presidency. In 1963, when asked whether they thought race relations between blacks and whites would always be a problem for the United States, or if a solution would eventually be worked out, 70 percent of blacks answered that they believed a solution would eventually be worked out. By 2001, this number had dipped to 32 percent. In August of 2008, however, when it was clear that Obama was the Democratic nominee for president, the percent of blacks who saw an eventual solution had bounced up to 50 percent. This is, of course, reflective of the sense among many blacks (and persons of other races) that the substantive changes they desired might be achieved. Yet just over a year later, when Obama had settled into the office of the president, black optimism had dropped back down to 42 percent; reality had set in (Newport 2009).

The few areas in which African Americans have clearly made and maintained headway are racialized specialties—those working within or directed toward the black population—yet these fields have limited influence. In particular, African Americans have become increasingly visible as officials and administrators at the state and local level. In response to civil rights policies implemented in the 1960s and 1970s, African Americans—many of whom were previously active in the civil rights movement—have been disproportionately drawn into professional posts in government and corporate offices dealing with equal employment opportunity, civil and human rights, and affirmative action (Durr and Logan 1997; Collins 1997). Likewise, African Americans have spent considerable energy electing viable black candidates.

Between 1970 and 2001, the total number of black elected officials in the United States went from 1,469 to 9,101; within city and county offices, the jump was from 715 to 5,452 (Bositis 2002). Although the significant increase in black officials is a triumph in and of itself, it is clear that this paradigm has not worked. Social science researchers have suggested a variety of reasons for the inefficacy of black leadership (Guinier 1994; Cunnigen 2006; Kraus and Swanstrom 2005), but for our purposes, it is only critical to acknowledge that it has been inadequate. The visible impotence of much of the contemporary civil rights legislation and judicial behavior is a key piece of evidence. One need only consider two recent political catastrophes that had disproportionately negative ramifications for African Americans to appreciate this point: the Florida general presidential election of 2000 and Hurricane Katrina of 2005.

On November 7, 2000—the year in which our participants entered college—Americans watched spellbound as the news media made projections and counterprojections of the Florida popular vote. When all was said and done, George W. Bush received Florida's 25 electoral votes to win the presidency. But while Bush and his supporters began celebrating, a crisis was unfolding: massive voter irregularities across the state which disproportionately affected Florida's African American population. What was eventually revealed by the media, the US Commission on Civil Rights, and even Governor Jeb Bush's Select Task Force on Election Procedures, Standards, and Technology, were multiple instances of black voter disenfranchisement in the months leading up to and the day of the 2000 presidential election. Among other things, voting machines in black precincts invalidated ballots at a higher rate than those in predominantly white precincts; thousands of voters in Palm Beach County mistakenly voted for Reform presidential candidate Pat Buchanan because of an indecipherable butterfly ballot (Wu 2002; Wand et al. 2001); and African Americans were erroneously placed on purge lists at a significantly higher rate than Hispanic or white voters (Hines 2002). When these irregularities were ultimately overlooked, Bush won Florida by only 537 votes—a margin of less than 0.01 percent (Phillips 2001).

Two months later, on January 6, 2001, at a joint session of Congress, electoral votes for each state were officially presented and tallied. During the presentation of electoral certification for Florida, 13 members of the House of Representatives, most of whom were also members of the Congressional Black Caucus, rose to object. Al Gore, then acting in his capacity as president of the Senate, repeatedly asserted that the objections could not be heard on account of an 1877 law requiring such protests be signed by a member of the Senate. Despite repeated calls, no senator, those from black populous states or elsewhere, would join the objection (Walsh and Eilperin 2001). George W. Bush was sworn in on January 20, 2001.

Four years later, on August 29, 2005, Hurricane Katrina landed on the Louisiana coast. Despite warnings, there was markedly deficient preparation for this catastrophe. Mayor Ray Nagin ordered evacuation prior to the storm, but tens of thousands of predominantly poor black people remained behind, in most cases because of a lack of or inadequate transportation and finances to leave (Kellner 2007). What eventually became clear was that Michael Brown, head of the Federal Emergency Management Agency (FEMA) under the Bush administration, and numerous other Bush-appointed officials had failed to do their jobs. In the end, thousands of residents in New Orleans alone were left homeless and jobless while hundreds of thousands from the Gulf Coast area remain in exile.

This leaves us at the point at which the participants in this study embarked on their careers. The first step in this direction, one which is critical, is the formulation of aspirations. What becomes clear throughout this study is that many of the same dynamics shaping the incapacity of these young adults to organize a new movement are those that inhibit them from entering a variety of careers that are now, at least ostensibly, open to them. The lack of progress within the black middle class, due in no small part to faulty legislation, minimal enforcement, and destructive judicial decisions kept many black parents from pursuing professional jobs. Likewise, white racism and declining economic well-being prohibited black families from moving into more affluent, occupationally better connected neighborhoods of the kind that offered their white peers countless opportunities. Simultaneously, awareness of racism, that experienced by older and past generations as well as their own daily experiences, limited the motivation of black students to pursue predominantly white, mainstream careers. The resultant reliance on racialized jobs, ones frequently oriented toward black welfare and black communities, therefore have become increasingly but erroneously accepted by youth as the most effective and valuable for changing the position of African Americans in this country. As I explain throughout this book, while community-oriented jobs are extremely valuable, even indispensable, they are not, on their own, sufficient to significantly lessen black inequality.

3

FAMILY EFFECTS

Is It Really Just a Matter of Money?

This book is not about the average black child, middle or lower class. It is about African Americans who have made it to prestigious universities and therefore represent a very specific subset of the black population. There is no doubt that their families, nuclear and extended, played a significant role in getting them there. Across all races, families are the first conduits of upward mobility for children. They are the first set of agents to develop children's capacity to learn and set goals, and they maintain considerable control over the ways in which children evaluate the social order and contextualize events and experiences. But the ways in which black families in this study were able to support their children, once in college, differed dramatically from their white counterparts.

Such differences concern not only economic welfare, but the respective social and cultural capital of African American and white families. Even in the midst of the civil rights movement, it was evident that if significant measures beyond ensuring basic civil liberties were not implemented, black families would face major obstacles for years to come. In his 1965 report to the president (United States Department of Labor), Daniel Moynihan wrote, "In this new period the expectations of the Negro Americans will go beyond civil rights. Being Americans, they will now expect that in the near future equal opportunities for them as a group will produce roughly equal results, as compared with other groups. This is not going to happen. Nor will it happen for generations to come unless a new and special effort is made." This was not an indictment of African Americans, but rather a warning that major efforts were necessary to ensure equality of achievements. As discussed in chapter 2, this warning was not heeded. Not only did the government not make "new and special" efforts, but the very legislation intended to provide basic civil rights was ineffective. Between 2008 and 2009, approximately 47 percent of African Americans fourth-graders in public schools attended high-poverty schools[1] and 11 percent of black children had an incarcerated parent. This is in contrast to 7 percent and less than 2 percent, respectively, of white children (Aud, Fox, and KewalRamani 2010; Western and Pettit 2010). Aside from the injustice reflected in these figures, numbers like these are indicative of the obstacles black children face in attending college.

These are not, however, the last stumbling blocks confronting the African American family seeking upward mobility. Today, Moynihan's warnings not only extend to educational achievement but to occupational access as well. Surely, a lack of financial stability profoundly impedes the ability of African Americans to attend college. Yet once in college, black students, lower and middle class, find themselves uninformed about many of the opportunities available to them, ones overlooked in part because of their parents' lack of familiarity with these options. Indeed, the responses from the students who participated in this study suggest that differences in social capital enable white parents to offer career advice and other support that is more insightful and more effective than the support provided by black parents.

Background Characteristics

Because socioeconomic status is the dominant factor used to account for the achievement gap between African Americans and whites, my discussion of the ways in which families influence occupational aspirations begins here. As a whole, neither the African American nor the white families referenced here fit a particular stereotype. The white families in this study were not more cohesive than their black counterparts, nor were black families any more maladjusted than white families. Recent research (Lareau 2003) suggests that black and white childrearing strategies, particularly among the middle class, are, in fact, quite similar. The majority of students interviewed—both white and black—had married parents, and most mothers, regardless of race, had careers and/or had never stayed home with their children for long periods of time. And like their white counterparts, African American students came from a variety of states, small towns and large cities, professional, blue-collar, and jobless families.

There was, however, one notable difference in students' backgrounds: family income. Whereas white students reported an annual median family income of $120,000, African Americans reported a median family income of only $70,000.[2] This disparity appears to be part of a trend among students at highly selective institutions. Not only are the African Americans attending these schools from families with significantly lower incomes, but their families have also accrued considerably less wealth to cushion them after college (Massey et al. 2003; Charles et al. 2009). The impact of these differences cannot be overstated.

Economic inequalities such as these translate to both the quality of education available to children and the time and ability of parents to intervene in their children's education (Lareau 2000). Social scientists frequently explain racial differences by referencing African Americans' lower average family income, decreased time for parental involvement, and unstable, single-parent households. Statistical analysis of the composition of class cohorts in highly selective schools suggests that black students are, in fact, considerably more socioeconomically heterogeneous than their white counterparts and that black immigrants are overrepresented among black students, particularly among those who come from more affluent backgrounds (Massey et al. 2003)[3]

Once socioeconomic variables are controlled for, however, racial differences in achievement—whether measured as college admission, high school graduation, college enrollment, or some other factor—should diminish. Indeed, once socioeconomic status is held constant, African Americans are actually more likely to attend four-year institutions than their white counterparts (Charles et al. 2007) and are more likely than whites to go to highly selective institutions. Moreover, native blacks and immigrants with similar economic backgrounds are equally likely to attend selective institutions (Bennett and Lutz 2009). Given the disparate rates of attendance at college between blacks and whites, particularly at highly selective institutions, it is evident that socioeconomic status has a profound effect on admission.

Yet the question relevant to this study is, How are students admitted to these highly selective schools influenced by their economic situation once in college? It is clear that the students in this study were affected by their social class, but, as I demonstrate in the remainder of this chapter, basic social class differences are overly simplistic and inadequate to explain the differences in occupational aspirations of black and white students. Socioeconomic status and family support are, of course, important to all college students regardless of race. Yet the ways in which these factors affect students appear to vary by race.

One of the ways socioeconomic status seems to have impacted student aspirations is actually contrary to what we might anticipate following conventional models of social mobility. Specifically, the larger debts African American students accrued in college[4] and their perceptions of their responsibility to support their families financially after graduation actually encouraged some black students to pursue nonracialized careers that have larger financial payoffs.[5] In contrast, not only was the average class background of white students higher, but some white students whose families expressed a concern about money, especially those at Berkeley, often experienced considerable pressure from their families to constrain their educational aspirations, and in some cases those students relented.

Although some African American students from low-income backgrounds chose to take on part-time work to pay for their tuition or living expenses, many still had significant debts to repay. Likewise, several of the white students I spoke with estimated that they too would be in personal debt at the time of their graduation. Such debts have a tendency to weaken academic performance for students of all races due to stress or the need to work during college (St. John et al. 1994; St. John 2001; Nora, Barlow, and Crisp 2006). African Americans were more likely, however, to cite repaying those loans or wanting to take care of parents or extended family members (most often those who they believed had in some way financially or developmentally contributed to their lives) in the near future as rationales for pursuing more lucrative occupations.[6] The effect of this debt and sense of responsibility, therefore, is contrary to traditional mobility models, which allege a negative association between socioeconomic status and aspirations. That is, debt or family financial instability actually propelled black students toward more profitable endeavors rather than hindering their upward mobility.

The response given by Paul, who planned to go into business and eventually take a senior position in government, was characteristic of low-income African American students (especially men) who were going into profitable, mainstream jobs. Having received a generous financial aid package from Stanford and several outside scholarships, he estimated the amount he would need to repay in loans upon graduation at only $5,000. Thus Paul's debts were minimal. But when I asked if there was anyone in his family he would need to provide for, he reported,

> Well, it's not necessarily have to provide for, but it's definitely that I want to give back financially. My grandma, I'll definitely want her to be freer from the financial strings of her husband, and my mom, I'll get her right. And then, as far as my brothers, I'm going to help them out, but they're grown men . . . I can scoop them up a little bit; give them a boost.

Paul further explained that he might have had other aspirations had he come from different circumstances and not been financially constrained. He openly acknowledged that were he less indebted to his grandmother in particular, were his mother and brothers more financially stable, he might have given serious consideration to other occupational pursuits like teaching.

Another student, Jason, directly associated his interest in working for corporate financial services to his low economic background. "Primarily it would be the financial security; that would be the drive because my family doesn't really have any. I think it's the daily grind of worrying about credit cards, worrying about getting your money on time from jobs. I'd like to be in the position where that's not a problem. If I didn't do it for money, it [his career] would be civil rights law."

Jason cited wanting to provide for his parents and his future family as well as to be able to donate to black communities as reasons this type of financial security was crucial to his aspirations. African Americans have amassed significantly less wealth than their white counterparts, due in no small part to racist practices that have impeded African Americans from purchasing homes and continue to do so (Oliver and Shapiro 1997). If Jason's parents had owned their home, which they did not, if they had any additional money to invest and accrue for retirement, which Jason assured me they did not, he might not have felt the need to consider them in calculations for his future. But Jason's parents could not transfer any wealth to him, so Jason had to consider his own initial finances and those of his future family in his career decisions. There was no safety net for Jason; rather, he was to provide the safety net for the rest of his family. Most significantly, Jason was not an exception in this study or in the greater population of black college students. The difference in income between black and white homes is enough to distinguish their respective capacities to save for their own and for their children's futures. Once we consider inequality in assets that come from home ownership and other forms of investment between African Americans and whites, the disparity in the options of students like Jason is notable.

As Jason and Paul suggest, the need and desire for economic stability had a direct relationship with their aspirations. Students who believed their loans were a burden or who wanted to contribute significantly to their family's well-being often cited financial stability as a reason for their disinterest in more community-oriented, racialized occupations. Thus, a primary reason that some lower- and middle-income African Americans planned to enter mainstream professions was the desire to take care of family and be economically secure, a burden borne by few white students, middle class or otherwise.

Influence of Significant Others

Despite the relatively strong influence of lower socioeconomic status on some African Americans described above, the interaction between race and class had several negative impacts on black families' abilities to help their children understand their career options and attain their goals. While white and black students both came from largely supportive environments with high expectations, the capacity of black families to aid their children in familiarizing and gaining them entry into a diversity of career fields was hindered by current financial inequalities and by a legacy of occupational and residential discrimination.

Family Expectations: Racial and Class Differences

African Americans and whites in this study differed in several respects, including parental income, parental education and parental occupations (white students doing better on all counts), yet black students fared better in one major regard: parental expectations. It was, in fact, rare to find an African American student whose family had not been exceedingly supportive and pushed them to attain the best education perceived possible. This characterization of black parental expectations is consistent with studies which have critically examined the claim that African Americans are not as positively oriented toward achievement as whites. Such investigations refute the enduring portrayal of black families as "inefficient vehicles for the positive socialization of Black youth" (Allen 1978, p. 232; Wilson and Allen 1987; Carter-Black 2001). Kao's research (2002), for example, reports black parents as possessed by high aspirations for their children that in turn, positively impact students' aspirations. Indeed, black students in this study, regardless of class background, were "expected" by their families to go to college; for them, the only choice was where. Kyra, for instance, described her parents' expectations of her attending college as one that "was ingrained in my head from the time I was two."

Paul, referred to earlier in this chapter, exemplified the lengths to which African American families had gone to educate their children even when it was well beyond their financial means to do so. His mother had been in and out of his life since birth because of drug addiction and he had never met his father. Paul, along with three siblings, was brought up primarily by his maternal grandmother. She had retired early in his life but had spent a sizeable amount of her retirement money on raising the children. In the midst of dealing with a drug-addicted daughter and raising four grandchildren, this woman had managed to enroll Paul in a private boarding school. Understandably, he credited her in large part for his admission to and attendance at Stanford.

Another African American student at Stanford, Dave, came from a lower-middle-class family. He succinctly described the role his parents played in applying to college: "Let me try to give you an idea about their involvement with the application process. They were in it. They were always like, 'Where's the applications? Where's the applications?'" Their expectations after college graduation were no less. As he put it, "They want me to do, go the highest possible." These students couldn't think of any reasons their parents or parental figures would have accepted their not pursuing a college degree. Like many white parents, African American parents or relatives frequently encouraged their children to apply to prestigious colleges, saved for their children's education, or were resourceful enough to find them scholarships and help them into prestigious boarding schools or their current university. Yet while black parents like Dave's uniformly expressed a desire for their children to get the "best" degree possible, white parents had more variable expectations, particularly along institutional and correlated class lines.

In this study, not only did Berkeley have a higher proportion of white students from working-class homes, but their parents were also more likely than those of any economic class at Stanford to have expressed to their children one or both of the following sentiments about college selection: first, that they should apply only to schools in-state (thus limiting the number of elite or prestigious schools to which their children could apply), and, second, that their children should or might consider entering a junior college before transferring into a state university or not attending college at all. While this may well be a simple reflection of the socioeconomic profile of the two schools, no students at Stanford—African American or white—expressed that doing anything but attending a four-year institution would have been acceptable to their parents.

Sarah presented a story that was repeated several times by white students at Berkeley. Her parents were lower middle class and had less education than most white parents of Stanford students. Her mother had finished her bachelor's degree recently at a small, local, private Lutheran school, and her father had only completed high school. When asked if it would have been acceptable to her parents had she not gone to college, she gave a fairly common response. "It would have been okay. It would have been completely fine to go to junior college also. Looking back, it probably would have saved a lot of money, but when I got into Berkeley, I was like, wow, okay, I have a chance to go to a great institution; I want to go there. So that was how it worked out."

For the most part it seems very little of Sarah's academic accomplishment and motivation derived from her parents. While Sarah had been thrilled at the prospect of Berkeley and recognized it as one she could not turn down, her parents were comfortable with the prospect of her transferring after two years at the local community college. She admitted that most of her career aspirations and comprehension of the job world had come from her networks and experiences at college. Sarah noted, "It's funny because I hear friends saying, 'Oh well, I have to go to get my JD' or whatever, 'I have to do this.' And I'm like, oh, my parents just want me to get by at Berkeley, so they'll be happy with that."

In this case, her parents had very little to say about her educational interests. They offered no advice about which schools she should apply to, what college to attend, or how to select her major. Her mother was apparently supportive of her attending college, but Sarah felt no pressure or encouragement from either parent to perform well or do anything at all when it came to her academic life. This type of response is perhaps reflective of the high transfer rate from junior colleges at Berkeley.

In fact, for several white working-class Berkeley parents, the concept of a liberal arts education appeared foreign. The white transfers at Berkeley described relatively competitive high school records that might have gained them admission as freshman. The reasons they had not attended Berkeley directly from high school seem to have had more to do with tuition or a lack of encouragement about college than an inability to gain admission. That is, their parents frequently encouraged them to save money by attending junior college. Many of these same students said that their parents saw college as a degree that automatically increased their earning potential rather than an experience in and of itself.

On the other hand, white middle-class parents at both universities were generally more active in supervising their children's schooling relative to white working-class parents, and their methods of supervision were more effective. That is, more affluent, better-educated parents provided more efficacious advice and acted as stronger advocates for their children (Lareau 2000; Useem 1992). For example, one study (Useem 1992) found that the insider information available to highly educated parents provided their children with significant advantages in math placement in middle school. In our case, lower-income, less-educated white parents had been less involved in their children's education and frequently provided poor advice in the college application and selection process.

In contrast, regardless of class, black parents of students at Berkeley and Stanford, saw the name of the schools to which their children were applying and being admitted and pushed hard for immediate entrance. Janelle described the pressure she received to attend Stanford as coming from all angles.

> I chose Stanford because, I don't know, I mean there was a lot of pressure from others, like my parents and my teachers. Because it's like "you got into Stanford. You have to go there. How could you not go there?" So definitely a lot of pressure from my mom, teachers, people I know. I guess there was just kind of this expectation I felt from others. Like I got in, so . . .

Janelle and other black students may have come from families who, like their white counterparts, did not have the background to understand the experiential value of a first-rate education. These parents may not have had any idea of what a "core curriculum" meant or how access to Nobel Prize–winning professors would concretely impact their children. Black families did, however, have some conception that all education is not equal, that names like Stanford and Berkeley meant better prospects than community colleges or less elite universities, and thus they encouraged if not pushed their children wholeheartedly to apply to and attend the most prestigious institutions to which they could gain admission.

Sociocultural Resources

Although black students grew up with parents, relatives, and others close to them encouraging them and maintaining high expectations, the lack of concrete guidance African American parents and family were able to provide their children was clearly a liability for black students of all class backgrounds. Prior research has demonstrated that regardless of the degree of their involvement, minorities and lower-income parents are less effective at helping their children achieve academically. That is, they "get less for their involvement" than higher socioeconomic, white parents (McNeal 1999, p. 136). The experiences of the students featured in this book suggest that the lower efficacy of minority and low-income parents in directing their children's success applies to career direction as well.

Like financial wealth, cultural capital is an asset. It is inherited, non-meritocratic, and to a great extent, invisible. While African Americans and whites both have varying degrees and types of cultural capital, the white students in this study tended to have greater access to capital relevant to upward mobility, particularly those in the middle and upper classes. Because of the newness of the black middle class (Landry 1987) and the extended history of discrimination described in chapter 2, African American families and the communities in which they live have been less able to offer substantive direction relative to career mobility. A true middle class for African Americans developed only after the civil rights movement had triumphed and equal employment opportunity laws had been implemented in the late 1960s and early 1970s. In 1960, only 13 percent of black workers held middle-class jobs; in contrast 44 percent of all white workers occupied middle-class positions in that same year. A decade later, new opportunities in this portion of the class structure meant not only that educational prospects for African Americans increased, but also that such opportunities did not have to translate into traditionally black occupations such as teaching and social work. Yet because opportunities to gain cultural capital and social capital were denied to African Americans through decades of de jure and de facto segregation, African Americans still lag far behind their white counterparts.

The conditions limiting the communities in which African American students could live are the same conditions restricting the practical advice black parents could provide to their children: a cycle of residential segregation that has significant consequences for African Americans (Massey and Denton 1993). When black parents live in residentially segregated areas and have themselves grown up in residentially segregated neighborhoods, it is challenging for them to transmit to their children the cultural capital necessary to give them the same advantages many white students, regardless of socioeconomic status, have in career decisions (see chap. 8). As Fryer and Loury (2005) explain,

> When some racial segregation exists among communities, the intergenerational status transmission mechanism differs substantially for the two racial groups. In essence, an intragroup externality is exerted through local public goods provision, by the lower income of black families who share a community. Because the racial composition of one's community depends (in part) on the choices of one's neighbors, this effect cannot be completely undermined by an individual's actions. Since social clustering by ethnicity and race is empirically relevant and has been observed since the dawn of its measurement, equal opportunity from this point forward is unlikely to assure racial equity. [P. 154]

During the interviews, it became clear that many white parents had presented their children with explicit suggestions about their careers while black parents often struggled to provide anything but abstract recommendations. White parents, with the exception of some from Berkeley who had discouraged their children from attending four years at the university, recommended specific subfields within professions and offered a wider range of recommended occupations than did their African American counterparts at all levels of income. Joe, a white student at Berkeley who aspired to become a bioengineer, described the advice his parents had given him about preparing for his career. They told him repeatedly, "Try to be with the best people. Try to work with the best people [in your field]. Take classes, not necessarily the ones that you'll get A's on, but the ones that will help you learn the most. And just, yeah, work with the best people in the field that you want to go into."

Although neither parent was an engineer, as physicians, both were familiar with biotechnology and science education and had provided their son with what he referred to as "simple but good advice."

Similarly, Kelley, a Stanford student aspiring to work in the recording industry portrayed her interest in business as stemming from her mother's influence. Referring to her mother, Kelley explained, "Yeah, I mean, I think, I guess being around someone who's been in business all the time, since I was really little. And being around my mom, and watching her do business, I guess that's been a big influence on me." Her mother, a real estate broker, had worked nonstop since Kelley was born. Yet she had pushed Kelley to succeed on her own merits, to take jobs since she was fourteen, and even to get her real estate license so that Kelley would have a background in business. Her mother had also pushed her to pursue multiple musical instruments, something Kelley indicated had steered her toward the recording industry. As in Kelley's case, white families—even some of the same working-class households who had exhibited very little interest in their children's college education—frequently discussed job options.

African American parents, however, were generally either unable to offer occupational advice or were unable to offer advice that was sufficiently specific. The careers African American parents desired for their children most frequently were doctor and lawyer, two well-known, and broad occupational categories. Kyra, who aspired to become an editor for a women-of-color magazine, was acting contrary to the wishes of her parents. Her father, himself a production supervisor at a major manufacturer, cited financial reasons for his hope that Kyra would pursue a legal education but could provide no concrete advice or preferences. "As long as I get the law degree and make a lot of money, that's all I know . . . I feel like that's my dad's general reason for the law degree: making sure I have a stable job, making sure that I have a strong income." So Kyra was left only with a sense that she should make money. Unlike Kelley, whose mother frequently discussed business with her,

Kyra knew only that she was supposed to go to law school to obtain a degree that provided entry into a profession about which her father could provide her with few specific insights.

Even black parents who were more affluent did not provide precise, concrete occupational suggestions. Will, a student at Stanford, hoped to own some sort of technology-related business and credited his father as being a significant influence on his career interests.

> You know, my father, he's an attorney and he ran his own law practice for well over thirty years now, and he's done fairly well. He's always kind of stressed to me that you could learn to do for yourself and have something for yourself and not depend on somebody else or an employer to make sure you and your family are doing okay. And if you work for yourself then you can do what you want, you can set your hours and make things happen the way you want them to happen. You don't have to be dependent on someone else.

What his father could not tell Will, however, was which business, which sector, which field would be best suited to his interests or how to enter the one in which he expressed interest. Will's family lived in a small, all-black section of town, so his father had a generalist law practice, serving the entire black community and all of its needs. He did not have colleagues from different types of law firms (corporate, patent, environmental, estate, civil rights, etc.) to which he might refer his son, nor did he have friends in a variety of other professions. There were few professionals in that part of town at all—just enough to keep it running—and like his father, they were generalists. As I discuss in detail in chapter 8, this community, like many other black communities, also lacked connections to major business and corporate sectors. This presents a paradox for black students. While middle-class African American children were strongly encouraged to go as far as possible, they were often shut off from exposure to occupational options that would allow them to do so.

This problem was more pronounced for lower-income African American students whose parents had virtually no suggestions for their children's careers because the world of professional work was beyond their understanding. Steve, a Stanford student headed into the business world, described the lack of comprehension his family had about his education and future career options. He explained,

> What I'm doing is so out of context for [my mother], it's beyond her comprehension, the whole notion of going to Stanford. She's excited, but it's not

something she can completely understand because it's something that my family's never done. My dad is more with it, but again, it's kind of beyond his level of understanding too. He has this thing about going to Harvard and being a doctor, so in his world, I'll be a doctor, I'll be in pre-med. But he thinks that I should be getting that PhD, and the JD, and the MD.

Certainly Steve's parents were encouraging about his pursuit of a professional career, even resourceful. Despite having a combined family income under $30,000, Steve's father had always made certain he had a computer so that Steve "could be this engineer of sorts." Yet according to Steve, what he was doing with those computers was, "Again, stuff that no one in my family could ever understand, not even my dad." His parents did take an interest in his career, but in large measure because of their own lack of education—a high school diploma for his father and an eighth-grade education for his mother—they simply could not comprehend or guide him toward his options. Referring to discussions with his parents about careers, Steve noted, "They always ask, and I was never able to answer, because I don't know . . . I don't know what's feasible . . . I tried to give them bits and pieces, but I realize that they can't understand most of it." Here again, it is clear that while African American parents saw a real value in education, even in obtaining advanced degrees, the jobs their children could get with these degrees were largely unfamiliar.

When lower-income African American parents did have suggestions, they often encouraged their children to enter traditionally high status yet broad occupational categories like law or medicine. These suggestions provided students with encouragement to perform, but no information on how to attain these careers or even why they might be suitable for them. Toni's mother, like many other low-income black parents, did not fully understand what went on in college but did recognize its value. Toni gave a typical account of her mother's career advice. Specifically, get the most advanced degree and become a doctor: "Mom is still kind of confused on what urban studies is, so, she's like 'What are you doing?'. . . All she wants me to do is just to keep going with my education. She doesn't want me to stop . . . I told her early in the beginning when I first came to Stanford, I'm not going to be a doctor. I'm not on the pre-med track, so just get that out of your mind. But she's still like 'Are you sure?'"

Like all the other participants in this study, Toni was in her junior year of college, too far along to declare a pre-med major. Her mother's insistence that she become a doctor was well intentioned, but not especially valuable. This is the primary conundrum for the black students. Those attending elite or selective schools such as Stanford and Berkeley are likely to come from homes that place a great deal of value on education; some are from professional families while others are not. Yet as they climb the ladder of mobility, it becomes increasingly difficult for black families who have limited exposure to professional occupations—even if they themselves are professionals—to provide beneficial advice about what to do next.

Occupational Standards for Men and Women, White and Black

Among white students, the exposure within their own homes and educational communities to professionals was enough to provide them with sufficiently clear understandings of their options. Likewise, their parents' own professional backgrounds offered many of these students viable role models and concrete advice for how to meet their aspirations. There was one notable distinction, however, in the type of advice provided to white men and women. A small number of white women from both schools expressed feeling pressured by their mothers about their careers. Specifically, these students recalled their mothers having expressed a desire, if not actual coercion, to enter predominantly female, or pink-collar, career fields, often having cited the rationale "you are so good with children."

Molly, a Caucasian woman who aspired to be a neonatologist, did not receive encouragement from her mother to pursue that career path despite having grown up in a family that was relatively scientifically and technologically oriented. Both of her grandfathers were nuclear physicists, and her paternal grandmother and aunt were engineers. Contrary to her mother's ambivalence if not outright opposition toward her intended career path, Molly's father, a mechanical engineer who grossed over $500,000 annually, was very influential and supportive. He had frequently taken her into work with him on weekends in addition to special take-your-daughter-to-work days during high school. Despite her father's enthusiasm for her pursuit of a career in science and her extended family's propensity toward professional careers for women, her mother, a homemaker, remained far more concerned about Molly's ability to raise a family. She recalled,

> The only thing my mom has ever said to me [about careers] is to make sure I have a life outside of medicine, and take time to get married and have a family. She said, "You know you can do what you want, but keep that in mind when you're doing your residency. And surgeons are on call a lot more than other types of doctors, so keep that in mind."

Given her mother's work as a stay-at-home mom, the situation is fairly easy to interpret. Clearly family was one, if not the greatest, priority for her mother. Her mother's expectation was for her daughter to maintain the same value of family life she had and evidently felt it would be difficult for her daughter to do so with a demanding job in neonatology. This was the general trend in the logic of those mothers who pressured their daughters toward pink-collar careers. Moreover, those who encouraged their daughters most strongly to pursue such occupations, or actively discouraged them from pursuing predominantly male occupations, were themselves stay-at-home moms or pink-collar workers.

This stands in direct contrast to the experience of black women whose mothers and fathers generally hoped they would obtain a PhD, JD, or MD. In no cases did black women's mothers, regardless of their own careers, attempt to steer them toward pink-collar occupations. Rather, in some cases, when African American women reported interest in nonprofit work, their mothers and fathers repeated their desire for their daughters to become doctors, lawyers, or some other sort of professional. For example, Beth, a young lady at Stanford who intended to go into architectural design, mentioned that both of her parents had initially pushed her to major in computer science. When computer science was clearly no longer an option, Beth's father, a radiologist, advocated strongly for her to go into medicine. Both parents, however, urged Beth to do something other than become a designer, the first career in which she expressed interest. Their reason: financial stability. Citing her father's rationale, Beth explained, "There would be two things. One of them is financial security, cause he figured if I do something with computers or I'm a doctor, I'm always going to be needed. And also those were the two areas that he was really interested in."

Similarly, Beth's mother hoped her daughter would be secure.

> She definitely, definitely is concerned with financial issues because she knows what it's like. Because she makes a lot of money [as an attorney], but she has so many places that the money is going. And she just, that's a really huge issue for her, and it's a big source of stress. So she wouldn't ever want me to ever have to handle all that. So she definitely wants me to make money and stuff.

The difference in the tendency for white and black mothers to encourage their daughters to go into traditionally female fields may be the result of at least three issues. First, it is possible that black mothers whose daughters were able to make it to selective universities were simply different from white mothers or black mothers with less academically successful daughters. This may well be a sample distinct from the general population. Second, black women have traditionally been forced into working in pink-collar jobs and may be resentful of the limitations forced on them. That is, historically, black women were limited to pursuing work in childcare, nursing (at the nonprofessional level), and later teaching. Having taken up such fields out of necessity rather than choice or having had mothers and grandmothers who did so may have prejudiced black women against these fields. Finally, past research has demonstrated a difference in the socialization of African American and white girls toward working because of the role race plays in dictating social inequality (Hill and Sprague 1999; Hill Collins 1990).

While white male income has often been sufficient to maintain a household, the significantly lower earnings of black men means that black female earnings represent a substantial contribution to total family income and are often necessary to maintain economic stability within a household (Choi 1999). The need for African American women to participate in the workforce has made female domesticity difficult and the presence of African American women in the workforce has resulted in a greater regard for gender equality among African Americans (Hill and Sprague 1999). In a study of black and white women in management and professional occupations, 94 percent of black respondents from both upper- and middle-class backgrounds affirmed that their parents had stressed the importance of an occupation to them while only 70 and 56 percent of middle- and upper-class white women, respectively, did so (Higginbotham and Weber 1992). The rationales these women provided, much like those in the present study, suggest that black women are encouraged to pursue occupations for their own security and for the sake of black upward mobility, whereas white women face greater pressure to get married and place childcare before their careers. Although working is seen as an implicit part of caring for a family among African Americans, it may be considered antithetical among whites (Hill Collins 1990).

Conclusion

Black students in college, ones who have made it through a pipeline of success, have already overcome many of the hurdles we typically conceive of for minorities. These students may well not match the profile of their counterparts who did not go to college or ones who attended less selective institutions. Once we allow that this is a select population and that career aspirations may not be influenced in the same ways as other forms of achievement, it is evident that both race and class have strong effects on these students' options. The trouble for black participants was not a lack of support or poor academic preparation. Some lower-income students actually cited their socioeconomic background as a rationale to pursue lucrative, mainstream careers. Instead, the primary obstacle facing working- and middle-class African Americans appeared to be a dearth of concrete exposure to opportunities and paths to careers—during and prior to college. Black families' often lesser ability to provide their children with cultural and social capital beneficial to occupational mobility reduced some of the strong positive effects of their high expectations.

As we will see in the chapters that follow, the structural barriers of race, not class alone, affect African Americans in ways that white students never have to consider. Although we cannot immediately change the situations in which these students are growing up without restructuring social inequalities, we can change how these students see their abilities, opportunities, and locus of control. While in college, we can better moderate the options and opportunities to which African Americans are exposed. The idea is to dodge the status quo of presenting only a sociology of failure; myriad studies already present cogent reasons and descriptions of the disadvantages of racial minorities. I do not discount these hardships. But it is equally important to consider what strategies have been used by students who experience the same disadvantages but are able to overcome them. This book repeatedly asks the question, what is it about some African American students—beyond their financial background—that allows them to succeed where others fear to tread? Families are the first place to start.

Having faced conditions very different from those their children face and in some cases having little understanding of what they will confront in college and beyond, many black parents or caretakers may find themselves at a loss about how they can help their children make the best occupational choices possible. Yet, basic awareness of a problem and the fundamental elements of how to alleviate that obstacle can be extremely powerful. The same loving and encouraging parents and loved ones that pushed these students to excel can also alert them that they need to aggressively seek out and pursue opportunities available at college. Equally important, they can remind students that the same intellect and talent that got them into such select institutions can be applied in college and as they develop their aspirations and make choices.

4

THE ROLE OF THE UNIVERSITY

For Toni, getting into Stanford was one of the greatest thrills of her life. Stanford was her first choice, and she and her mother had been quietly praying that she would be admitted. With a broad smile, she recalled the moment she found out:

> I never thought that I could go to a place like Stanford. I came home and my mom was kind of nonchalant about all the schools that I got into; we were both kind of secretly, not secretly but silently wishing that I got into Stanford. And I came home one day from school and the envelope was face down, so the only thing you could see was "Congratulations" in red. I dropped my books; I remember it was right there on the dining room table. I dropped my books and tried to hold it in. I'm like "Thank you Lord," cause I knew I had gotten in, "Congratulations!" And then I'm jumping up and down; I'm rolling on the floor. I mean my neighbors were like, "Girl, what's all the noise coming from over there?" And I was screaming, you know like crying. And I'm like, "I'm going back to wake mom up! Mama!" and you know, of course she knew. And she's back there crying and telling someone else on the phone, "My baby is going to Stanford; I gotta work five jobs! My baby got into Stanford!" She was not emotional about any of the other schools; we were both kind of waiting for Stanford.

This was indeed a tremendous feat. Toni grew up in South Central Los Angeles in what she referred to as the "poor inner city," although her mother had managed to get Toni enrolled in a preparatory high school program at a California university. Toni's mother, a preschool teacher and data entry clerk, raised her, and Toni had little knowledge of her father. In the spring of her senior year, Toni had already been admitted to a number of other prestigious schools including Yale but was far more enthusiastic about Stanford because of her perception of the racial climate at Yale. "I could have gone to Yale, and honestly if you're going to think in terms of the name, Yale is a better school, but I didn't want to go there. It was a whole lot of white people at Yale, and that was scary."

In contrast, her visit to Stanford had reinforced her desire to attend and set the tone of her college experience. "I came here and loved it; I just absolutely loved it. I had so much fun Admit Weekend. I saw the black and brown communities gather and unify. I saw causes over and over again."

Stanford also provided Toni with a "full ride"; at that point, she made her decision. Once she got to Stanford, she immediately immersed herself in the black campus community, spent considerable time at the black theme dorm, and committed herself to community service activities, all closely related to her desire to own a nonprofit organization dealing with inner-city schools. Given her interests, her social circle, and her major in urban studies, her aspiration to work in the nonprofit sector—an area in which African Americans are significantly represented—running an organization geared toward minority populations made perfect sense.

Like Toni, Jane was a native Californian. She grew up in Oakland in a predominantly black and Latino, lower-income neighborhood in the San Francisco Bay area but attended a local preparatory school. Unlike Toni, Jane's parents were still married although their combined income was quite limited. In some respects, Berkeley was Jane's first choice. She had attended a small liberal arts school for one year and then transferred to Berkeley after braving one New England winter. The transition, however, had been relatively simple. Berkeley provided Jane with a good financial aid package, and she was able to take advantage of in-state tuition; the $15,000 she estimated she would need to repay after graduation was far less than it could have been.

Once at Berkeley, Jane became friends with a racially and nationally diverse set of students and chose to major in development studies, both of which were in keeping with her aspirations to work as a diplomat, an area from which African Americans are visibly absent (for more see Krenn 1999). As she explained,

> My love of history, my love of people, and my desire to experience things outside of the confines of the United States [helped shape my aspirations]. I had

one professor who took an interest in me and he was like, "You really should look into the Foreign Service, especially since you have that interest, especially since you're open minded about new experiences. This is something you should check out." And he directed me to the website and was like, "focus, focus, focus." And so I think that helped me look for an opportunity.

Jane, in fact, went out of her way to explore her career options. "When I think about my experience, most of it was self-directed. I sought out people who I thought would be able to help me." Her ultimate goal was to become secretary of state—a notably nonracialized job with considerable power. To determine the best route to that position, Jane had been very aggressive. "I'm very assertive. I don't know if it is rude or brash to ask people, 'What exactly do you do?' and I joke with people all the time and ask, 'Can I have a shadow day with you, just to see what it is you do?'" There is no doubt Jane had leadership potential. She had been the president of a large black women's alliance on campus and made every effort to say hello to everyone with whom she had even a remote acquaintance.

How did two young black women with similar backgrounds at highly selective schools wind up with notably disparate college experiences and occupational aspirations? Certainly, their experiences prior to college helped shape their interests. Yet to get a comprehensive picture of the source of these differences, it is also important to recognize the significant disparities between Stanford and Berkeley. While both are advantaged schools, representative of the types of education available to academically accomplished African Americans (DuBois's Talented Tenth), they are distinct from one another in many ways including racial diversity and the support mechanisms provided for students of color. There is indeed a terrific irony in these differences. By doing its best to bring in, educate, and support black students, Stanford has created a situation in which their black undergraduates enter a smaller range of occupations than they would had they attended an institution which places a lower priority on racial diversity[1] and interests such as Berkeley.

Institutional Differences

Stanford is one of the most elite private schools in the world, with an endowment of $7.6 billion. Its undergraduates comprise approximately 47 percent of its student population and have an average class-year size of 1,680. Admission at Stanford is exceedingly competitive; the university admitted only 13 percent of those who applied for the 2002/3 freshman academic year and only 8 percent of transfer applicants. Resultant cohorts are extremely accomplished; close to nine-tenths of the students enrolled in 2002/3 were in the top 10 percent of their high school classes and over three-fifths entered with math or verbal SAT scores between 700 and 800. Stanford is also racially diverse, particularly when compared to many other universities, including Berkeley. African Americans and Hispanic Americans each comprise roughly 10–12 percent of the undergraduate student body; Asian Americans make up 24 percent; and whites hold just under 50 percent of the seats (Stanford University 2003).

To accommodate its African American students, Stanford built a large black theme dorm (which includes an eating hall) as well as a black community center, and even holds an independent black graduation. In terms of basic infrastructure and representation, Stanford is clearly committed to enrolling and retaining black students. The result is a strong Black Community (henceforth capitalized for its organizational nature), which encompasses a close-knit group of students who maintain extremely tight social networks through social activities, living and dining arrangements, and organizational affiliations. This community is also highly segregated—both from students of other races and from African American students who are not a part of it. The students in this group hold many seats in official black organizations on campus and are more outspoken than the average college student, black or white, about political, social, and economic issues affecting African Americans. Although an outsider may not have any way to discern who belongs and who does not, African Americans on campus—regardless of their affiliation with the Black Community, know who is in and who is out.

Despite Berkeley's standing as one of the top universities in the country, the average scores of its students fall well below those of students at Stanford. Just over one-quarter of students came in with SAT verbal scores 700 or above and under half had math scores in that range. Berkeley also has a notably smaller black undergraduate population. Asian Americans are the largest population, occupying over 40 percent of the more than 20,000 undergraduate seats; whites claim 30 percent; and, aside from international, American Indian, and Hispanic American students, African Americans are the least represented. They comprised only 4 percent of the freshman class during the year of this study (University of California Office of the President 2007) although they represented roughly 7 percent of the 2002 California high school graduates (Reed 2005).

The racial difference in the student populations of Stanford and Berkeley can be partially explained by recent changes in the State of California legal infrastructure and federal judicial challenges. California is one of a growing number of states that have revised their use of racial preferences in admissions and employment. In 1995, the Board of Regents of the University of California system voted to eliminate affirmative action in hiring and admissions, effective the following January. The result was a 53 percent drop in the number of African American applicants admitted to the University of California Berkeley between 1997 (the year prior to Prop 209) and 2002, and a 41 percent decrease in the proportion of African Americans in the admitted class (University of California Office of the President 2007).

Berkeley not only has a substantially smaller proportion of African American students than Stanford but also does considerably less to support its students of color on campus. At Berkeley an office devoted to African American students is located within their multicultural center, and its black theme housing is home to just over 50 students. Effectively, physical spaces reserved for black students are relatively insignificant entities on Berkeley's campus. Although Berkeley provides African American organizations with space to meet and organize (as it does for most formal organizations on campus), there is no one place large enough for a significant number of black students to congregate on a regular basis; more important, there is no single place in which African American students are consistently separated from the rest of the campus.

While Berkeley does have a Black Community, the size of the black population and capacity of black students to maintain segregated social worlds are notably different at Stanford. There are hundreds of student activities at Berkeley, more than thirty of which are targeted at African Americans; they range from the arts, to academic, to preprofessional, to community service, just as they do at Stanford. And while these organizations at Berkeley meet on a regular basis, the students involved in them are compelled by institutional constraints to interact outside the classroom with persons of other races.

Coupled with the isolation generated by low proportions of minority peers and faculty, a lack of diversity restricts the types of interactions students have in and out of the classroom. These interactions, in turn, help shape the ways in which black students see the world, form their values, and cope with adversity. To understand the impact of Black Communities on African American students, however, it is important to appreciate why black students at predominantly white universities maintain segregated social networks and what these networks look like.

College Segregation and Social Networks

When African American students attend colleges that are not historically black, it would appear they have far more opportunities to comfortably integrate their social circles. That is, there are enough people of other races for them to have at least some daily interracial interaction, and there are enough African Americans with the same level of education and on the same type of achievement track for black students to feel less isolated or marginalized by making friends outside their race. But this did not prove to be true for all of the African American students in this study. Some maintained racially insulated social networks and were wary of students with more integrated relationships, particularly at Stanford.[2]

While past studies have shown that students engage in segregated or integrated social networks based in part on their prior experiences with diversity (Saenz, Hoi, and Hurtado 2007)[3] or their socioeconomic backgrounds, the actual dynamic proved to be far more complicated. Black students in segregated social networks came from small towns and large cities, predominantly white prep schools and all-black inner-city schools as did their peers with integrated social groups. And, although African Americans had a lower scale of family income than their white counterparts, African American students with segregated and integrated networks came from a similar range of socioeconomic circumstances. White students reported family incomes that ranged from $43,000 to $650,000 annually with a median of $120,000. In contrast, African Americans with segregated and integrated networks reported family incomes ranging from $20,000 to $120,000 and from $14,000 to $300,000 respectively, and both had median incomes of $70,000.

Although family income did not appear to play a role in whom black students befriended,[4] a number of factors seemed to influence their openness to diversity and social integration, including courses, housing arrangements, extracurricular activities, the institutional support of segregated activities, as well as purely personal preferences and experiences. Moreover, the type of counseling students had received at home about racial matters, the support or lack thereof from peers in dealing with racial antagonism, the environment in which these incidents occurred, as well as the students' own predilections, all interacted with one another to shape the outcome. In effect, openness was a "cumulative result of a set of interrelated experiences sustained over an extended period of time" (Pascarella and Terezini 1991, p. 610), not any one experience.

Today, predominantly white universities and colleges continue to be challenging environments for black students. African Americans attending these institutions encounter discrimination, stereotypes, low expectations, and negative attitudes among other things by their peers, faculty, staff, and administrators alike. The amount and degree of racial antagonism on campuses may well be surprising to some who picture universities as bastions of liberalism and political correctness. Thus, the experiences of black students within a university are often qualitatively different from those of their white peers. In general, a significantly greater proportion of students of color view college campuses as "racist," "hostile," and "disrespectful" and report significantly more harassment than do both male and female white students (Rankin and Reason 2005).[5]

Although white students also varied in terms of whether their social circles were segregated or integrated, the ramifications of this did not appear to have an obvious relationship to their occupational aspirations. In fact, only a few white students had predominantly nonwhite social networks; most whites had purely white social networks or ones with a single nonwhite member.[6] Certainly, the benefits of diversity for students of all races has been well documented including increased cognitive function and improved problem-solving abilities (Gurin et al. 2002; Chang, Astin, and Kim 2004; Levin, van Laar, and Sidanius 2003). Moreover, in order for there to be segregated social groups of other races, white students themselves have to be relatively segregated. The difference is that while the absence of students of other races in their social networks has implications for their opinions about race, whether they are in diverse or segregated networks, white students in university settings do not feel marginalized on account of racial antagonism against them. Black students, on the other hand, do face feelings of ostracism and must find ways to cope.

One way African Americans handle this sense of social marginality on predominantly white campuses is to form predominantly African American social groups (Fisher and Hartmann 1995; Feagin 1992). Black student groups are frequently defensive responses to racist campus environments (Feagin, Vera, and Imani 1996). As Jodi, a black student at Stanford explained, "I think African Americans in general have a tendency to gravitate toward one another simply because of all the stigmas and stereotypes that are out there, either toward us, or that we have as a community toward the way we're viewed."

Within racially segregated groups, students may develop solidarity, live together amicably, celebrate their cultures, and find relief from oppression. "As long as they cohere, they need not feel too much haunted by their problem" (Allport 1979, p. 149). In fact, one of the primary reasons African

Americans in this study gave for maintaining segregated peer groups in college was their expectation of discrimination. What segregated social groups provide to students apprehensive about or tired from dealing with racism is essentially a safe haven—a place in which they are unlikely to face racial antagonism.

Chapters 5 and 6 address at length, the racist and discriminatory incidents that most of the African American students endured prior to and during college. While most black students were cognizant of experiencing some form of racism in the past, particularly within academic environments, these prior negative experiences were likely to be exacerbated or triggered within a college environment. A multitude of academic research gives light to the numerous everyday racialized experiences faced by black students on white campuses (Feagin 2006; Feagin, Vera, and Imani 1996; Bonilla-Silva and Forman 2000). Even in situations in which students of other races, frequently white students, believe they are acting liberally, their behavior may be racially offensive. Consider, for example, Leslie's recount of an incident involving the boyfriend of her roommate:

> My roommate freshman year, her boyfriend was like, I think it was a race/ black/gender thing. He was kind of hitting on me and alluding to sexual stuff. It was racial, because when I first met him, he was like, he's from New Hampshire, so no black people, right? So when I first met him, he was like, "Oh, I take African studies classes," and I was like, "So? I don't care; get out of my face." And he was like, "Oh, I really identify with the black experience . . ." and it was like, "No you don't, you're from New Hampshire and you're white. You don't even know real black people." And he just said a lot of ignorant stuff.

She evidently was agitated by what her roommate's boyfriend likely believed was innocuous if not open-minded behavior. Leslie and others were faced with a sort of liberal racism disguised as or mistaken for progressiveness in which black people are considered an "exotic" other.

Chris explained that the most "frustrating" part of this sort of racist treatment was the offenders' refusal to recognize what they had done or said as racist. As a relatively forthright person, Chris generally attempted to address each incident she observed by calmly telling the offender that what they had said or done was insulting. Their responses, according to Chris were, "Denial, which is like always the reaction: denial that they didn't mean that, and that's not what they mean, and that I shouldn't have interpreted things like that."

Black students also contended with blatant bigotry on both campuses.

Jason referred to the "racially questionable dialogue" he encountered frequently at Stanford. As an example, he recalled a joke he heard.

> There was this joke that some people, some nonblack people said that, you know a person on an airplane, and there's too many people on the airplane and they start tossing people, sort of weight issues. So they start calling out, "oh, let's have the African Americans," and a few people would go. And now the blacks, and now the colored, and the darkies, and yadda, yadda, yadda, and they just go through the list. And there was a dad and a kid who were just not standing up. And the kid asked, "Why aren't we going?" And the dad says, "Well, for today son, we're niggers." And they'll tell this joke and I'm like . . .

For Jason, however, this type of joke was minimal relative to other things he had experienced both on and off campus. "I know, it's like that joke you think, 'Oh my God,' but that's not the thing that's going to make my life more difficult. What's going to make my life more difficult would be being judged and denied social opportunities . . . It's more like the systematic stuff. It's not the things you'll forget in ten minutes."

Paul, a Stanford student, pointed out that he saw racism on campus, "damn near every day" in a variety of contexts. One type of incident occurred repeatedly during walking tours of Stanford. He explained that a common feature of such tours is "impromptu" conversations with Stanford students, yet the guides frequently avoided approaching him if there were white students available.

> Just, just little ways. I feel like I would say from the littlest ways like tour guides walking by our house. And I'll be sitting there, maybe with a little do-rag on or something, you know. And then there'll be someone else sitting in the yard, and they'll [the tour guide] kind of walk up to the other person and ask them [to speak to their group].

These events, coupled with the general perception of many white students (and others on campus) that African Americans displaced more deserving whites in admissions, created an air of intolerance. Consider Clegg's claim that "Implicit in the praise for diversity is the notion that we shouldn't have rules or standards, and shouldn't require people from other cultures to conform to them" (Clegg 2000, p. B8).

In response to the large and small, implicit and explicit racially antagonistic experiences that black students face on campus daily, some turn to segregated social networks as a coping mechanism. Toni clearly believed the sizeable Black Community at Stanford's campus made a difference in her comfort level. "I think that because the black community at Stanford has such a large presence, I don't ever feel like I'm in a minority here. And also with the classes that I've chosen to take in my department there are a lot of people of color."

In fact, Toni actively avoided organizations, classes, and social activities that were not majority black. At the time of our interview, Toni was dropping a class on technology in the Islamic world because, "I'm the only black person in there. And there's a disproportionate amount of white males. I'm dropping that class. When I think about it, my comfort level when I'm there is, I don't feel comfortable in that environment."

Thus Toni immersed herself in racially segregated social activities, chose classes based partially on racial composition, and selected activities that were both rewarding to her and safe: all things she could do with relative ease at Stanford.

Janelle, another Stanford student, believed it was particularly important for her to socialize with other African Americans and felt she had lost out by not living in the black theme dorm. Since freshman year she had made an effort to be sure she made black friends by attending, "primarily black events, or events sponsored by black organizations . . . And yeah, interacting with other black students in different ways, either in classes, or through organizations, or socially, just by hanging out."

She cited the closer connection she felt to black students as part of her connection to the Black Community on campus. "I've felt more comfortable with African Americans here at Stanford. I guess maybe because I feel like we have similar goals in terms of our future, what we want out of our futures, and academics and things like that."

Part of the reassurance she felt in getting to know African Americans with similar experiences and goals, however, had also reinforced Janelle's feeling that on Stanford's campus, having black friends was essential to her well-being. While there, she maintained an all-black circle of friends and counted herself among the members of the Black Community.

Another—but not extraneous—appeal of segregated peer groups, particularly at Stanford, was the social activities and strength involved in many of these groups, in particular, the organizational characteristics of the Black Community on campus, which often functions as an informal organization. Though there are many small networks within this community, the Black Community constitutes an umbrella network of African American students who primarily participate in exclusively black social groups. At Stanford, unlike Berkeley, this network is relatively large given the higher proportion of African Americans on campus (despite Berkeley's greater overall student population).

As noted at the start of this chapter, Toni had based much of her decision to attend Stanford on the Black Community there. She commented: "One of the reasons why I chose Stanford [was] because when I came here on Admit Weekend, I saw the strong, very out there black and brown communities that I dealt with in my high school, and I'm like, yes!" Similarly, Leslie explained that her primary reason for attending Stanford was the appeal of its Black Community. She had lived in a predominantly white neighborhood prior to college, and attended predominantly white schools. Her friends growing up, however, were mostly African American, attributable in large part to the racist attitudes she felt were pervasive in the area in which she lived. Leslie had visited the university shortly after being accepted and believed her exposure to the Black Community on that trip had been a deciding factor in her ultimate college choice: "When I visited, I stayed at Uj [or Ujamaa, the black theme dorm], and there was such a stark contrast compared to my high school; it was a black community—one existed here and it seemed really close. It was very visible, and I felt like I could go here and not feel isolated from other black people."

As Leslie suggested in her account, it isn't simply a matter of there being enough African Americans for black students to feel welcome at Stanford. Instead, there is a thriving, autonomous community that provides a very different campus experience from the mainstream Stanford arrangement. While there was also a Black Community at Berkeley, its size did not offer students the same sense of solidarity that existed at Stanford. Hence, its appeal was primarily limited to students trying to avoid or cope with racial antagonism.

Not all African American students at either university felt they needed a safe place, however, and not all African American students who desired some same-race friends expressed an interest in maintaining an exclusively black peer network. Indeed, those involved with integrated social groups had a significantly different outlook on their experiences confronting racism. Students who shied away from segregated networks felt they did not need the protection of or exposure to other black students provided by these networks. Jane actually cited diversity as something that made her feel secure. "Race is not a determining factor of my comfort level, but there is some comfort to be within a diverse group of people. I mean with diverse backgrounds, diverse viewpoints, and diverse experiences. It's just comforting because you know that everyone has differences."

The insulation of segregated groups was, in fact, frequently a deterrent to students who had more integrated social circles. Shelly, an African American Berkeley student who hoped to become a travel writer or journalist, described her aversion to racially segregated groups. "Being in a group that segregates themselves is just, is bothersome to me. I've been . . . You know, I'd feel uncomfortable in that. Yeah, I mean, I have friends here who are African American, and I hang out with them sometimes, but I don't necessarily hang out when they hang out."

Similarly Roger, despite having had a predominantly black social circle prior to college, felt that being part of the larger segregated black network at Berkeley would have meant acting contrary to his own nature. He was clearly aware of the minimal number and proportion of other African Americans on campus, lamenting, "Sometimes I go wow, there aren't that many black people here, you know, and I feel kind of weird when there's very few." Yet Roger also felt out of character participating in the Black Community.

> Up here I don't hang out with that many black people, and I feel kind of weird. So going to college, I don't know, I just don't know if I want to do that. It would be not myself, and I'd have to put on more of a front of being blacker than I am, and that's what I do not, another reason why I didn't want to have to worry about that, and another reason I didn't want to go to a seriously black college.

While clearly some students with integrated networks found segregated communities problematic, it also meant that they had to approach racial antagonism in a different way, that is, without the support of this sort of group. John, a student at Stanford who wanted to be a pilot and engineer in the military, had a philosophy on dealing with race issues somewhat characteristic of those African Americans who had a racially integrated social circle. In discussing race relations at his high school in Texas (one in which there were very few African Americans), he observed that he was discriminating in the racial problems he chose to address.

> We were pretty well integrated into the school setting. And for the most part, there really wasn't a problem, but at the same time, it is the southwest. You've got your racists is what it boils down to. And you'd figure out who they are, and you deal with them as little as you have to, and you go on about life. And sometimes there'd be points changed, and other times they don't. Most days [racial tension] was very low key. Obviously though, if people were drinking a little bit, it'd come out a little bit more. But at the same time, a lot of times it wasn't directed at me. I was sort of the accepted one. After you spend a year or

six months in the system, you are one of the family for the most part. And so they didn't really look at you as black.

Although John's later point about not being seen as black may be contrary to the experiences of other students, his initial commentary gets to the core of the thought processes of many African Americans with integrated networks. While most maintained a concern about racism in the broader picture—belonging to black activist student groups, volunteering within lower-income black communities, and maintaining memberships in national organizations—on a day-to-day basis, it was not a consideration. When racist incidents did arise, however, students with integrated social groups faced them and then continued on with their lives. They did not generalize their experience with persons of other races and were therefore able to sustain interracial friendships, dealing with each person they met individually. In general, these students might be considered "balanced" (Grant and Breese 1997). They are aware of race, frequently proud of their racial heritage and struggle, but are able to interact with people from different groups comfortably.

The disparity in the belief systems of these students is perhaps most evident in the answers students provided about their views on race relations. During our interviews, participants filled out a form identifying how they characterized the way they thought about racial inequality and selected from among several possible answers. Their options were: "You're as good as anybody else," "Recognize that all races are equal," "Blacks don't have the chances that whites have," "None of the above," and "Other." Students had the option to check as many as applied. African American students with segregated social networks on campus most often chose "Blacks don't have the chances that whites have," whereas black students who had more integrated social networks, like most white students, picked "Recognize that all races are equal" or "You're as good as anybody else" most frequently.

Not only does this suggest that different coping mechanisms among black students are related to different attitudes about white society and predominantly white spaces, but it implies that a primary source of these mechanisms lies in the degree and type of racial segregation or isolation experienced by these students while in college. Those students who had considerable anxiety about their position as underprivileged minorities or otherwise marginalized persons had or developed a stronger need to avoid potentially aggravating situations by segregating their social networks. Conversely, those who had a balanced outlook were more capable of sustaining friendships and interactions within a more integrated social group. Thus, "the more students interact with diverse peers and the greater the extent to which such interactions focus on controversial or value-laden issues that may engender a change in perspective or opinion, the greater one's development of openness to diversity and challenge" (Pascarella et al. 1996, p. 188).

Hence, regardless of the ways or reasons by which students decided to engage in segregated social networks, the effect was both to reify the benefits of that group—celebration of blackness coupled with protection from outside hostilities—while cutting off the possibility that interactions with individuals from outside could sway their perceptions about those groups. Prior research (Sidanius et al. 2004) has shown that while a sense of victimization or presumed conflict do not significantly influence the likelihood of students joining ethnic specific organizations, membership in these groups produces a significant increase in the sense of victimization and zero-sum conflict between ethnic groups. Moreover, attributing negative experiences to prejudice actually increases the salience of racial group membership and motivates people to become increasingly dependent on their own racial group to build a positive self-concept (Branscombe, Schmitt, and Harvey 1999; Crocker and Major 1989).

Having grown up in what she described as "a pretty mixed" neighborhood and having had friends from a "variety" of races, Laurie, a Berkeley student interested in nonprofit work, concluded that her interactions with segregated black networks had heightened her awareness and concern about race. She asserted that this trepidation had grown as she'd "been at [Berkeley], just because I've been able to interact with some [social] groups that are ethnically specific. I've become more aware of it." This was, as she explained, not something she had felt prior to college.

> Like I was saying, when I was younger in high school, I was trying to always hang out with the people who were, who looked like they had some kind of inside connection with the teacher or seemed like they were going somewhere: they were going to college. I would be hanging out with them. So I wasn't really worried about being the downest, you know, black person. I never kind of was interested in that.

She termed her newfound consciousness a "psychological thing" which she believed had arisen during a retreat sponsored by an African American student organization—one dominated by students with segregated social groups. As Laurie described it, "they were always talking about, you know, 'we have to, we're a black community.'" Although her association with this particular group had tempered after her freshman year, she felt that it had had a lasting effect.

> [Race has] become a lot more important since that high school weekend, that black senior weekend. Sometimes I wonder if I just came to Cal, would it have been the same experience if I hadn't been part of that organization. I don't know. But I guess because of that, when I first got here just meeting all, a whole bunch of black students when I got here and the whole black community, that made me want to be a part of it. And so now it is important.

Similarly, Beth, an African American student at Stanford, described how concerns about racism and her discomfort around persons of other races had become increasingly significant since she was at college. "It is important at least to have, I would say, other minorities, preferably African Americans around. I think so. And I might not have said that before, but I think as I get older, I start to notice more things that actually do bother me that I thought didn't bother me before."

Despite Beth's initial contestation that her lack of nonblack friends was entirely unintended, I gathered it was more than a coincidence that she had made no Caucasian friends (or friends of other races) over the course of her residence in an almost entirely white dorm.

Although Beth had not requested to live in the black theme dorm her freshman year, she had been randomly placed into it. In her second and third years, however, Beth did not get her first choice in housing and had to move elsewhere. As she pushed herself to understand her lack of white friends, she struggled with her own responsibility for this outcome. Race, she declared, "Wasn't even something that I thought about before . . . I'm not the kind of person who would think about stuff like that." By "before," Beth was referring to her years in high school during which she had maintained a diverse group of friends; when she entered college, however, she placed into the black theme dorm and quickly found that all her friends were African American. Reluctantly, Beth acknowledged that for her, the ultimate priority in selecting friends was in feeling safe. Referring to her lack of white friends she stated, "I don't even know if it's discrimination [on her part], or if that's a bad thing. Besides, my greater concern is that I feel less comfortable in white environments than I used to." This type of increased anxiety about interracial interactions is actually relatively common. Prior research confirms that having fewer out-group friends heightens anxiety about being around people of different races later in college (Levin, van Laar, and Sidanius 2003).[7] Thus Beth's freshman year in the black theme dorm made it less likely that she would befriend students of other races in subsequent years.

This book does not seek to establish an exact process by which African American students in segregated networks and those in integrated groups arrive at certain perceptions or values. While some students may have entered college with them, the dynamics within these groups may also lend themselves to certain beliefs and behaviors. The point is, there are divisions among black students with segregated networks and integrated networks that appear during college, and these differences have implications for occupational aspirations.[8]

Social Networks and Aspirations

So how did students' aspirations vary by race and social network? There are significant contrasts in the occupational aspirations of African American students with integrated networks, African Americans with segregated networks, and white students (fig. 7). On one extreme, white students reported a wide range of occupational aspirations, none of which had any racial focus nor a high percentage of African Americans in the workforce. In contrast, black students, particularly African Americans with segregated networks, often chose occupations in which African Americans are highly concentrated and/or racialized occupations (Collins 1997). The eleven African Americans with self-reported segregated social networks professed career aspirations including nonprofit employees, a social activist/social worker, a civil rights attorney, an editor of a women-of-color magazine, a principal, and a business owner. Those aspired to by the nineteen black students with racially integrated social circles included a medical researcher, a strategic consultant, a video game programmer, an engineer, and a senator.

While these figures are far from definitive, they do suggest a basic difference. While some of the African American students with integrated social networks aspired to racialized careers in fields such as nonprofit work, civil rights law, and careers in which African Americans are more represented, a greater proportion of students with segregated social groups were drawn to racialized careers and occupations with relatively higher proportions of African Americans (fig. 7). The emergent trend is that black students with segregated social networks are selecting occupations that directly target the black community and ones in which they will not feel isolated. In contrast, those with integrated networks are choosing a more varied set of careers

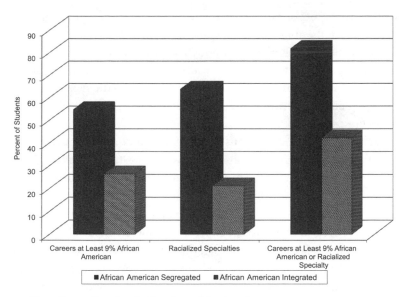

Fig. 7. Occupational aspirations by social network

which are generally higher-paying and higher status with less of a direct emphasis on African Americans.

Of the eleven black students with segregated networks interviewed, seven showed a preference for a racialized specialty within a broader career field (such as nonprofit work for African Americans, black product marketing, civil rights law, etc.) and six aspired to fields in which African Americans are more strongly represented including nonprofit or social work. In the end, only two of the eleven African Americans with segregated social groups selected occupations that were not either or both racialized specialties or at least 9 percent black. The numbers for African Americans with integrated networks are considerably different. Only five of nineteen with integrated social groups planned to work in fields that were at least 9 percent African American, and four aspired to racialized career fields. In the chapters that follow, I explore the ways in which concerns about racial antagonism, values, and social capital result in the considerable racial and network differences in the occupational aspirations of students (see fig. 7).

The Black Community at College

Given the differences in the aspirations of students, not only by race but by social network, it is important to consider the role universities play in students' social groups. Most germane to this book is the significant difference between the ability of black students to maintain segregated social groups at Stanford and Berkeley. Although some of this may be due to differences in the students attending these institutions, it is also attributable to the numbers and proportions of African Americans on the two campuses and the administrations' respective responses to black student groups in the past and present.

At Berkeley, African Americans are 3–4 percent of the population. Although this equates to roughly between 720 and 960 students in any given year, their visibility is minimized by the enormity of the undergraduate population alone. With approximately 24,000 undergraduate students, 720 African Americans spread across a large campus are barely visible. Many get together because they need sometimes to feel like less of a minority or outsider. But size itself is actually a major deterrent to isolationism at Berkeley. Black students are hindered from having strictly segregated social networks because Berkeley's black population is such a small portion of the student body. Conversely, at Stanford, many people cite the large and active Black Community as the reason they were attracted to the university. Since African Americans compose approximately 12 percent of the population on campus, the Black Community serves not only as a shield from racism but as a visibly active group. Whether African Americans (or students of other races) at Berkeley choose to have segregated social groups is not in question. Some do so; they eat at predominantly black tables in the cafeterias or sit only with other black students in classes just as many white students do with other white students. But at Berkeley, there is little space that can accommodate black students' preferences to meet, eat, or live consistently based on race. The Black Community is not reinforced by institutional support and its grasp on black students is relatively smaller.[9]

Stanford, however, does have amenities that permit a physical separation of African American students from the rest of the campus. Approximately 94 percent of students live on campus in a variety of dorms and houses, including the black theme house. The goal of the theme house is to provide social and educational opportunities centered on African American culture. Stanford first established ethnic theme dorms in 1970 under pressure by the Black Community Services Center and the Black Student Union, within a cyclone of debate. The first black dorm, Ujamaa, a name it was later given, was followed by Asian American, Chicano American, and Native American theme houses in 1971 (Devasher 2002).

The house proved to be particularly significant in the formation of aspirations of African American students at Stanford and is examined more in later chapters. Although Ujamaa (commonly referred to as Uj) houses only

131 students—half of whom are black—annually (just over 10 percent of the black population),[10] its impact on the Black Community extends well beyond basic accommodations for that 10 percent. Because the house emphasizes the African American culture, priority for assignment to Uj is given to African American students; the result is a 50 percent African American and 50 percent non–African American racial composition. As a consequence of Stanford's housing assignment system, the majority of black students in Uj elected to be there. Yet for the majority unable to get housing at Uj, there are many opportunities for socializing, particularly at mealtimes. Not only do students who live in the black theme dorm eat there, but many other black students not living in Uj also eat and socialize there regularly. It accommodates far more than the 10 percent of the black population that is assigned to live there at any given time and thus serves not only as a residence but also as a center of African American student socialization. Black students can effectively maintain separate social lives from others at Stanford, and those in the Black Community exercise their right to do so. To be clear, however, it is not the racial and ethnic organizations (whether professional, academic, artistic, social, etc.) that appear to have a relationship to students' aspirations. Although some students may join them for the same reasons they have segregated networks or are active in the Black Community, many students who participate in racially specific organizations have well-integrated groups of friends. Rather, it is the ethnic theme dorms, the center of the Black Community, that are associated with occupational interests.[11]

Given its institutionalized nature at Stanford, the Black Community, not surprisingly, has a stronger hold than it does at Berkeley. Leslie, who identified closely with Stanford's Black Community explained the reactions the community had to people they might refer to as "incogs."[12] "As long as you participate in something, it's okay. But if we never see you in the Black Community, then people assume automatically that person doesn't want to be black, or doesn't realize that they are."

What is most salient here is the expectation of participation on the part of the Black Community at Stanford; it is a force that students who wish to be at least somewhat active in black-oriented activities must contend with as it calls into question their racial identity. Jason gave a detailed description of the pressure he saw coming from the Black Community:

It's a pressure to hang out with them and them alone. And particularly if you're not spending time with them, you're not being authentic to the community. It's almost like you're not, without them, if you just do your thing and try to survive at school; that's not sufficient. You have to go to certain black activities too; otherwise it's like you're not acting on your implied validation to hang out with them. I think the other pressure is you need to fulfill certain roles . . . Those are the pressures. And if you're not, if you don't fulfill those traits, you're not authentic as being part of the community. So that part's like, you're selling out, because you're being more politically white.

This pressure to participate, however, sometimes scared African American students away. Carol, a Stanford student described how she felt about the Black Community.

There are times where I've been affected by what black people have to say; the whole incog thing really spun me for a loop when I first got here. That was like the biggest thing, because I already came in with this issue about not being black enough. I always felt like the black kids were like "Oh, you're not black enough," because I was the only black kid in most of my classes.

She explained that the stigma associated with being an incog intensified the pressure to participate; if you do not get involved, "it means that, you know, you're selling the idea that you're better than." Yet despite the pressure, the obligatory nature of participation drove her off. She felt insulted by having to prove her blackness, something other African American students noted as well.

Linda, another Stanford student, attested to the pressure referenced by Carol and Jason and indicted it in the underperformance of black students on campus.

There's a lot of emphasis put on, you know, not just going undercover and being a student and sort of working your way in anonymity, but actually being an active part of the community. Like that is a really big deal that bothered me about that. I think there's a lot of pressure on people to really deal with that, and I think it's unfortunate because it's really hard. There's a lot of people at this university that don't do anything but study, you know. You don't see them because they're always studying. But there are also people that do things, like I sang for two years and I did other things, like I did the competition last year for architecture, and I did a play my freshman year. And when you do other things that puts you at a disadvantage. And I think they put pressure on members of the community to be really, really, really involved in the community at risk of being, I don't know, exiled or something. I think that's unfortunate, because a lot of people end up doing not that well in school. And I don't think it's because they're not smart enough; it's because they spent like twenty hours organizing the BSU meeting, or the NAACP meeting. And I think that, yeah, I think that some people need to be the ones who are out in the classroom, like busting the curve and pulling people along. I just think they're just serving the community in that one way.

Linda did, however, have close friends who were black. She did not disavow the importance of race or associating with other African Americans, but she made it clear that race was not a primary factor she considered in making friends.

I have black friends that I value a lot, and I found all my friends are minorities, and many of them are black, but I didn't pick them that way, and that wasn't important. And I don't think I would ever say that I would try to become friends with somebody because they're black . . . I don't think I've ever based any of my really close relationships on anybody's race, ever.

Instead, Linda had participated in a minority mentoring program, a singing group recognized for its racial diversity, and attended events sponsored by the Black Student Union and NAACP. Her six closest friends included an Asian American, two African Americans, and four persons of mixed race. But according to Linda, the races of her friends had not been a factor in their friendships, at least not a conscious one.

While smaller and less visible, the Black Community at Berkeley exerted the same type of pressure but to a lesser degree than the one at Stanford. Referring to the definition of a sellout she attributed to the Black Community, Laurie observed, "I feel that's the kind of pressure that the Black Community puts, or some parts of the Black Community put on people who aren't necessarily always down with everything, and partying, and doing stuff [like] that; I can't, I don't know if I can say majority or not, but a good portion of the Black Community."

Similarly, Jane explained that she felt considerable pressure from other black students to participate in the community, but she had managed to maintain her own sense of what was important. "Yes, I feel it from certain groups very specifically to get involved on campus. But I think for me it's more important that oppressed groups have a voice and that policies are directed to leveling out inequalities. When I see people or groups that don't encourage that kind of leveling out, I feel like they're selling out." Rather than adhere to what she saw as hollow demands, Jane saw participation in a diversity of jobs and activities, not social groups, as important to what she referred to as "leveling out."

The primary difference between the two Black Communities, therefore, did not appear to be in substance; Jane and Laurie described an outlook by students in the Black Community at Berkeley similar to that at Stanford. Instead, the distinction was in these communities' different capacities to exert pressure and enforce their values on their members or the black populations at their respective campuses.

The main finding here seems contradictory to the relative prestige of each institution and the degree of importance they confer on diversity. Given the higher status of Stanford over Berkeley as an academic institution as well as the degree of support Stanford provides its students of color, one would expect the aspirations of black students at Stanford to be more diverse than those of their Berkeley counterparts. That is, students at Stanford, ones who by any measure represent the best and brightest of all races, should feel encouraged to participate in a variety of academic disciplines and to seek out a diversity of career options given the commitment and support Stanford provides for their success. But because of the strength and force of the Black Community at Stanford, the outcome is contradictory. African American students at Stanford involved in the Black Community faced three major disadvantages. First, they are involved in a community large enough to exert considerable peer pressure. As discussed later in chapter 7, this pressure is often focused on active participation and avoidance of selling out (often defined as working in careers not directly related to the African American community). Second, Stanford's students were frequently preoccupied with racial disadvantage and contended with magnified and often unenlightened fears about mainstream careers. And, third, because students' social networks were constrained to other African Americans, the limited resources and social ties of their friends, which mimicked their own, restricted their social capital further. Less pressure and smaller numbers resulted in the need to associate with other races at Berkeley, even the incapacity to do otherwise. Thus, African American students at Berkeley were more likely to consider a greater diversity of job options than their Stanford counterparts.

Conclusion

As noted at the start of this chapter, the role played by a university can be significant in students' formation of career interests. Black students at predominantly white universities face an obstacle with which white students do not have to contend: their race. Regardless of their socioeconomic background, family support, religion, or educational interests, black college students, like all black adults, face a burden that they feel both in extreme instances of racial antagonism and in their daily lives. In college these students are challenged not only with the academic rigor confronting all students but also with a constant battle over their social identities and the perceptions of these identities by others. How a university helps students face these challenges can, therefore, have a lasting impact on their future.

Segregated social networks are a draw to some black students at predominantly white universities. They function not only as places in which their culture(s) can be celebrated and acknowledged but as sanctuaries from the many forms of intolerance, ignorance, and hostility endemic to such institutions. Whether it is a matter of avoiding the feeling that they must serve as constant representatives of their race, as educators to uninformed peers, or as the scapegoats of problems on campus, their concerns are real and understandable. Although African Americans at any university can opt to maintain segregated social networks, my findings indicate that the ways in which universities recognize, accept, and support this may impact other aspects of students' lives.

Several black students in this study did maintain segregated social networks at Berkeley, but the majority did not. By revoking the use of race in its admissions considerations, the University of California's Board of Regents has shown relatively little support for a diverse atmosphere, especially at its flagship schools. Yet the university itself does support the black students on its campus in some ways. It does so largely through affording space in the multicultural student center, offering assistance through the Black Student Recruitment and Retention Center, funding student organizations, and providing such organizations with formal recognition. On the other hand, the drastic drop in faculty of color in previous years, the awareness and effects of Proposition 209 looming, and a small black student body can hardly be said to foster diversity or provide a supportive environment to black students. Thus, African American students at Berkeley find mixed support for their experiences and interests. Clearly, however, the university provides minimal institutional sponsorship of physical segregation of students by race, thereby inducing students to find information through mainstream campus mechanisms.

Stanford is significantly different. Like Berkeley, there are myriad activities—academic, extracurricular, and professional—targeted at black students. Unlike Berkeley, however, there is a large African American student presence, and university-sponsored living quarters and dining facilities provide a portion of this student body the option to live and socialize differently than they otherwise would on the mainstream campus. And, while the purpose of this and other chapters is not to assail the rights of minority students to self-segregate in college or the rationales of universities to aid students in doing so, institutional support of this behavior, however judicious, must also be thoughtful.

The debate over theme dorms is nothing new. During their inception in the 1970s and 1980s, they came under considerable attack and have been at regular intervals ever since. For instance, in 2002 the conservative think tank, the New York Civil Rights Coalition, presented a scathing report of what it deemed separatist and paternalistic practices on campuses across the United States. Aside from ethnic theme dorms, the report took issue with minority affairs offices, academic courses on minority issues, multicultural centers, and minority mentoring programs. Referring to minority academic centers, the report claimed that, "In a not-so-subtle way, some colleges tell students of color that they as minority students need special help to succeed in a competitive environment" (Afshar-Mohajer and Sung 2002, p. 18).[13] Furthermore, "By giving each minority separate support systems, the college suggests that ethnicity-specific support is preferable to general student support services. Paternalism is clearly at work" (p. 23). Similarly, referring to multicultural curriculums, Schlesinger (1992) asserts that:

> The militants of ethnicity now contend that a main objective of public education should be the protection, strengthening, celebration, and perpetuation of ethnic origins and identities. Separatism, however, nourishes prejudices, magnifies differences and stirs antagonisms. The consequent increase in ethnic and racial conflict lies behind the hullabaloo over "multiculturalism" and "political correctness," over the inequities of the "Eurocentric" curriculum, and over the notion that history and literature should be taught not as intellectual disciplines but as therapies whose function is to raise minority self-esteem. [P. 17]

Detractors of multicultural or racially targeted programming also cite the lack of similar white-oriented student programs. Dinesh D'Souza, for example, argues that, "White students generally have no desire to set up their own racially exclusive unions, clubs, or residence halls" (1991, p. 238). Of course, charges such as these are without merit; white students, by their very predominance on campus, have a variety of informally racially restricted associations and physical spaces including college fraternities and sororities. In fact, desegregation since the 1960s has not brought fundamental changes in the character and cultural norms of white institutions. For the most part white regents, administrators, faculty members, staff and students have shown little willingness to incorporate black values, interests, or history into the core of campus culture. At predominantly white colleges most campus activities reflect white student and faculty interests and traditions . . . This situation encourages black students to congregate in their own groups and plan their own activities, a reaction that often brings white condemnation. [Feagin and Sikes 1994, p. 95]

This book does not, in any way, concur with criticism that special minority-focused programming is problematic. Multicultural centers, academic and social advising, non-Eurocentric curriculums, and programs aimed at campus diversity are all fundamental to successful minority and white experiences on campus and later in life.[14] The reality is that some minority students do need special support—not remedial instruction—to navigate through an often racist environment at a time that is confusing to anyone their age. However, multicultural theme dorms perhaps one of the greatest institutional structures impacting the social interactions of black students in this study, despite being supportive environments, do appear to have secondary effects that should be addressed.

Theme housing such as fraternities and ethnic program dorms actively inhibit students' exposure to diversity—racial, economic, political, or cultural—a claim that remains undisputed by its proponents. Instead, an increasing body of work demonstrates the wide variety of benefits diversity has for minority and white students both during and after college. For example, prior research shows that informal interactions with peers of other races has significant positive effects on the intellectual engagement and academic skills of black, white, Latino, and Asian students alike. Likewise, classroom diversity positively influences these students' active thinking and intellectual engagement (Gurin et al. 2002) as well as their self-reported intellectual ability, social ability, and civic interest (Chang, Astin, and Kim 2004). Interracial interactions on campus also help quell racial animosity by decreasing ingroup biases and intergroup anxiety (Levin, van Laar, and Sidanius 2003).

These types of results can have profound effects on students' lives after graduation as well. Over half of black respondents and close to 50 percent of whites in the 1989 cohort studied by Bowen and Bok (2001) report that racially diverse interactions in college had contributed positively to their abilities to get along with people of other races, providing them with useful skills at work, civic activities, and at home. (For an overview of the effects of diversity in organizations, see Milem 2003.)

Given the recognition many university administrators accord the significant role diversity plays in shaping the cognitive, intellectual, and social abilities of young people, it is important that they consider its impact on the aspirations and choices of black students after college. If universities such as Stanford are supportive of segregated arrangements such as ethnic theme dorms, they must also recognize that information flows into those spaces differently than it does to the rest of the campus and influences the way students experience and perform while in school. As I discuss in the following chapters, information about careers, jobs, and job-related opportunities may not make its way to a space separated from the rest of the campus or may be interpreted differently. Likewise, these residences may impact student perceptions and expectations of racially diverse environments. Supplementing segregated networks and the spaces they inhabit, therefore, is the least an institution that purports to value diversity can do to provide students with the full benefits they need and deserve.

5

MAJORITY RULES

Apprehension, Racism, and Racial Representation in Occupations

Over the past several years, political pundits and academics have pondered whether we are now a postracial America, that is, one in which race is no longer significant. And since Barack Obama's election to the presidency, that speculation has mushroomed. The term itself began appearing with frequency in the mid 1990s in response to the O. J. Simpson verdict, the Congressional reelection of two African American politicians (Sheila Jackson Lee in Houston and Eddie Johnson in Dallas) in minority black districts, and Tiger Woods's rise to fame. Yet America is assuredly not postracial, nor was it at the time of my interviews. The recollections of students in chapter 4 alone remind us that racism remains a reality, even for black elites. One need only observe the protracted debate over affirmative action or the persistence of residential segregation to recognize that racism is an institution in the United States that will not die quickly. African Americans are undeniably the most systematically avoided group in this country. This aversion to blacks is evident in the extreme measures taken to block residential integration such as redlining, insurance and mortgage discrimination, racial steering, and white flight (Massey and Denton 1993). Perhaps equally telling, African Americans are the racial minority least likely to marry outside their race (Fu 2007; Qian and Lichter 2007).

While Obama's election did signal a shift in the degree and type of racism within the United States that should not be taken lightly, it was not a transformative event like the passage of civil rights legislation forty years earlier. Part of Obama's appeal to whites was his "postracial persona and political stance" (Bonilla-Silva and Ray 2009, p. 178). Although white perceptions of African Americans may well be shifting, especially among younger generations, the reality for most black people is that race and racism are of immense importance to their experiences and prospects. Instead, perhaps the most important signal from Obama's election was African Americans' perception that change is possible. This is reflected clearly in the record 66.8 percent voter turnout by blacks, one that surpassed the prior 58.5 percent record of 1964 (Bositis 2008). Yet even the meaning of Obama's election among blacks suggests that African Americans see substantive change as a long-term process. According to surveys taken shortly before the election, blacks believed this change was largely symbolic whereas whites saw it as just the opposite (Hunt and Wilson 2009).

In chapter 2, I detailed the significant discrepancy between white and black perceptions of racism. Civil rights and affirmative action legislation may well have led whites to believe that African Americans now receive preferential treatment; yet African Americans experience daily the lack of impact much of this legislation has had. While blacks remain acutely aware of racism and racial inequalities, whites believe we live in a far more progressive, meritocratic society. This is apparent in the dissimilar perspectives on affirmative action in college admissions. A 2003 Gallup Poll that asked whether individuals favored or opposed affirmative action programs for racial minorities yielded patent differences in opinions. While 70 percent of African Americans favored affirmative action, only 44 percent of whites did so. Similarly, when asked in 2006 who would be accepted if equally qualified black and white students applied to college, 64 percent of whites believed the black student would fare better, while only 4 percent of African Americans agreed with them (Gallup 2005).

It is also clear that whites see the preferences they believe exist for African Americans as unfair. When asked whether applicants should be admitted solely on the basis of merit or if an applicant's racial and ethnic background should be considered to help promote diversity on campuses, the vast majority of whites, 75 percent, said that merit should be the only consideration (Gallup 2005). Hence, the very presence of African Americans on campus draws skepticism among whites.

At the same time that students are forming their career aspirations, African Americans suffer exposure to situations in which their merit and presence is questioned by peers and professionals. Coupled with their earlier experiences with racial antagonism as well as understandings of race and racism passed on through parents and friends, black students must grapple with what they will face in the future. Several of the black students in this study based their career aspirations, in part, on their desire to avoid racially antagonistic situations. For some, concerns about racism in occupations were influenced by their social networks, whether those networks emphasized the omnipresence of racism in the workplace or stressed the benefits of diversity. For others, the relative importance of economic struggles played a greater role, shaping both how African Americans chose to deal with racism and how significant it would be in their futures.

Coming from Personal Experience

By the time they entered college, most African American students had experienced some degree of discrimination or racism, and they continued to encounter it in their university. In fact, almost all African Americans recalled with ease, several specific stories of racial antagonism during our conversations. Regardless of which state students hailed from, what socioeconomic background they were raised in, or what type of primary or secondary schools they had attended, all African American students had experienced racial antagonism. The only way such characteristics seemed to vary was in how students experienced it—overt versus genteel, with the police or with teachers.

Jane, the Berkeley student referred to in chapter 4, classified the racism she had encountered throughout her life as "a blunt reminder of how hard it is" and went on to describe a situation she confronted during her senior year of high school at a predominantly white prep school in California. "I don't know how the conversation came up, but we were all on the morning bus going to school, and some kid made this statement. I think I was complaining about something, and some kid made this statement like, 'Yeah, well we didn't ask you to come here.' And I was like, 'Excuse me? What?'" Although it was not an isolated incident, Jane had taken this confrontation in stride. Yet as the spring of her senior year rolled around, and Jane and her classmates became aware of their college options, her peers voiced doubts as to why schools such as Berkeley admitted Jane. "There were the comments like, 'Oh, you're only getting into these colleges because you're black' . . . different things like that where people kind of second-guess why you're there or how you got there, and are very quick to scale it down to a matter of race or gender instead of your own abilities and intellectual capabilities." Jane's experiences represent the type of everyday racism that African American students, especially those who attended integrated schools, are exposed to frequently. Such encounters serve as persistent reminders that black students are not welcome in a particular environment and that others second-guess their accomplishments, presuming that their success was handed to them because of their race.

Another African American woman, Janelle, had grappled with racism in her high school as well. As part of a community service requirement at her boarding school, many of Janelle's classmates had involved themselves in a tutoring program for underprivileged children. Emphatically she described what had ensued.

> There's a community service requirement and a lot of the kids who come in [to be tutored] are black. And [white students] called [the children] "Niglets"; other people doing the community service called them "Niglets." When I found out about the "Niglet" comment, I was really upset. I wrote a letter to our newspaper and I wanted someone to do something. And nobody did anything. The reasoning of the house who put on this program was "Well, we're not even the worst. You should see what the guys in the other house say." Just that kind of incredible insensitivity.

For Janelle this experience reinforced feelings of both marginality and impotence. Not only was she now aware that referring to black children as Niglets was considered only a minor offense on the spectrum of racism among her peers, but her attempts to reprimand those guilty of the racist acts proved futile. The "Niglet" incident was quickly swept under the rug by students and administrators alike; Janelle, however, did not forget it.

Other students questioned the way teachers or counselors had steered them. Sandra, the child of Nigerian parents, both of whom held graduate degrees, had attended a predominantly white science and math magnet high school and had performed quite well academically. Over the years, she made many friends but had become extremely close with Clara, an "Amerasian" student who had attended school with Sandra since the fourth grade. By senior year, the two were neck and neck in terms of GPA and class rank. Yet although the counselors and teachers encouraged and expected Clara to apply to Georgetown and other prestigious universities, Sandra believed they anticipated far less of her, based in part on their recommendations of a number of less competitive state schools. Referring to the contrast in expectations of herself and Clara, Sandra noted that, "Everyone was really supportive and kind of just expected that of [Clara]. But I don't think they thought of me the same way." Notwithstanding her high grades and scores or the myriad activities in which Sandra had participated, school officials never recommended Stanford or any other elite universities. Instead, despite dissuasion from her counselors, she applied to Stanford at the insistence of her parents, strong in their belief that her abilities and qualifications had been disregarded by the very people who were paid to appreciate and encourage them.

Unfortunately, for most black students exposure to racial stereotyping continued in college. Sharon solemnly recounted her first and only visit to a professor's office hours. When she introduced herself to this particular professor, an older white gentleman, his first response was to ask which athletic team she belonged to at school. Yet Sharon was not an athlete, nor had she been one in high school. She was a woman of average physical build whose manner of dress indicated, if anything, an artistic flare. There were no markers that would imply that she was on any team—no team uniform, sportswear, or athletic musculature—except that because she was black, she fit a stereotype: an African American whose only reason for admission could be explained by athletic prowess.

Sharon's experience of being stereotyped was not unique among black students in college. Dave's black persona was often judged, both by Stanford affiliates and outsiders. He recalled a specific incident in which a fellow passenger on his flight to Stanford during admit week had casually applied a stereotype of black college students to him. "I was on the plane out here, well it was either on the 29th for admit weekend or on the plane back, I think it was up here. And this woman was sitting next to me and she was like, 'Where are you going?' And I was like, 'Yeah, I'm headed for Stanford,' or something. And she was like, 'Oh, you play basketball?'"

But Dave, like Sharon, was not an athlete. Nor was this an isolated incident. When he and his roommate moved into their dorm earlier in their junior year, there appeared to have been some confusion about just what type of students they were. The two had first been assigned to a relatively small room on the third floor of their dormitory but later found that a larger room had become available on the first. According to Dave, the higher floors are coveted by students who tend to socialize more frequently and with more vigor, while the first floor is often inhabited by more scholarly students. Evidently, this difference was apparent to the residential assistant, a middle-aged white man, who felt it was only appropriate to point out to the two young black men that they might want to reconsider the switch since the first floor was likely not "the kind of place [they] would feel comfortable."

Experiences of Past Generations

Over the years, the African Americans with whom I have discussed the types of experiences and concerns mentioned above have offered varied reactions. While younger African Americans tend to express sympathy for these students and their unease, older people often scoff at the gall these students have to complain about what they view as frivolous inequities. Those who were part of the civil rights movement tend to express scorn that the students profiled in this book have such "thin skins" and argue that the African Americans of their generation endured far worse with considerably more fortitude.

It is therefore ironic that the concerns expressed by African American students were based not only on their own experiences, but on those of their parents, grandparents, and others who were part of the movement— both active and passive—and have been a part of the black workforce for years. Indeed, many African American students reported that their parents or close family members had spoken to them frequently about their own experiences with racism as they were growing up and that such conversations had directly impacted their career aspirations. Moreover, the most significant feature of these stories is that they usually pertained to the job discrimination faced by these older generations.

Jane, for example, grimly described a common theme of household conversations about her father's career:

> My dad has talked about experiences where, you know, a company will allow him to educate [other employees] . . . He was like one of the first people in the architecture world to get into CAD technology and [his employers] kind of pressed him to get that knowledge and learn it, but it was like, "Okay you can train these people," and then those people would be promoted over him.

Although Jane had managed to remain firm in her intent to pursue a career that was predominantly white, her father's frequent comments appeared to have increased her apprehension about future discrimination. Reflecting on her father's experiences, she stated, "in that sense, yeah, I definitely get more upset" about potential discrimination and explained that one of her priorities in choosing a career was to avoid having to work for others lest she be passed over for reasons other than her abilities.

Jackie, the daughter of a Korean mother and African American father, also grew up hearing about her father's encounters with racism. Born in 1942 and raised in rural Georgia, Jackie's father had been ineligible to vote in 1961 when he joined the army. His high school diploma was the last degree he received, and aside from an unrewarding career as a serviceman in the army, he had managed to find only temporary retail jobs in the years following Jackie's birth. The paradoxical nature of being able to serve his country in the military while not being permitted to vote, along with a number of other setbacks he attributed to racism, left him bitter and resentful. As Jackie was growing up, she and her father often discussed race in reaction to news reports of current events. His response was consistently one of anger toward whites, and, though comical, her description of her father's "muttering" was also telling. "Have you ever seen the Chris Rock thing, where he talks about how he's got an uncle that hates white people? That's my dad, he hates white people. My dad is very power to the people. Yeah my dad was like, 'Arr, arr, I hate white people!' You know, 'This country is so blah blah racist.'" Compounded with her own experiences of racism, Jackie's expectations and aspirations for her future contended with the anxiety implanted by her father's outlook on race relations.

Jane and Jackie's observations are just two examples of the many instances in which students referred to reflections on discrimination as common household topics. Indeed, this sort of attention to racial problems is common among black families. Of the thirty black students interviewed, Jesse, an engineering student with plans to extend his education to the doctoral level, was the only one who could not recall his parents having discussed racial antagonism or personal experiences about race. It is worth mentioning that both of his parents were Nigerian expatriates who had lived the majority of their lives outside the United States, away from the type of racism endemic to this country.

The emphasis on discrimination common among black families is generally intended to prepare children for life as black people and to provide them with tools to cope with racial antagonism (Lareau 2003). It became clear, however, that anxiety about the possibility of racial antagonism was an unintended side effect of these discussions. Jackie, for example, listed racial diversity as one of the most important things she sought in a career. Specifically, she desired a place that valued diversity enough to promote its minority workforce. As Jackie phrased it, "I want to work somewhere that values diversity more than just, you know, diversity they can put in a picture. Somewhere that actually likes to hear opinions. I feel like people say they want diversity, but they really just want you to be there for when they have to take pictures to put on the company's website." She was cynical about the possibility of finding such a job in mainstream corporations. Although she retained a positive attitude about her own abilities, she said she could hear her father whenever she became too positive about her prospects: "It's just sort of like my dad talking to me, like, 'Oh, they might say xyz, but . . .' That is, you can come, but what's it going to really be like when you get there?"

White Experiences

Such concerns, however valid, were nonexistent among white students. Perhaps not surprisingly, white students and their parents had very little experience on the receiving end of racial antagonism. White women, however, had often felt the sting of sexism and contended with misgivings about it in much the same way that black students contended with racism.

Sarah, a white student at Berkeley, had at one point considered going into business but was now interested in a career in travel fiction or possibly in diplomacy. She described an unpleasant incident of sexual harassment that had occurred during her internship with a prestigious investment bank the previous summer and made it clear that this ordeal had influenced her career interests significantly. Over that summer, Sarah was repeatedly harassed by a supervisor who referred to her as "the cute blonde one." On one occasion, he interrupted a conversation between Sarah and a male coworker to question the young man's sexual intentions toward Sarah. This incident was a turning point for her. Detailing how she handled the situation, Sarah acknowledged, "I didn't make it a big deal. It was . . . I said I had to leave because I'd found another job on campus. I just didn't like it." Referring to the type of environment she would now like to work in, she said, "What I do not want is what was at [Firm X], which was all old white males. I couldn't handle it . . . it was just so horrible." The experience was, in fact, pivotal to Sarah's career ambitions. And while such encounters did not make Sarah or other white women more apprehensive of racism, it did correlate to a greater sensitivity to black concerns relative to their male counterparts.

The experience of white men in this area was drastically different from those of African Americans or white women. With only one exception, Jonathan, a Jewish student who described having a classmate in junior high school repeatedly use the word "kike" in jokes, white men were unable to recollect any events of actual racial antagonism. Instead, when asked if they had ever experienced any form of racial discrimination or hostility, white men were likely to recount incidents in which they felt "uncomfortable" when they were in predominantly black situations, but without exception, the situations described by these men were always nonconfrontational.

Joe, an affluent, white Berkeley student, described such a scenario in which he and his girlfriend missed the last train out of the city back to school one night.

By now it's like 5:00 in the morning when we get there, and we just missed the connection to get to [school], so we have to sit there another hour. And so luckily the driver decides to stay there so we don't have to wait outside in the rain. But then all these people start getting on the bus. And it's Saturday, 5:00 in the morning; I'm wondering, "What the hell are these people doing out?" And it's a bunch of black people, and it's me and my date, who is this short Filipino girl. And this gang of people just walks in, and they're all like, "Who are you?" You know? And it was just the weirdest thing I've ever . . . They were just out for the whole night, I guess. And then this really old black guy steps in and starts talking to the bus driver about his life and smoking a cigar in the front of the bus. I just, I thought it was weird. I mean that did kind of freak me out. But then all these guys, there were maybe ten of them; they sat in the back of the bus. And I could really feel like, all right, this isn't my place here, because you know, obviously, physically we stood out. Obviously I didn't want to be there, I wanted to be at home. And they had just gotten there; they wanted to be there. And yeah, I . . . I didn't feel unsafe. I didn't feel like, "Oh my God, they're going to beat me up and rape my girlfriend," I didn't feel like that at all. But I did feel like, you know, a level of . . . uncomfortable.

Without prompting, Joe insisted he was only uncomfortable and not fearful of rape or assault. He presumed to know the motivation of the other bus patrons, whom he described as a "gang," yet he had given no thought to the possibility that the African Americans entering the bus at the same time were, in fact, on their way to work. It was after all five in the morning, a time many working-class people head to their jobs. Moreover, he had not considered that he and his girlfriend had also been "out the whole night" and that the others riding the bus, who he assumed "wanted to be there," may have found themselves trying to return back to their homes in Oakland or Berkeley just as he was. This sort of defensive strategy is often used by whites who presume they are being attacked or threatened by minorities (Feagin 2006).

Because like Joe, most white people have not had to confront racism in any serious capacity, racial representation within a job or classroom is not necessarily salient in this context. They do not have to be concerned (for the most part) that they will face any racial discrimination, although some white men did express concern about confronting reverse racism. For most whites, racism is the "prejudiced behaviors of individuals" rather than an institutionalized system of advantages that benefit them (Tatum 1997, p. 95). On the contrary, African Americans have very real concerns about the racist incidents that have often transpired in their lives or those of persons close to them by the time they make their career and academic decisions.

Connecting Race to Careers

Considering their personal experiences as well as those of family and friends, the African American students in this study had justifiable reasons to anticipate some degree of racial antagonism in predominantly white environments. Prior empirical research on occupational discrimination suggests that lost opportunities—personal or communicated—can depress minority abilities and motivation in the workforce (Greenhaus, Parasuraman, and Wormley 1990). Unfortunately, understanding that discrimination is more prevalent in occupations where blacks are less represented could give way to anxious expectations that discrimination would be endemic to those fields.[1] Thus, some students became wary of predominantly white occupations; some saw occupational racism as yet another hurdle they would have to face but could handle, and still others saw it as incidental relative to what they had already overcome.

Regardless of how they approached occupational racism, however, it was clear that most African American students had given serious consideration to how race might impact their careers and some were able to detail exactly what aspects of their work would be affected. In response to whether he was worried about being discriminated against, Dan, a Berkeley student answered simply, "Yes . . . I am concerned about that," and went on to describe his consternation about encountering discrimination in his future career as a doctor. Although Dan did not identify the specialties he was referring to, he noted that this apprehension had impacted which fields he was considering. On the top of his current list was general practitioner, the most common field of medicine among African Americans (Arcidiacono and Nicholson 2005).

Similarly, Jeanette, a black Stanford student who planned to be an OB/GYN explained, "If my goal in the future still remains to be to open up my own clinic, there's a lot of respect and perceptions that can affect your clientele, and how respected your practice is. And so being a female as an OB/GYN isn't a big deal, but being African American, I think, would be a bigger deal in terms of what people think of reputation." When prodded about her choice of specialty she mentioned that she had considered dermatology and orthopedics but that, "I don't think I'd ever do it . . . I don't think I'd do very well, because it's male, white male."

Yet, while Dan and Jeanette clearly attributed part of their career choices to potential racial antagonism, others did not openly admit to doing so despite their preferences for racialized occupations. Jackie, whose father had told her repeatedly of his personal experiences with racism and who now planned on going into black product marketing, grappled with how much power race had in her life. On one hand, Jackie regarded others' reactions to her race as significant to her potential for success. Race is "important, only because it's important to the people I will be around, and what I will be trying to do with my life in the future."

Her reflection closely resembles Beverly Tatum's observation that, "The parts of our identity that do capture our attention are those that other people notice, and that reflect back to us . . . that which sets us apart as exception or 'other' in their eyes" (1997, p. 21). Yet on the other hand, Jackie fought vigorously to retain some control over the role race and racism played in her life. While she acknowledged the consequence of race in people's perceptions of her, she also felt that she maintained some agency in the importance of race because her chosen career was targeted toward the African American population. "But [race is] going to be important because I'm going to make it important, not because it has to be important . . . It's not the end all be all." Of course it is hard to decipher what role racism played in Jackie's choice. She had dealt with racial antagonism in the past but retained a considerable concern about its role in her future. As discussed earlier in this chapter, her father's experiences with discrimination echoed in Jackie's head whenever she considered her career prospects. It is arguable that Jackie's desire to choose a racialized subfield was in some way related to her father's warning that working for others, particularly whites, was the wrong path to take. Likewise, Jackie's later commentary in chapter 6 on her choice of college major and her concerns about being stereotyped had a considerable amount to do with both how she believed others thought of her and how she chose to respond to those perceptions. In effect, race matters for African Americans both because society deems it significant and because African Americans value their heritage and connections to other African Americans (Lacy 2004).

Like Jackie, Jesse, an African American student at Stanford, had difficulty capitulating to racism; nonetheless, he had ruled out the military as a career option. Although he had been in the ROTC during high school and previously considered joining the navy as his father had, his dad's past employment with the navy was enough to discourage him. As he put it, "You'll never get promoted there." And while Jesse currently had aspirations to go into product design, a subfield in engineering in which few African Americans work, it became evident that his choice involved (in his mind) a limited potential for discrimination. He premised this notion largely on his expectation of working independently and having limited exposure to the client. When I asked if he was concerned that his college name, something into which he placed great trust, would not overcome others' prejudices, he responded instead that, "Unless they can tell by the name, they may not know at all . . . the client may not see me, so they won't know." Although Jesse repeatedly evaded my question concerning the possibility his degree from Stanford and intent to work independently would not prevent potential racism, he continually pointed to choosing a career in which he would not be seen. As his comments suggest, in some ways Jesse was choosing an occupation with a lower risk of racism. The way in which he sought to avoid any conflict was by becoming invisible—taking a job where his race would be unknown to clients and perhaps to supervisors rather than confronting the racism he acknowledged existed in other parts of the workforce.

These students are just four examples of those who voiced concerns about their potential for success in predominantly white career fields. Regardless of what strategy they chose to apply to avoid racism in an occupation, black students consistently identified racial antagonism in employment as a reality. This was reflected in their answers to direct questions as well as topics not explicitly related to racism. In fact, when I asked African American students whether it was important to work in an environment with persons like themselves, an intentionally vague question, most asked whether my query was in reference to their race. When told it was in reference to "anything," many African Americans answered that chief among their priorities in an occupation was an environment with other African Americans. Will, a black Stanford student stated simply, "As I've gotten older, I think that everything I do as an African American is very important, so it is very important to me having someone I can share my experiences as an African American with, you know?"

This type of response stands in contrast to the reactions of white participants who unfailingly assumed the question referred to anything but race. For example, Jonathan, a white student from Stanford explained that "Forming some kind of meaningful relationship with the people I work with is a criterion. And that would include being like me in terms of similar level of intelligence and similar place in life. I wouldn't want to work with a lot of older people."

Another man, Craig, who hoped to become a physics professor said that he wanted to work with others who shared his interest in science. "I'd like to have at least one person around who knows what I'm talking about . . . I would like to work someplace where there's at least one other person I could yell at, 'look at this cool thing.'"

As these quotes imply, for white students, personality type, general interests, and a variety of demographic characteristics were things they considered potentially important. Sharing experiences with other members of their race or having a strong white presence in a career, however, were evidently not a part of this calculus. Although this may be the result of being part of the majority (or close to the majority) on campus and in the workforce, most of the white students seemed unaware of this or other advantages of being white. This likely reflects the nature of whiteness as "unmarked" (Brekhus 1998) or inferred through the "other," so that whites are unable or unlikely to see their own advantages (Frankenberg 1993).[2] Some scholars (e.g., Bonilla-Silva 2003; DiTomaso, Parks-Yancy, and Post 2003; Frankenberg 2001; Omi and Winant 1994) argue that this lack of awareness of privilege is part of an ideology that appeals to whites, in part, because of its disavowal of white privilege. Others (Lipsitz 1998) assert that the normative nature of whiteness and the absence of racial disadvantages among them renders whites oblivious to their advantages or the disadvantages of others. Regardless of the causes, however, the omission of race in the list of characteristics that appeal to them as well as the absence of inquiry into whether my question pertained to race reinforce assertions that the disposition of "whiteness" itself has considerable impact on the thoughts and actions of white people. Indeed of all the students I spoke with, only a few white women were able to identify the existence of white privilege.

Linda, a white Stanford student interested in working at an NGO with refugees, explained:

> I think that I've definitely had opportunities that have been easier for me to get, that allow me to pursue things that other people might not have been able to pursue, because of my race and ethnicity. And I also think that I can have a platform to speak on to the majority, being a member of the majority, If you were a minority person you might get labeled just a special interest.

Deborah, a Berkeley student, echoed Linda's comments stating: "I think I have, um, I mean based on what I've learned in classes and certain diversity trainings and such, I know I'm privileged because I'm white. And so I think even going into a job interview, I would probably be able to land a job better based on the way I look. I think that will definitely have a hand in things."

In contrast to Deborah and Linda, who openly acknowledged the role of white privilege in their lives, many white students did not believe racial hierarchy had anything to do with their success or others' lack thereof. Instead, racism remained a minority issue to them just as sexism has been characterized as a woman's problem (McIntosh 1993). Whites and people of color tend to have different definitions of racism (Bonilla-Silva 2003); while people of color generally characterize racism as something systemic that pervades most aspects of life, whites typically make no distinction between racism and prejudice. Race played a marginal and sometimes positive role in most white students' interpretations of their experiences and aspirations, often going entirely unnoticed. It therefore had little if any conscious function in their occupational goals. Paradoxically their occupational interests may reflect and reinforce their own privilege, as most of the occupations they showed an interest in were predominantly white.

Coping with Racism

While all black students were aware of the existence of racism and the vast majority of African Americans could recall numerous racially motivated incidents or conversations with their parents or other adults on the matter, not all African American students indicated a significant concern about confronting racism in the workplace or a substantial need for racial representation within an occupation. Two areas in particular seemed to mediate the desire to work in fields or occupations explicitly related to or commonly held by African Americans. First, it seems that participation in segregated social groups encourages students' concerns about and perceptions of racism. And, second, contrary to what is commonly seen as a double negative—being poor and black—lower-income African Americans maintained a healthy confidence in their ability to overcome prejudice and a lack of familiarity with racial antagonism related to academic or occupational realms.

Social Networks as Sanctuaries

Although this study does not focus on the reasons African American students initially formed segregated or integrated social groups, my interviews revealed differences in the reactions to and expectations of racism between black students based on whether they belonged to segregated or integrated peer groups. One way such differences manifested themselves was in the significance placed on working with persons of the same or other races. While all African American students believed race was a significant aspect of their identities and most felt having other blacks around would be beneficial, black students with integrated social groups, like whites, did not tend to see the racial composition of the job as a key factor in determining their future career. Instead they often saw their experiences as ones tied closely to the benefits of diversity.

For example, Dave, a black man from Stanford, wanted to own a graphic design studio. His closest friends were African American, but he was part of a broader, more integrated social circle. He reasoned that, "It's real important [to have black friends] but it's important to associate with other races too, though. Maybe even more to associate with other races."

Likewise, Theresa, an aspiring attorney, asserted that being in a diverse workplace was a priority for her. "I would love to have African Americans around. But I just think diversity is good in general." In fact, one of the appeals of Berkeley was the racial diversity. In reflecting on her choice of school, she explained, "I really liked the diversity, just the overall diversity. I like having the ability to have white friends and have black friends."

Contrary to the experiences of other African Americans, however, African American students with segregated social groups tended to focus on their identities as marginalized minorities and how that might impact their careers. For instance, Janelle, who had dealt with the Niglet incident, was interested in starting a nonprofit organization focused on the public health of minority adolescents and felt that associating primarily with African Americans (at school and at work) was extremely important for her to overcome feelings of discomfort with other races and the challenges brought about by being black. "I think it's going to be really important. Especially to have people to look to for support or advice. Especially when you get into situations where you might be discriminated against or feel alienated because of your race. It's definitely important because you want to have those people to identify with and share your experiences with." When she looked to the future, she perceived the work world as one rife with bigotry and was concerned about the gender and racial discrimination she might face. Referring to discrimination in her career, Janelle observed, "Yeah, like it's always, always been a concern. Like maybe, definitely more so than in the past . . . as I get closer to, you know, thinking about what I want to do, that's definitely something that remains as a concern." Having a career with other African Americans was important in handling what she saw as inevitable. For her, nonprofit work brought with it not only the advantage of serving other African Americans but also an environment with enough black people to lessen the chances of experiencing racial antagonism and to allow association with others experiencing similar obstacles.

Notwithstanding the comfort segregated social networks promote, certain aspects of these groups may also maintain or intensify concerns about potential racism among students like Janelle.[3] Because segregated groups are formed partially in reaction to experiences and perceptions of racism, these social networks may actually heighten expectations of racial antagonism among some of their members or at the least not lessen them. Equally important, segregation does not allow for disconfirming experiences and may therefore perpetuate the need for avoidance. The heightened awareness of race could actually become a preoccupation for some students. In particular, stories and incidents of actual discrimination within job fields were sometimes communicated in such a way that they became something like urban legends; no one knows who it happened to exactly, or when it happened, but everyone is aware of it, and it was awful.

Stanford student Brandy, who was interested in social work, articulated precisely the anxiety some students felt about what they saw as chronic and pervasive racism in predominantly white occupations:

> Just hearing stories of what happens, being black in a majority white work-force, and even if I [get] more education, I still don't have enough if the places I work will most likely be majority white. So I guess one of the main things I'm worried about is glass ceilings, and also people, I don't know, thinking I'm not as smart as I am, or not respecting me or not thinking I know what I'm talking about because I'm black.

Far less anxious about potential racism, African Americans with integrated peer groups tended to be what some have called "balanced" (Grant and Breese 1997). As I mentioned in the previous chapter, these students expressed an awareness of race as well as an ability to navigate among different groups comfortably and without much thought. John, an African American from Stanford who wanted to be an engineer and pilot in the military, had a philosophy on dealing with race issues somewhat characteristic of those African Americans who had maintained a racially integrated social circle. Although he had many stories of discrimination and hostility from childhood and adulthood to share, he seemed relatively unfazed by the possibility of discrimination in his future. When I asked him whether he was worried about encountering racism in his future job he replied:

> No, it's one of those things that I know exists, and the day I face it is the day I'll figure out how to overcome it. But there's no point in worrying about it, cause then I'm just going to start seeing it everywhere. And more than likely, I'll actually be just creating it rather than actually seeing it, and it's just going to hamper my effectiveness . . . My mother always drilled it into my head that as far as I'm concerned, when I walk into a room, I'm the best person in the room. Whatever it is we're doing, I'm the best. It's up to everybody else to prove me different. The burden of proof is on them. So in terms of achieving

in engineering, in terms of going for my pilot's slot, that's the way I approach life. I'm the best, and if somebody wants to prove me wrong, then go ahead. I'll come back about five days later, and I'll be the best again.

This does not imply that John was unaware that discrimination was possible. He described the relationship between his race and his future as potentially strong. Discussing the possibility of experiencing discrimination in his professional life he commented,

> It's hard to say cause you know, I mean the [military] is still a good old boys network. The majority [of officers], the majority are white, Caucasian. Advancement, yeah, it might have something to do with it down the line. Like I said, there's only one black four-star in the entire [arm of the military]. At the same time, by the time I really get to that level, life may have changed.

Thus while confident in his ability to handle discrimination, John did not dismiss the probability that he would experience it in his career.

Jason, an aspiring CEO, also recognized the likelihood of confronting racism in the future but acknowledged that other factors would contribute to his comfort level at work.

> It's not about the race of people there, or even gender, it's more about what they do. I've had environments with all black people, and I've been totally miserable. And heck, when I go home for winter break, that's a miserable experience. I know; that's just sad saying that. It's gotten better since when I first got home from college, but it's not like I'm having fun, either. It's more about what the environment is than about who is there.

It is perhaps not surprising that Jason was less apprehensive about whether his future career would be populated by other African Americans given his experiences growing up. It seems, however, that he had found a comfort zone in having a multiracial social group and believed, based on encounters with people of a variety of racial groups, that the race of individuals was less important than their behavior.

Low Income as a Source of Strength

Like social groups, for some students economic background appeared to be related to perceptions of racism and occupational aspirations. Although low income could be a considerable handicap for some African Americans in handling the rigors of college, others students found strength in reflecting on all they had overcome. While acknowledging the potential for discrimination, these students recognized it as one among many things they would have to face and were capable of surviving. Paul, an African American Stanford student, stated simply: "I personally think you gotta just, you gotta keep going when it's going to be there." Raised in Ohio by his impoverished aunt and grandmother because of his mother's drug problems, Paul spoke at length of the sacrifices his family had made for his education. He believed that he owed his interest in the CIA to "big dreams" and had chosen to be optimistic about any problems he currently faced, having seen the situations many people from his hometown had to confront. He explained, "I've just seen a lot of extremes. So I've learned to twist that into a positive angle and just go with it." In general, Paul handled racism by disregarding it as best he could. "I think that at this point in my life that you kind of screen it. You screen it, so once you do see it, you screen it so you don't see it. And then in that sense, I don't even get upset over it, at all . . . I don't, I mean I don't even think about it. I notice it, like I could point it out to someone else, but there's no point in me thinking about it."

Paul's outlook on weighing the relative obstacles of race and class is very much in keeping with assertions that the life chances of lower-class African Americans have more to do with their class status than with their race. That is, movement out of the underclass is hampered more by lack of education than by racial discrimination (Wilson 1978). Given the extensive hurdles lower-income African American students like Paul have had to overcome in order to end up at schools of this caliber, it is perhaps understandable that they possess such self-assurance. Yet their confidence in their ability to handle racial discrimination in their careers may also be attributed to having endured what some distinguished as a harsher form of racism growing up. That is, black students from low-income backgrounds were more likely than middle-class African Americans to report having been arrested or involved in racially motivated physical altercations. Paul described one such incident:

> At home, in my town, it's bad with the police. Like every time I go home, everyone's just like, "Don't get in trouble." Cause you just, you get pulled over right off. Like when I went home this time, we were supposed to go to my cousin's graduation, who is my Aunt Diana's son. And we were driving the next day, and then that night we got pulled over. My brother's car got towed; he got arrested for nothing. Straight up nothing. But you just don't have the,

you don't have the lawyer fees and stuff to fight anything like that down there, so you just deal with it.

Having dealt with such overt antagonism, Paul had developed a lackadaisical approach to handling what he believed was a less virulent form of racism at school and among professionals. "Here it's [race] kind of just being discussed; it's not like things get called out all the time. People see things differently. I don't know. It's just not a concern for me here at all. And this is just like a la-la land." Yet despite his assertion that Stanford and the elite world presented less of an obstacle than his childhood environment, he had faith in his ability to handle whatever came up.

> I'm a survivalist, so whatever's presented in front of me, I just take it on. So this really didn't change much. This is like a fairy tale world at Stanford . . . it's just a lot different. Like I said, to me it's like a fairy tale where I need to get caught up on all the things that I'm missing, but I need to just enjoy it and be happy while there are no worries here. There's nothing wrong, there's nothing wrong. Like don't go looking for things wrong.

Accordingly, the race of other people in his future career was of little import to Paul. "I mean, as far as I'm concerned, if I'm in an office with another black person, just because he's black doesn't mean anything. He's still a geek off the street, especially at Stanford. The color thing is just so far beyond me personally."

Still other students, like Toni, who was originally from a low-income neighborhood in Southern California and now attended Stanford, actually saw income as a greater obstacle than any form of racism. Though she often used race interchangeably with class during our conversation, Toni made a distinction between poor and working-class African American students like herself and middle-class black students. When I inquired if she believed the disparities in student behavior at Stanford were based more on economic than racial differences, she answered, "Definitely, I think definitely. I mean, there are some very wealthy African American students here that don't work, that don't have to worry about anything . . . If I don't work, I don't send money home to my mom. If I don't work, I can't pay my bills."

She explained that poor black students had appreciably different options than their middle-class counterparts. In fact, according to Toni, poor white students had more in common with poor black students than middle-class black students. "To me," she continued, "it's more about class than race.

Because there's some, like I've said, there's some really poor white students. I've seen poor whites act like they were struggling just like me, work just like me. And they don't have those options either."

For Toni, middle-class African Americans were so unlike poor African Americans that they, unlike their poor counterparts, could not sell out since they had no connection to poor blacks.

> So what if you're black middle class? Let's say you work for a corporation, and you're black middle class. And you know, there's a black person that needs help and you're not going to help them. But then racial relations don't connect. I think that, I think there's just a difference; class plays a big part in terms of how you see each other in terms of race. And if you're black middle-class, and you've always been black middle class, you never had any relations with lower-class black people and just won't be able to connect that. I don't think black middle-class people have a responsibility to black poor. I think that [selling out is] just remembering your roots.

This type of outlook is consistent with prior research findings that African Americans from low-income backgrounds perceive themselves as being appreciably different than their more advantaged counterparts (Smith and Moore 2000). Such perceptions are often based on the belief that higher-class status insulates other African Americans from many of the problems their low-income peers face. Hence, middle-class African Americans tend to be more race conscious than lower-class African Americans and lower-class African Americans are more class conscious than middle-class blacks (Durrant and Sparrow 1997). Thus, like Paul, Toni perceived race to be less of a hindrance than class. And, while Toni acknowledged that she initially felt as though other students questioned her belonging when she entered Stanford, she "eventually got over it. I'm not as sensitive because I know that I'm supposed to be here, and I have way more confidence; I'm like, 'I'm just as good as you.'" For low-income students like Toni and Paul, the upshot may be that overcoming material disadvantage likely depends on, and in turn reinforces, a strong sense of efficacy, which leaves these achievers far less anxious about the threatened loss of control occasioned by racism in the workplace. Put another way, low-income students who make it into such selective universities are part of a special pool that has managed to overcome significant hardships. By Toni's own recollection, she, not her high school counselors, was the force for her applying to highly selective colleges such as Stanford: "I was always in [the counselor's] face like, 'I need, I need, I need.'"

There is, however, another explanation for the disparate concerns of low-

and higher-income African Americans: the context of racism. That is, while low-income African Americans have experiences that are perhaps more brutal and certainly more violent and though they bear the brunt of structural inequalities built on a racist system, their experiences are generally not directly relevant to occupational racial antagonism. And although this exposure to violent and structural racism may, in the long run, strengthen their resolve, it may not leave them with the same consciousness or expectation of antagonism and discrimination in the workplace. On the other hand, middle-income and affluent African American students have more exposure to racial antagonism within the academic sphere and have adults in their lives who caution them about the perils of workplace racism. When such reminders are combined with personal experiences, middle- and upper-class African American students, who in most other regards would be considered more fortunate than their low-income counterparts, may be at a disadvantage. Unfortunately, as I discuss in chapter 8, the low-income African Americans who did maintain the resolve to exclude potential racism from their career decisions often lacked the social networks to develop or pursue less traditional occupational aspirations.

Conclusion

This chapter suggests that African Americans students' social-psychological reactions, though reasonable, can be complicit in reproducing the gap in occupational achievement. What is important to remember is that students are making decisions in college, both about career paths and about routes to a more satisfying life. Some feel anticipated racial hostility is a legitimate factor to consider in their evaluations of occupational options. However, these perceptions and the responses to them do have ramifications that are worthy of concern. While racism is not an imagined issue in the lives of these students, the tendency to expect it in predominantly white settings may deprive them of opportunities that they might otherwise find attractive. Some African Americans in this study looked to the proportion of their numbers in a career as an indicator of the racial climate. In doing so, they ruled out careers and specialties in which African Americans are currently underrepresented and instead turned to occupations with a higher proportion of blacks or mainstream careers with a focus on black markets.

Social network composition and economic background help explain why some African Americans are less concerned with potential racism than others. Just over one-third (eleven) of the black students interviewed in this study maintained segregated social networks, and while these groups may be beneficial in some ways, they also inhibit African Americans from interacting with whites (Fisher and Hartmann 1995). Although "self-imposed separation" may well be comforting because of the sense of belonging and group worth intrinsic in these circles, inattention to out-group norms and denial of possible similarities, can be harmful and preclude members of marginalized groups from "capitalizing on the opportunities that may actually exist" (Branscombe and Ellemers 1998, p. 259). African Americans who regard themselves as upwardly mobile have to take seriously the importance of getting along with the white majority (Bowen and Bok 1998). Given the racial structure of occupations, the value of learning to handle diversity may be considerable for students in their occupational pursuits. Moreover, "it is not clear that attributing negative outcomes to perceived racism will consistently result in self-esteem protection among disadvantaged group members. In fact, the use of such attributions may provoke problems of a different sort; in particular, some group members may be especially likely to reject devalued group members who voice prejudicial explanations for their outcomes" (Branscombe and Ellemers 1998, p. 259). While the nature of this research precludes me from providing a definitive cause for the heightened sensitivity to racism observed among students with segregated social groups, I offer the following argument for consideration: segregation and sensitivity to racism have a reanimating relationship. That is, anxiety about racism—often informed by first-hand experience—promotes the avoidance of integrated situations that, in turn, reinforces the salience of the issue and therefore the necessity to segregate.

This chapter also highlights the fact that for some participants, low income could be a source of strength. Despite the many drawbacks related to poverty, the students in this research represent a subset of low-income youth who have made it through a pipeline of achievement and survived. Consequently, the drive which allowed some African Americans to persist in situations in which they were deprived of many of the benefits other students—African American and white—took for granted, appears to be a utility in maintaining their career aspirations. Moreover, for some students, the awareness that they had achieved so much, given their background, seems to have instilled a confidence that they could survive other handicaps—such as racism—when faced with them in the future.

Given the concerns most students had about racism in the workplace, the implications for the continued use of affirmative action in both college admissions and occupational hiring are considerable. Although affirmative action is usually rationalized for its contributions to diversity and providing opportunities to those who have been disadvantaged, my findings indicate that affirmative action has a third, equally important role. According to the students in this study, the low proportion of African Americans in many occupations and academic disciplines deters black students from considering them as career options. Therefore programs that increase African American representation within financial, corporate, scientific, technological, and engineering occupations and majors may decrease the perception of racism in those fields and increase their appeal to black students. Put simply, increasing the number of African Americans willing to consider a career by increasing the number of African Americans in that career may be, as one African American student described it, "a natural evolution."

6

STEREOTYPE THREAT

Where Have All Our Scientists Gone?

In March 1999, the year most of our research participants entered college, Jesse Jackson arrived in Silicon Valley and announced that he and his organizations, the Rainbow Coalition and Operation Push, were going to buy stock in the largest tech firms in the valley in order to end discriminatory hiring practices pervasive in the Bay Area. Jackson encountered mixed reception by those in executive positions including a particularly antagonistic retort by the CEO of Cypress Semiconductor, T. J. Rodgers, who challenged him: "I invite Jackson to send me the resumes of those disenfranchised people who've received training from 'the best universities.' With 115 open positions, we could use them. We hire 500 people per year and still never fully meet our needs—just like most other Silicon Valley companies."[1]

Rodgers's response was reinforced by a number of studies of the valley's "workforce gap" that showed, among other things, that the shortage of local high-tech employees had cost Silicon Valley firms approximately $4 billion annually in recruiting and lost productivity. As a result, approximately 160,000 jobs, roughly one-third of the valley's high-tech workforce—were filled by workers from outside the region or went unfilled (Evangelista 1999). According to Ben Smith, a principal with the management consulting firm A. T. Kearney who assisted in preparing one such study, the "gap" cost employers in the area approximately $6,000 to $8,000 a year per vacancy (Evangelista 1999). A *New Republic* article similarly concluded that "By 2000, 60 percent of all U.S. jobs will require technical skills. There are currently close to 200,000 unfilled jobs in the computer industry alone—a field expected to generate more than a million new openings by 2006. No wonder the industry wants to import more foreign workers" (Jacoby 1999, p. 29).

Although Jackson's claim of discrimination within Silicon Valley is not without merit, the relatively low number of qualified minorities, those with degrees in science, math, and engineering, suggests that discriminatory hiring practices are not the only culprit for the dearth of African Americans in high tech fields. In 2004, the year in which participants were expected to graduate, African Americans accounted for 7 percent of the baccalaureates awarded in math, science, and engineering and only 3 percent of doctorates in those fields (National Science Foundation 2007a). In the year prior, blacks comprised only 4 percent of the science, technology, engineering, and math (STEM) workforce, not including social sciences (National Science Foundation 2007b). Such low figures are highly problematic, not only because they are indicative of the lack of African American occupational diversity, but because the STEM industries hold an increasingly high share of this nation's wealth and stability. That is, fewer African Americans in technological and scientific fields mean a smaller minority share in the wealth of the scientific and technology industries. In 2003, for example, 11 percent of federal budget outlays went to science and technology development and training (Government Printing Office 2005).[2] This number does not include outlays to natural resources, defense, or energy, all of which rely on persons trained in science, math, and engineering. Moreover, the scarcity of black scientists negatively impacts the types and amount of attention African Americans as a group receive in scientific (especially medical) research. That is, the lack of African Americans in scientific and medical research is mirrored clearly by the lack of research conducted on diseases, health issues, and environmental concerns that disproportionately or differentially affect African Americans. The manifest white maleness of these fields guarantees minimal consideration will be given to such fields in the future, for research tends to have an autobiographical slant.

Explaining the Workforce Gap

The dearth of science, technology, engineering, and math professionals is closely related to the low rate of black majors in these academic disciplines. As Elliott and others (1996, p. 706) point out, "You can't play if you don't stay, and leaving science or premed for education or history usually means leaving science or premed forever." It is virtually impossible to pursue a graduate degree or career in STEM without majoring in a STEM field. Regrettably, the number of African Americans who major in STEM fields is considerably smaller than the number who express interest in such fields prior to or at the

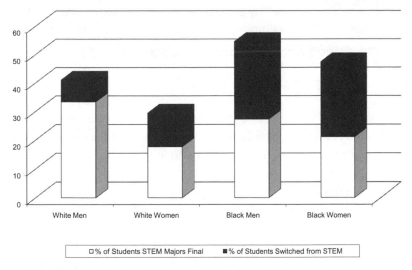

□ % of Students STEM Majors Final	■ % of Students Switched from STEM

Fig. 8. Percent of black and white men and women switching out of STEM majors

start of college. In a sample of four Ivy League institutions, only 34 percent of African Americans who initially expressed an interest in science persisted as science majors relative to 70 percent of Asian and 61 percent of white students (Elliot et al. 1996). National estimates follow a similar pattern; in 2004 the ratio of entering white freshman who intended to major in STEM relative to white STEM grads was 0.76 but the figure for African Americans was only 0.57 (National Science Foundation 2007a).

Stanford and Berkeley are no different. Not only were black students more likely to express interest in STEM fields initially, but they were also more likely to leave those fields over the course of their college careers (fig. 8). By the time of my interviews, nearly one-third of black women and men in this sample had moved from science, math, or engineering majors to disciplines within the social sciences or humanities.[3] Of the fourteen black students initially intending to major in STEM fields, only seven ended up pursuing such degrees. Although the low proportion of white women initially interested in STEM (five out of seventeen) and their high rate of attrition were also notable, it was not as extreme as in the African American sample. White men, however, were a different story.

In contrast to both white women and African Americans, only one white man left a STEM major and one white man transferred into one at the start of his junior year.[4] This attrition rate is all the more puzzling given the schools from which these participants graduated. Stanford is the epicenter of Silicon Valley and through its graduate programs and alumni is largely responsible for the technology industry explosion in Northern California. It has received hefty donations to forward its technology agenda from such grand names in high tech as Hewlett Packard (a record donation of $400 million in 2001) and Gates ($6 million in 1992), as well as high-profile donors such as Philip Knight of Nike ($150 million in 2006).

To explain the scarcity of black STEM majors, most research has focused on the academic deficits of African American students (Elliott et al. 1996; Stangor and Sechrist 1998). Educational statistics do indeed indicate that a considerable amount of the racial disparity in initial STEM interest can be attributed to inequalities in primary and secondary education. African American and white students have notably different educational opportunities; in particular, strong differences in teacher quality, curriculum, class size, and school size are correlated both to race and academic performance (Darling-Hammond 2004). Yet, while academic preparation does account for part of the loss of black STEM majors, as research attests, considerable variation in the degree of preparation and socioeconomic background at each level of performance remains (Aronson, Quinn, and Spencer 1998; Steele 1997; Steele and Aronson 1995). Such findings are compounded by unsupported claims that the deficit of African Americans in STEM is based on differences in aptitude. This is an illogical position; even the black students in my sample who dropped out of STEM majors had to be academic stars to have gained admission to Stanford or Berkeley. As Stangor and Sechrist (1998, p. 111) point out, "Since many students choose their final majors after their first year in school, it seems unlikely that aptitude is playing a large part in determining them." We must therefore consider alternative theories to explain the dearth of African Americans in STEM fields.

The Missing Link: Stereotype Threat

The observations of the African American students in this study suggest that their sensitivity to prejudice and discrimination within the fields of science, math, and engineering, largely dominated by white males, poses a significant obstacle. Previous research attributes the underperformance of black college students to perceived discrimination by faculty, peers, and administrators (Allen 1992). Moreover, despite showing an initial interest in science and taking courses in scientific fields, many black women, like the students in this study, feel unwelcome and intimidated in these disciplines (Hanson 2009). Indeed, the majority of black students, especially African American women in this study, referenced their anxiety about other's perceptions of their race as a major impediment to their success in STEM fields. These concerns closely correspond to the symptoms of a phenomenon known among social psychologists as "stereotype threat."

Defined as the social-psychological threat arising from a situation or activity for which a negative stereotype about the actor's group applies (Steele 1997; Steele and Aronson 1995), stereotype threat has been used to explain the underperformance of minorities and women in a variety of domains. Specifically, it is the anxiety individuals from stigmatized groups have that their behavior might confirm—to others or even to themselves—the negative stereotypes imposed upon their group (Spencer, Steele, and Quinn 1999). It is a complex phenomenon that has multiple explanations (Steele, Spencer, and Aronson 2002). On one hand, stereotype threat undermines achievement by interfering with performance on mental tasks by, among other things, increasing blood pressure (Blascovich et al. 2001) and reducing working memory capacity (Schmader and Johns 2003). Stereotype threat also drives students to defend their self-esteem by disengaging from the domain in question (Aronson, Quinn, and Spencer 1998). Disengagement is triggered by expected or actual threats to identity in a given area (Major and Schmader 1998).

In 1995, psychologists Steele and Aronson performed a series of clinical studies that have been replicated with similar results numerous times on racial and ethnic minorities as well as women (e.g., Schmader 2002; Schmader and Johns 2003; Obrien and Crandall 2003; Smith and White 2002; Kiefer and Sekaquaptewa 2007). In one case, students were broken into two groups: one was told the exam was based on cognitive ability whereas in the other group, the exam was presented without reference to ability. African Americans performed worse than their white counterparts when the test was presented as a measure of ability, but performed equally to whites when the test was presented as reflective of something else. In another study, groups were divided into two categories, one in which students were required to list their race prior to taking the test and the other in which students were asked to list their race at the close of the exam. African Americans in the first group fared worse than any other group, but African Americans in the second group performed equally to whites (Steele and Aronson 1995). The results of these experiments indicate that the simple consciousness of race and, one assumes, the associated racial stereotypes are sufficient to reduce African Americans' intellectual performance.

African Americans are acutely aware of the stereotypes held about them. Black students are not only susceptible to negative stereotypes but are frequently accurate in their perceptions of such stereotypes. A study of University of Pennsylvania undergraduates found that white students consistently held racial stereotypes of African Americans as criminal, violent, poor, and intellectually inferior. Moreover, white students maintained college-specific stereotypes of African Americans as unqualified for the university and able to attend only because of affirmative action quotas or athletic ability. In turn, more than 75 percent of African American participants believed that most whites assumed they were the recipients of preferential treatment and incapable of being accepted on their own academic merits (Torres and Charles 2004). Similar findings indicate that the belief that such stereotypes are accepted and acted upon by their peers and instructors increases the burden students feel in academic settings which, in turn, results in lowers grades (Charles et al. 2009).

What makes stereotype threat particularly important to this study is that it has its strongest influence on the vanguard of negatively stereotyped groups. That is, it has the greatest impact on those individuals with the skills and self-confidence to aspire to enter fields in which negative stereotypes about their group are particularly salient (Steele 1997). Moreover, this effect is likely to be especially powerful in learning situations where students are prone to be inexpert and make mistakes. If students fear that what is a normal part of the educational experience—asking questions and learning from mistakes—will be evaluated more negatively because of their race, it may undermine feelings of self-efficacy.

Throughout my interviews it appeared that the reputation of math, science, and engineering as hostile environments for African Americans and the subsequent expectation of racism in these fields provoked African American students to grow estranged and withdraw from or underperform in these majors. Consequently, some African Americans entered school with considerably different goals than those with which they would leave, many of whom expressed concern about being stereotyped.[5]

Perceptions of racial antagonism among black STEM majors, such as those described by Janelle, were not uncommon. At the time of the interview, Janelle was a management science and engineering major who aspired to open a nonprofit for African Americans. But she entered Stanford with the plan to double major in genetics and human biology. While discussing her feelings about the racial composition of her classes, she related a story about her encounters when she was deciding on her major. "I took [chemistry] and I was one of three black people there, or something like that, maybe not even. And that, that didn't make me feel very comfortable . . . I sort of felt odd, I can't say that anyone ever said anything to me at all, but I sort of felt something, like I didn't really belong somehow." Unfortunately, her class performance reflected her discomfort with being one of only a small number of minorities in a class with over 100 students; she declared, "I did awfully . . . it was really bad." What ultimately led her to abandon a science major was her avoidance, specifically her avoidance of study groups. In the abstract, her rationale for not participating appeared nonracial. Janelle explained that she had been reluctant to join a group in which she knew no one. "They all knew each other. And I was just sitting there, and I didn't, I didn't particularly feel comfortable going, 'Hey, can I join your study group?' You know." While such an explanation could have come from any student, regardless of race, what made her feel uneasy about these strangers was telling. Janelle clarified that beyond feeling unhappy about the racial composition of the class, she detected that her classmates were not taking her seriously because she was black.

Whether the perception of prejudice described by students like Janelle is reflective of the actual feelings and beliefs of classmates and teachers is beyond the scope of this research. Yet, as W. I. Thomas theorized in 1928, "If men define situations as real, they are real in their consequences." Janelle had certainly confronted blatant racial antagonism by the time she entered college. As mentioned in chapter 5, her high school dorm mates casually referred to black children as "Niglets"; and many of those same white students attended the AP physics and calculus courses in which Janelle was one of two black women. Even her high school counselor believed she was being "overly optimistic" when Janelle apprised her of her intent to apply to Harvard and Stanford. What is definite, however, is that Janelle left the major, not out of a loss of interest, but out of apprehension and anxiety about discrimination—a sentiment no white male students expressed.

Beth, another black woman, also worried that other people had stereotypical expectations of her abilities. Her situation exposes the potential that students' past academic experiences may prime them to look for racism in educational settings. Beth spoke at length about experiences in high school and elementary school in which she believed teachers had exhibited lower expectations of her than white students. When I asked whether she felt that the professors or teaching assistants at Stanford expected her to perform poorly as well, her answer was a resounding yes.

> Yeah. I think that there definitely is an expectation. And when I go into a class, it's like . . . I'm taking a philosophy class on mathematical reasoning and logic, and it's part of the series that, you know, is supposed to be one of those difficult classes in the Math Department, Philosophy Department, and it's got all this baggage that goes along with it. And I'm actually doing really

well, which is exciting for me. But the first few times that I approached my professor, I definitely got the feeling that I had to overcome something to ask him a question, I definitely got the feeling he was expecting my question to be more simple . . . Oftentimes, there can be a simple form of a question I guess. And oftentimes I found that he would misunderstand what I was asking and assume that I was asking the simpler thing, and I wasn't. And I think that it's good, because now he doesn't do that anymore, and he knows my name, and he says hi to me when he sees me around. But there definitely was that element at first. And I find that a lot.

Beth's professor may well have assumed her questions were simple; however, it is also possible that she misinterpreted the general disinterest of faculty as lower expectations based on a negative stereotype about her race. Beth herself noted that there were no blatant signs of discrimination in her classes. "I felt really guilty, actually, leaving the Math Department because I really wanted to do it and I felt like, really I had this big thing to prove, cause I was the only black female in all my classes, and I think there's even a sort of sexist feeling to the Math Department. It's very strange. It's not overt, nobody ever says anything." However, research suggests that we should not be quick to dismiss Beth's assessment of the situation. In a study of fourth graders—an arguably less perceptive group than high school or college students—children were able to identify whether their teachers considered them smart or not, basing that assessment not only on what teachers told them and their grades, but also on more subtle indicators like the instructional practices applied to them and the overall classroom climate (Weinstein 1993). In fact, one investigation found that while teachers reported providing more emotional support to those students they perceived as low-achievers than those they identified as high-achievers, students perceived just the opposite (Babad 1995). Thus, "teachers' natural affection for the high-expectation students was interpretable by students despite teacher attempts to control this" (Rubie-Davies 2006, p. 538). When we consider college-age students at selective universities, the effects are much the same. Among other things, teachers' interest in students and recognition for their achievements have significant effects on determining those who major in STEM fields and those who do not (Hanson 2009).

The strength of effects such as these is not surprising. People interact with others based in part on expectations—derived from both objective indicators (e.g., past performance) and subjective cues (e.g., prejudices and stereotypes)—of how others will perform (Miller and Turnbull 1986; Trouilloud et al. 2002). One way in which this occurs is through perceptual

biases, as when teacher expectations predict grades because their evaluations (grades) are biased (Trouilloud et al. 2002; Miller and Turnbull 1986).
Teacher expectations may also impact student achievement by directly al-
tering student behavior (Jussim 1989). For example, a 2005 meta-analysis
concluded that between 5 and 10 percent of the variance in student achievement could be accounted for by teacher expectations (Jussim and Harber
2005). Such expectations affect student academic achievement as well as
academic productivity on a long-term basis (Weinstein 2002). Whether low
expectations are plain or subtle, the result is the same. Students who are
expected to achieve poorly perceive their interactions with teachers as less
positive than students who are expected to succeed.

These effects appear to be strongest for minority and low-income students (Gill and Reynolds 1999; Jussim, Eccles, and Madon 1996), and the
accuracy of these teacher expectations tends to be significantly lower for
African American students than for white students (Murray 1996; Downey
and Pribesh 2004). Studies based on classroom observation show that white
teachers give African American students less attention, less praise, and more
criticism than white students (Casteel 1998; Ferguson 1998). Recall the experiences of Sharon in chapter 5 whose professor presumed her attendance
at Berkeley was due to her imagined athletic prowess rather than her intellectual abilities.

As a result of such experiences, African American students are well aware
of the negative stereotypes about them and carry those stereotypes with
them whenever they enter class. Their negative effects are certainly not
limited to explicit situational reminders. Beth did not need her professor
to tell her he thought her questions were stupid because she was black or
inform her that he expected less of her because of her race for her to experience anxiety. Instead, stereotypes may be implicitly activated in domains
in which the stereotypes are well known. For example, one study (Chavous
et al. 2004) found that African American students exhibited significantly
higher levels of stereotype expectations for traditionally male-dominated
majors. Another study found that students who entered college with an el-
evated sensitivity to racial rejection reported higher levels of anxiety about
reaching out for academic help and lower attendance at academic review
sessions later in their college careers (Mendoza-Denton et al. 2002). In essence, susceptibility to stereotype threat requires only that individuals are
aware of negative stereotypes about their group and that they recognize the
potential that they will be judged on the basis of those stereotypes (Steele,
Spencer, and Aronson 2002; Wheeler and Petty 2001).

Jodi, a political science major who previously intended to go into engineering, agreed that the concern about playing into a stereotype needn't be a conscious one. While she generally did not think about how her performance, particularly poor performance, reflected on other African Americans, she pointed out that, "When I speak in class, I feel like it does . . . It's just something I feel. But not overtly like: 'I must represent my people!' But sometimes, you know, you just kind of feel a little, hmm . . ."

The awareness of these stereotypes, however, may well have substantial effects. Jackie, a student at Stanford, attested that the perception of negative stereotypes frequently precluded black students from staying in more rigorous STEM majors. At the time of our interview, Jackie was a psychology major and had plans to go into marketing for black consumer products. She said that she had sold herself short in her academic life and described the prevalence of this phenomenon among black students.

> Psych . . . has, I would say, a lot of blacks, maybe. Just because it's, it's not an ability major, and I feel like a lot of black students here may be, may be doing what I did, which is selling themselves short, basically. And also, it's a dump off major for [human] bio and a lot of the harder pre-med majors; people can't hang with it, so they end up there.

Several African American students affirmed Jackie's point and noted a concern about their initial preparedness. Yet, ironically, their response to feeling insufficiently prepared, unlike white students, was to avoid assistance. When I asked whether she had sought help when she realized she was performing poorly, Jackie explained that seeking assistance as an African American aroused a sense of angst.

> I'm the first one to say that as a black student, it's hard to get academic help, just because you don't . . . I don't want people to be like, "Oh, she's affirmative action," you know what I mean? So I feel like, yeah, in the section I would be more hesitant to speak up, unless I knew I knew the answer, or you know, I wouldn't ask the question unless I felt like it was a good question. Sometimes, there'd be little things I'd be unclear on, and thought, "No, I'm not going to ask that."

Leslie, an African American student at Berkeley, had used the same approach, lamenting that as a result of her insecurities she had abstained from classroom participation. "I wouldn't ask a question in a math class, because I'd be afraid that people would think I don't understand something, and then they would say, 'Well, she's black,' or 'She's a female,' so I wouldn't ask a question." As in many cases like Leslie's, her concerns about being stereotyped obstructed her class participation and, ultimately, her education. Despite having remained a math major, her performance was such that she believed a career in that field was out of the question. She acknowledged that she was "not doing stellar" but was going to pass. And although she had finally attended office hours when it looked as if she might actually fail, she still concluded that the apprehension she felt about joining a study group outweighed the benefits of what she admitted might be "the one thing" that could significantly help her grades. Her feelings were clearly strong; she preferred failure in the course and the loss of some occupational options over feelings of inadequacy based on potential racially antagonistic reactions to her appeals for help.

These experiences are not uncommon among African American students. For some, stereotype threat nullified their ability to perform well in science, math, and engineering. In other cases, however, fears of poor performance rather than actual performance failures were enough to drive the students out of the field. It is as Merton (1948) described, a "self-fulfilling prophecy." That is, "Once they have assigned some meaning to the situation, their consequent behavior and some of the consequences of that behavior are determined by the ascribed meaning" (p. 149).

Black Males' Experiences of Stereotype Threat

While African American men also dropped out of science, math, and engineering, they were less likely to attribute their attrition directly to stereotype threat. Instead, those who left expressed some of the same basic concerns as black women—that they were uncomfortable participating in class and concerned with how others would see them—but did not directly offer racism as a cause. For example, Jason, a student at Stanford, reported that he had chosen to major in political science as a last resort: "I don't like the major, but it's the most feasible thing I could do, because engineering is completely unfeasible. Econ is simply . . . everything else is unfeasible." He described the choice as a "process of elimination," which began with math, then economics, and finally came down to political science. He felt he could not keep up in other majors but—unlike white students—had been too anxious about attending office hours or joining a study group to succeed.

Similarly, Brian, who now hoped to become an attorney, had entered Stanford with the intention of majoring in physics. He explained that he initially felt he could not handle the most common route in physics and decided instead to take an easier set of courses despite his advisor's advice to the contrary. He ultimately felt he was off track and would be unable to continue because of his initial choice of courses and feelings of inferiority in the class. "These people all have one up on me," Brian explained. He eventually declared an independent major in social science. In retrospect, however, Brian believed he could have handled the more difficult track. Yet as a junior, he was too far behind to change majors. In this case, Brian literally psyched himself out of pursuing his interests. Although presumably some white students also enter college with less preparation than others, none of the white students in this sample allowed this to hinder their progress.

Roger, a math major at Berkeley, had a comparable experience in science. When I asked him if he participated in class discussions, he explained that he was generally less outspoken in his science courses than in others. As he put it: "If you ask a question, it has to be relevant to the discussion; it has to be something that you know, I don't feel, I don't want to ask stupid questions." Because Roger's responses were similar to those of the African American women I had interviewed previously, I was curious whether he could articulate the relevance of race to his experiences in the classroom. My inquiry confirmed that race was a notable influence. In reference to whether he believed having an African American professor would make a difference in his achievement, he responded yes and commented enthusiastically on a computer science professor whose class he was currently taking: "My computer science teacher is African American this semester. I thought, wow, this is cool because I haven't seen any African American professors, definitely not in computer sciences. But this semester I was like wow, okay, I want to meet him." This was especially significant since Roger had never attended the office hours of any other professor. His perception of the importance of African American faculty emerged not only in our discussion about his own academic performance but also in more abstract conversations about the black population. Talking about the future of black mobility, Roger identified scientists and professors among the most important occupations for African American achievement: "Black professors, that's one important thing, because professors do a lot of research and it encourages black students . . . Uh, what else is there? Scientists, that is another career that is important: to diversify the sciences."

As Roger's observations indicate, race was definitely a substantial issue for him and other African American men academically, even if they were only able to relate it indirectly to their own experiences. It is perhaps no coincidence that while only 22 percent of baccalaureates awarded to African American men in 2004 came from historically black colleges or universities—institutions with a far greater proportion of black faculty—32, 36, and

32 percent of baccalaureate degrees awarded to black men in mathematical, physical, or biological science, respectively, were from historically black colleges and universities (National Science Foundation 2007b). This suggests a link between the proportion of African American faculty and students, and black male STEM attrition that deserves further examination.[6]

There are at least three possible reasons for the inconsistency in the responses provided by black men and women, however. First, because this sample had fewer men than women, a larger sample might have rendered more similar responses between the two groups. Second, studies have established that stereotype threat is both conscious and unconscious (Bosson, Haymovitz, and Pinel 2004) and therefore men may find it more difficult to recognize and report than women though men may experience the same degree of anxiety and negative effects as their female counterparts undergoing stereotype threat. In particular, because the perception of being the target of classroom discrimination or at least recognizing the possibility is a sign of "victimhood," and "victim" is a feminized category (Donnelly and Kenyon 1996), black men may be reluctant to acknowledge, either to themselves or to others, the role it plays in their anxiety. Prior research indicates that even when students do not feel the burden associated with stereotype threat, the awareness that they are being stereotyped can undermine their motivation to perform and affect their grades (Charles et al. 2009). And, third, the hesitation of men to directly relate their performance and concerns to racism may reflect gendered differences in the perception of racism or may indicate an additive or interactive impact of women's concerns about sexism.

The awareness of group stigma may vary between individuals, and in these cases the variance may be along gendered lines (Pinel 1999). Prior research suggests that being female and a member of a racial minority may present a double threat that appears in more subtle forms of discrimination in academia such as being ignored in class (Chavous et al. 2004). The difference in the perceptions and behaviors of black women in this study is certainly not exceptional and may well be a matter of the interaction of race and gender. Consistent with previous findings, a higher rate of African American women than men in this study who expressed an interest in STEM left these majors. In general, African American women, in both secondary and post-secondary education, report higher grades and greater effort but lower degrees of self-confidence than African American men (Catsambis 1994; Hall, Mays, and Allen 1984). Such findings are particularly disturbing given the disproportionate representation of African American women enrolled in and graduating from college.[7]

It is certainly possible that black men who enter STEM fields are qualitatively different from both black women who do so and black men who do not. Bowen, Chingos, and McPherson's study of graduation rates (2009) found that white women, white men, and black women at flagship state universities across the country had significantly higher rates of four-year graduation than black men. Specifically, while 75 percent of black women and white women as well as 64 percent of white men graduated within four years, an astoundingly low 33 percent of black men did so. Of their sample of flagship schools, black men were the only subgroup besides Hispanic men in which more students graduated in five or six years than in four. There is evidently some dynamic that may extend beyond stereotype threat that influences black men's academic achievement. Yet among those students who graduate within six years, there appears to be a greater drive to do so in STEM fields among black men than any other subgroup. When socioeconomic status, high school grades, SAT scores, residency, and institution are held constant, black men are more likely to graduate with a degree in STEM fields than white men, while black and white women are statistically less likely to do so. Although this study cannot resolve this disparity, it does indicate the need for further investigation of the experiences of black men in college and STEM fields.

White Women's Experience of Stereotype Threat

Like African Americans, white women had a high rate of attrition from STEM fields. Yet as with African American men, they did not directly attribute their departure from these disciplines to the characteristic most salient to their attrition: gender. Instead, like black men, they voiced concerns about their competence and what others would think of them without mentioning their identity.

At the time of our interview, Trish was considering a career that integrated her newly formed interests in fashion design and business. Yet when she entered Stanford, she had expressed a strong interest in math. Throughout high school she had excelled in her math and science courses, and her counselors and teachers had encouraged her to continue to pursue these interests in college. But during her freshman year Trish took three math classes and did rather poorly. Her response to her grades: "I was like, no thanks! . . . then I just accidentally picked econ my sophomore year." While there is certainly nothing wrong with this choice of major, it appears that poor performance was enough to make Trish reconsider her identity as a math scholar.

Nancy had also excelled in science during high school and had entered

Stanford trying to decide whether to major in chemistry or math. Yet when she sensed she was not performing as well as she would like, she sought out another major. According to Nancy, "I just realized that I had exceptionally good chemistry teachers in high school that were really cool and also the same with math." In college, however, she found that she was "more stressed and less interested." She was less comfortable in her chemistry and math classes and, like many African Americans, withdrew from participation. She reflected, "At times I just felt like a complete fool, cause some of the stuff just seemed so solid to people, and it was just so abstract to me." Although Nancy's concerns mimic those voiced by African American women, she did not connect the relevant stereotype of women being bad at math to her expectations of looking foolish or being incapable of continuing as a science student. And while her concerns are certainly valid, it does not explain why women like Nancy would allow these concerns to dissuade them from continuing in STEM fields when their male counterparts who also expressed having difficulty with these courses at the start of college did not leave the majors.

What then can account for white women's attrition from STEM fields if they themselves do not recognize stereotype threat as the cause? Since stereotype threat can be an unconscious phenomenon (Bosson, Haymovitz, and Pinel 2004), these women needn't be able to identify their concerns about fitting a stereotype in order for them to face it. In fact, only a minority of the white women involved in this study could recall any encounters with sexism either before or during college and still fewer had mothers who had spoken with them about their experiences with sexism. Neither Nancy nor Trish had been able to recount any personal experiences with sexism and generally discounted the existence of sexism on their campuses.

Their lack of perception of sexism is not abnormal, however. Only a minority of adolescent girls report having experienced any type of academic discouragement by friends, peers, family, or other adults (Leaper and Brown 2008). Instead, as they mature, girls are far more likely to report instances of sexual harassment. Being only a few years past adolescence, it is therefore foreseeable that the young women in this study would still have limited awareness of any sexism happening to them or going on around them. Although myriad studies have documented the existence of sexism in and prior to college, it is possible that young women may not regard objectively sexist actions as such because they do not yet have a working understanding of what sexism is. They may recognize the negative impact of sexist activities, but without being able to detect the more nuanced and often subtle nature of sexism, their concerns about negative stereotypes may be on a subconscious rather than a conscious level. Thus, their inability to identify a relationship between their STEM attrition and stereotype threat is, to some degree, predictable.

Conclusion

Despite these disparities, the result for African Americans and white women who experienced some degree of stereotype threat was an underperformance or abandonment of academic and occupational interests. This loss can be exceptionally painful; in some cases, students were giving up on disciplines that truly enriched their lives. While discussing what she wants out of a job, Beth, who ultimately majored in architecture and planned to pursue it as a career, noted that, "Part of the reason that I like math and wanted to be a math major is that it makes me think so hard. I really love thinking hard, and I really love math . . . There's something inside me that's just not happy being an artist."

Their perceptions of racism and sexism, actualized or not, prevent students like Beth from experiencing their education with the same degree of involvement and sense of belonging as white male students. Yet previous studies (Rayman and Brett 1995) have shown that those undergraduates who remain math or science majors are likely to have had undergraduate research experience, received advice from faculty, or had a mentor during college. Not only does stereotype threat discourage students from pursuing a major by directly threatening their desire to concentrate in that academic field, it also inhibits them from participating in the very activities that would help retain them.

The observations of the students in this study provide evidence of the existence of long-term stereotype threat. In the case of African American students, stereotype threat appears to have a considerable role in the attrition of black students in math, science, and engineering majors. African American women, and to a lesser degree, African American men and white women, are greatly underrepresented in STEM and overrepresented in social science and humanities majors relative to their proportion in the general college population. Not only are the latter disciplines more racially and gender diverse in faculty and students, but they are more apt to address issues of race and diversity (through curricula and programming) than traditionally white male-dominated STEM fields (Chavous et al. 2004).

As others have demonstrated in clinical psychological studies (Aronson, Quinn, and Spencer 1998; Steele 1997; Steele and Aronson 1995), stereotype threat is a real phenomenon with considerable implications. In the long term, stereotype threat has its effect in at least two ways. Specifically, when students perceive themselves to be judged by their race or gender, it leads some to underachieve—either directly as a reaction to stress caused by this threat or indirectly by withdrawing from educational opportunities available to them. Contrary to claims that the race and gender of faculty are of little consequence to occupational outcomes (Cole and Barber 2003), the perceptions, if not the actual experiences of the African American students here, may depend on the racial composition of the class and teaching staff. Not surprisingly, students in historically black university environments exhibit higher objective and perceived cognitive gains and increases in disciplinary understanding than African American students at predominantly white institutions (Flowers and Pascarella 1999; Seifert, Drummond, and Pascarella 2006).

What is less evident is what can be done at the college level to mitigate the effects of stereotype threat. Creating identity-safe environments—ones in which stigmatized groups can enter without being reduced to a negative stereotype—should moderate the vulnerability of individuals from marginalized groups (Davies, Spencer, and Steele 2005). Yet this problem must be handled carefully. Stereotype threat is lessened when individuals are provided with situational explanations for poor performance (Brown and Josephs 1999). For example, recent work by Johns, Schmader, and Martin (2005) demonstrates that women who were informed about the negative impact of stereotype threat prior to taking a math exam performed as well as men while those who were not informed of this effect performed significantly worse than men on the same exam. Thus, informing members of stereotyped groups about the potential effects of stereotype threat may well buffer their performance on stereotype-relevant tasks. However, other studies pose the possibility that reactive messages reinforcing expectations of racism or sexism have the potential to exacerbate the negative effects of discrimination in adolescent well-being and are associated with greater numbers of reports of discrimination by faculty, administrators, and peers (Fisher, Wallace, and Fenton 2000).

Although historically black educational institutions currently provide a home to a large proportion of future black scientists and engineers, the prestigious nature and considerable funding of many predominantly white universities such as Berkeley and Stanford reinforce the importance of increasing the number of black STEM graduates at such institutions. That Stanford and Berkeley, two universities with decidedly renowned scientific departments and schools in the heart of America's technology corridor, should have a high attrition of black students from such fields is regrettable. These are the institutions where future Nobel Prize winners will be drawn from, major discoveries will be made, and tremendous funding will be provided.[8]

The considerable workforce gap T. J. Rodgers alluded to at the start of this chapter should be of serious concern to anyone troubled by the increasing reliance of the United States on foreign countries for human resources. In the past, the United States has been able to squander domestic talent because there was minimal competition for this talent in the world. Hence, a significant amount of US intellectual power could be drawn from international sources. For example, 26 percent of inventors or co-inventors on international patent applications in 2006 were foreign nationals living in the United States (up from 8 percent in 1998), and 41 percent of patents filed by the US government listed foreign nationals as inventors or co-inventors (Wadhwa et al. 2007). At the same time, however, global competition in the science and technology sector has increased considerably and the potential for a reverse brain drain has progressively become a reality. According to one estimate, approximately 20 and 30 percent of new legal immigrants and organizational principals, respectively, have, at the least, tentative plans to return to their home countries. Likewise, the visa backlog due to US immigration law is rising annually, further limiting the number of new immigrants (Wadhwa et al. 2007).

This vulnerability to international competition could be decreased considerably were the United States to cultivate the intellectual capital of students of color. Consider some basic numbers: in 2004, 57 and 36 percent of Asian and white doctorates were earned in science, math, and engineering fields. Only 17 percent of black doctorates were STEM; this equates to only 315 African Americans earning doctorates in these fields (National Science Foundation 2007a). If we changed nothing except the proportion of African Americans receiving their degrees in STEM to that of whites, the number of black doctorates would double. That is, 673 African Americans would graduate with doctorates in STEM fields. And, if blacks shifted to the Asian proportion, 57 percent, the number would nearly triple: from 315 to 1,065 black doctorates in science, math, and engineering.

Yet before we can consider advanced degrees in these fields, it is clear that the proportion of African Americans majoring in STEM at the undergraduate level must grow, an increase severely impeded by the obstacles posed by stereotype threat. In 2004, 16,400 African Americans, or 13 percent of African Americans receiving bachelors degrees that year, received degrees in STEM fields. This pales in comparison with the 25,758, or 30 percent of

Asians, and the 95,681, or 37 percent of white men (National Science Foundation 2007a). If we again raised the proportion of African Americans to that of Asians, we would produce an additional 20,385 persons with baccalaureate degrees in STEM. Similarly an increase of African American STEM graduates to the proportion of white men would create an additional 28,969 for a total of 45,369 African Americans graduating with bachelors' degrees in STEM. While increases of this size cannot possibly occur overnight, even slight changes in the proportion of black STEM majors would put a substantial dent in the current workforce gap. The research reported in this book presents an up-close look at the educational impact and the potential workforce impact of race- and gender-based phenomena that social psychologists have been studying in laboratories for over a decade: problems that cannot be fixed by improved secondary school preparation alone.

7

THE VALUE OF WORK

Careers That Matter

The media's incessant portrayals of black-on-black crime, black crack addicts, and misogynistic, irresponsible black rap stars comprise a considerable part of society's current image of young African Americans. At the same time, neoconservatives such as John McWhorter (2000) frequently claim that anti-intellectualism among African Americans stems from their pervasive sense of "victimhood" and inability to reason effectively. African Americans are depicted as seekers of immediate satisfaction who are incapable of basic cooperation amongst themselves. Such characterizations locate the source of black inequality in supposedly individualistic and opportunistic cultural values of African Americans—an unfounded assertion that is flatly contradicted by an extensive body of historical and sociological research that consistently underscores the collectivism fostered within black communities.

African Americans have a lengthy tradition of activism and community service that predates the founding of the NAACP at the turn of the twentieth century. This heritage is reflected in the success of the civil rights movement as well as the subsequent expansion of black professionals in racialized occupational fields like education, social services, community relations, and politics. The desire to improve the fates of African Americans is truly an enduring legacy. The majority of black students in this study articulated a strong desire to aid in black social mobility, and many students believed their career choices were closely tied to their desire to decrease black inequality.

The problem with this otherwise positive trend is that many of these students, particularly those with segregated social networks, believed that the only clear way to decrease black inequality was to work in racialized fields. Unfortunately, what was not only functional but necessary for the civil rights movement to be successful is no longer a sufficient paradigm for black upward mobility. The obstacles facing young African Americans as individuals and within communities are qualitatively different from those of decades ago. The primary hindrance to black advancement is no longer the denial of basic civil rights legislation; it is far more complicated. Instead, as I explained in chapter 2, civil rights without enforcement, proper application, or political backing equates to minimal efficacy. Contemporary racism is not only institutional; racial inequality is embedded in every structure of our society. Thus, laws which can only address intentional racial discrimination and only work when rigorously enforced are not enough.

Combating entrenched and often concealed antagonism necessitates different strategies from those used prior to and during the civil rights movement. It requires African Americans to build influence in all aspects of society, so that their perspectives have a greater likelihood of being heard and felt. Developing economic strength and representation within a variety of occupational spheres is particularly important and has been an effective strategy for other marginalized groups in the United States. Both Jews and Asians, for example, benefited greatly from strengthening their financial power (Brodkin 1998; Loewen 1988). While the situations in which Jews became assimilated as whites and Asians became the model minority were assuredly different from the situation of African Americans today, it is significant that a primary contributor to the upward mobility of both groups was economic advancement.

In this light, the choice of individual African Americans to take service-oriented, racialized jobs has substantial economic, social, and political consequences for African Americans as a group. Yet, the steadfast salience of race and the reliance on historical paradigms of social and political efficacy seem to have led some of the African American students who participated in this study to reject anything but full-time devotion to community service. Strong commitment to black equality, coupled with concerns about facing racism in mainstream careers not only led African American students to avoid some career options but also increased the likelihood that they would choose others.

What Is Valued: Black and White Differences in Priorities

The considerable inequalities—unemployment, housing, education, wealth, incarceration—between the black and white populations at every socioeconomic level mean that race is a primary determinant of the life chances of all African Americans (Wilie 1989). It is logical, therefore, yet often challenged, that African Americans tend to be more community-oriented than whites. Study after study shows that African Americans have a considerably greater devotion to the collective than do their white peers.[1] The longstanding black struggle against racism creates a shared sense of common destiny (Dawson 1994).[2] As a result, many African Americans are compelled to balance their own interests within a larger context of black society. In contrast, as relatively advantaged persons, whites can maintain a more individualistic belief system that emphasizes responsibility to the self and significant others and envisions the world as a meritocracy.

Given this trend and the persistence of racism, it is not surprising that the black students in this study showed a significantly greater interest in serving the community than did their white peers. This was apparent in the disparate ways in which black and white participants evaluated certain activities in terms of the importance of each to their future including having lots of money, getting recognition from work, having a family, spending time with family, working to correct social and political inequalities, and helping the community. They first rated these items on a scale of 1 to 5 (1 being not at all important and 5 being extremely important) and then ranked them in order of priority from 1 to 6. African Americans overwhelmingly rated working to correct social and political inequalities and helping the community 4 or 5 out of 5, regardless of how highly they rated the other activities. They also ranked working to correct social and political inequalities and helping the community among their top two priorities. In contrast, having lots of money and getting recognition were most frequently among the three least important items.[3]

Among the small number of black students who rated making lots of money or getting recognition from work above a three or those who ranked these items among the two most important, however, there appeared to be a significant degree of discomfort. These students frequently hesitated before writing their answers and often felt compelled to explain their rationales.

Janelle's response was typical of African Americans who assigned a moderate to high value to recognition or money. She first rated helping the community and working to correct social and political inequalities both a 5, and when asked which community she'd most like to help, she replied, "I'd really like to help urban communities, particularly kids in the urban communities, and low-income communities." This was a response very much in line with her proposed career of public health promotion for minority adolescents. But when she rated making lots of money a 3, something she seemed to be embarrassed by, she qualified her answer. "I'd like to feel like it's really not important how much money you make. For me, a reality is that the more money you have, the easier it's going to be for you to maybe get things. Maybe pay for school . . . But, yet I'm here, with the help of financial aid and stuff. That's where I would say it doesn't matter as much." To Janelle, money was something that served as a means to a very specific end, not an end in itself. Yet while she may well have planned to use her future earnings in the same ways as many white students—paying off loans, supporting her family, avoiding debt—she felt awkward admitting that money influenced her aspirations.

Similarly Grace, aspiring to become a corporate executive, initially ranked "having lots of money" among her top two priorities, but she could not bring herself to admit the significance she placed on it.

> I want to say five, but it's not the end all, be all. I feel like my family would be more important. But I don't know, one of my goals is to be one of the Fortune 500 execs, so probably, I would probably have to say, it's probably more, not a factor of it's not important to me, but I really, for whatever reason, I guess I don't feel comfortable telling you that it is . . . It's something that I have to think about it . . . I mean, I'm saying it, right, but I'm thinking about it now, "Why did five just come out of my mouth?" And I think this is something that I have to think about, why, why would I not, even though I know it's important, why was I not supposed to say it?

She defended her interest in money as a way to benefit other aspects of her life. Money was an uncomfortable necessity, not one she wanted to acknowledge.

Unlike their African American counterparts, white students were considerably more varied in their responses and expressed no discomfort or second thoughts about their answers. White women were more likely to prioritize success or money over community or society than African Americans and ranked family highly. There were, however, no other patterns in their priorities. White men, on the other hand, consistently rated having lots of money or getting recognition from work 4 or 5 out of 5; they often rated having a family highly, although they frequently rated spending time with family only a 1 or 2; and rarely did they rate helping the community or working to correct social and political inequalities above a 3. They prioritized money above other objectives while placing the lowest priority on helping the community and working to correct social and political inequalities.

Thus, a trend emerges suggesting that the black students in this study, like those in prior research, place considerable emphasis and priority on community and social responsibility whereas white students, particularly white men, accord more value to money and status.

The Salience of Race

Racial consciousness—the perceived significance of race—not only affects individual African American's belief systems about how they fit into a group, but it also influences the way they negotiate responsibility between acting as an individual and acting as part of that group.[4] Racial consciousness has two primary components: (1) an acceptance of an identity based on racial grouping and (2) action to redistribute the power between racial groups (Woldemikael 1989). The awareness of and commitment to both components among African Americans is well illustrated in students' definitions of selling out.

First, African Americans almost always defined a sellout in terms of race whereas white students ascribed a more individualistic meaning to selling out. Responses by black students to the question, "what is a sellout?" often resembled the one given by Chris: "Somebody who doesn't have an interest in black people, and I guess somebody who holds their own personal gain above the interest of black community at large." Chris was herself already heavily involved in predominantly black activities at Stanford, including membership in two black professional organizations, a black cultural group, as well as a volunteer program. For students like her, selling out meant evading a virtually intrinsic duty to help the larger black populace.

Toni attempted to articulate the link between racial consciousness and her own dedication to helping black communities.

> I think that at Stanford especially you're a part of what we call "The Community." And if you're a part of "The Community," you recognize that you have a position of privilege. So you want to give back to different communities. And that looks like you're sacrificing some time during the week to sponsor for a program, or something like that. That's what it looks like. So I think that your experience would be different. But in my personal opinion, a lot of white students don't recognize that they're in positions of privilege, and that because of their race, and because of their class, they don't have to worry about a lot of things that I will probably have to worry about, or stress about.

In fact, as Toni asserted, white people were incapable of selling out because they did not have a community. "But could a white person sellout? No, I don't think so . . . No. No. Selling out, I think, is if you come from a community, and I don't know . . ." According to Toni, the relative privilege experienced by white students meant a lack of the kinds of shared experiences that ultimately bound her and other African Americans to a community. Her distinction was based, in large part, on her perception of the advantage whites had socially and economically. Not only did she participate extensively in a local tutoring program, but she worked an average of 40 hours a week during the academic year. For Toni, the contrast between herself and white students whom she believed were afforded the luxury of not putting in these sorts of work hours created a deep divide wherein the shared grievances of being black inherently created a "community" that such a lack of injustice could not do for whites.

Consistent with Toni's assertions, white students never defined a sellout in terms of race or community. Instead, a sellout had much more to do with white students' own moral integrity and was commonly related to money. Common definitions were like the following: "when someone lets their beliefs be suppressed by their relations to money," "betrayal of stuff that you really believe in, in order to get something," "when you sacrifice some other, some sort of integrity, artistic, personal, et cetera, for the sake of financial gain," "putting money before your ideals," "going against your beliefs for money, or your, I guess your beliefs, or what you like, or you're changing for money." One woman even provided a caveat for those who had always been immoral. Her original answer, "giving up your original values so you can make money, or more money," was quickly followed by this addendum: "However, I think from a looser perspective, the term could be used for people who never really had anything to sell in the first place, and who were always unscrupulous when it came to money."

Another variation was based on the arts. Berkeley student Lynn, a self-proclaimed music aficionado from the suburbs, provided the following definition: "I guess I mostly hear it in terms of music. Like bands that, I'm really into punk, so people complain that some punk bands sold out because they're now, they're massive, they've changed their music style so now they're, they sold out their kind of 'punk principles' so now they're popular to a mass audience." In all these cases, selling out for white students meant sacrificing something individualistic, whether it was personal integrity, musical authenticity or beliefs, for another cause—most frequently money or fame. In no case did it mean anything about community or society.

Linking Values to Actions

So how does the salience of race concretely affect African American students' values? Jason put it succinctly: "I'd want to help people like myself: African Americans who find it really, really difficult to just survive. If I was a Bill Gates, I would actually write checks. I'd find kids and write checks. 'Here's 120K, yeah, you can go to Stanford.' That's what really my dream would be." The closeness he felt to other black people and his awareness of racial inequality provided Jason with a clear target for his aspirations. Similarly, Carol believed that race was a particularly important aspect of her desire to open a nonprofit organization. What she wanted most out of her future career was "a sense of satisfaction in terms of helping the community around me because I sort of feel like that's what my role is, or my goal is in life: to really be helpful to other people and to spring up any oppressed people, more specifically black people." Not only did Carol describe her racial identity as one of the most important aspects of who she was, but she also explained that her family's experience with race was one of the things influencing her to work toward providing education to other African Americans. During our interview she explained that,

> In the rural South, for example, that's where my family's from. I have this cousin, and she's so smart; she's going to Clemson. And she's doing really well there. But at the same time, I feel like she doesn't know all the options and what she could really do with her future. And I think that doesn't have, that's not necessarily a factor of income, it's a factor of her [racial] environment.

For Carol and others like her, racism, past and present, helped inform choices about the future. In this particular instance, Carol related what she saw as the racialized structure of her cousin's surroundings to her goal to help other oppressed black people.

Toni also articulated a clear understanding of what she had not been exposed to because of race. When I asked her what she thought had influenced her career aspirations, she described the community in which she had grown up:

> Well, I grew up in South Central L.A. and the school was, I mean you can go twenty minutes on the freeway [to the valley] and you see distinct differences between education, and it's awful [in South Central]. I mean, it was so bad; I really believe that I received one of the best educations that my surround-

ing community could offer. So again, that [is] my community: basically poor inner-city people.

Toni had managed to make it to Stanford by enrolling in a special academy for gifted, underprivileged students that exposed her to college campuses and opportunities outside her immediate environment. Her description of the academy sounded remarkably close to what she hoped to accomplish by opening an educational nonprofit that provided inner-city children with better educational opportunities: "We would go to Saturday school, and then we'd have people come in and speak to us about how to apply to college and [for] financial aid, so we were in a privileged situation from the beginning in terms of knowing how to work the college system." Having come from an underprivileged background, Toni was keenly aware of the advantages she had been given by attending a special school and now wanted to pass that opportunity to others like herself.

Leslie also recognized the role her race had in her aspiration to become a criminal defense attorney. Although she was raised in a suburb, she grew up hearing the word "nigger" used repeatedly by people on the street and by friends' parents. Her recollection of her move as a young child was that "people were like, 'Oh my gosh! Niggers are on the block!'" Leslie acknowledged:

> I think a lot has to do with just where I was brought up. I'm from the suburbs, and it was a white suburb, and my family was pretty much the only black family. So even though we weren't impoverished, we still had to go through different kinds of racism just because we were black. So if it's this bad for me, how much worse would it be for someone who has the economic problems to go along with it?

Although Leslie and Toni had experienced different forms of racial antagonism in their upbringings, for both, experiences of racial disadvantage ultimately bonded them to their identity as African Americans and their dedication to helping other black people.

Unlike their African American counterparts, however, white students never expressed a desire to help a cause focused on any racial or ethnic classifications. While this finding is ostensibly positive—that white students were not determined to aid white power causes—their omission of any race is also indicative of the relative insignificance of their race to whites in general. Hence, because racial identity is relatively weak among whites, they are unlikely to consider occupations targeting a specific racial group or racial cause.

Rather than describing an interest in any particular group, white students offered up a variety of philanthropic causes, but rarely anything geared toward minority communities, even indirectly. More important, white students, especially white men, showed little or no interest in helping anyone at all. When students who rated a desire to help the community at least a 2 on a scale of 1 to 5 were probed about what they meant, their community almost invariably was their locality or "all of humanity." A sample of responses to the question "Which community would you like to help?" from white students is suggestive of the lack of thought put into their intentions to help others: "wherever I am at the time," "I guess my immediate town where I live, or humanity," "just the town or country that I live in," and "this physical place, not like one specific group of people."

Claire, a white student at Stanford who came from a middle-class home in California had a particularly rough time defining the community she wished to help.

> I would say my work community, people and colleagues I'd be working with, my family, immediate family and then extended family. And then my neighborhood that I'd be living in, and depending on the size of the town, the town or the city, just the whole world. I don't really think of having a, I mean obviously, I have my neighborhood and stuff, but there's nothing that I feel that is, you know?

She did not discuss any type of social service work before or after this line of questioning, nor was she able to list any previous volunteer work when probed about her extracurricular activities. Instead, Claire's desire to help was an abstract one—something she might do in the future but for which she had no concrete plans.

This type of uncertainty was also consistent with the causes in which white students expressed an interest. When asked what cause they would most like to help, the majority of white students did not have one in mind. Instead, many of the responses were like the one from Lynn: "Probably doing something more public service related, like, gee maybe, I don't know, working on some political or social issue or something like that." At the time of the interview, she had done no community service and had no definite plans to do so in the future.

Craig, a white man from Stanford whose plans included working as a ski instructor and massage therapist for a few years after he graduated and eventually going into law, had given even less thought to how he might contribute. Coming from a very affluent home in Connecticut, Craig readily admitted that he had never been exposed to persons less privileged than himself prior to attending Stanford. He asserted that helping the community was not particularly important to him because his sister was "a good person." Smiling, he went on to explain, "My sister does that. So that sort of takes the burden off me." Given our conversation up to that point, it was not surprising that when asked what cause he'd like to help most in his life, he couldn't think of one. After a few moments of silence, Craig asked, without any indication of embarrassment, for some ideas.

There were, however, a small number of white women who were able to articulate their desire to contribute to the social welfare of others regardless of whether they had any minorities in their social circles. And, like black students, these women most often focused on a salient aspect of their own identity: gender. Sarah, the Berkeley student who had been sexually harassed at her summer job at an investment bank had become increasingly conscious of her gender and the disadvantages associated with it. She had begun to openly rebuke the stereotype ascribed to her, explaining: "I used to think that it was so cool, like oh, I'm blond and have blue eyes. And now I'm like, oh God; I'm not one of those sorority girl types." Far from that negative stereotype, Sarah hoped to help "diverse groups of young girls" in part because, as she said, "It was so hard for me to find a mentor, so I hope I can do that one day." She thought back to her time in high school and noted that she had not considered majoring in anything related to math because she had been deterred from showing an interest in it growing up. Sarah reflected that, "being a woman, growing up like that and hearing 'you're better at communication or stuff like that'" had steered her from opportunities she might otherwise have considered. Together, her encounters with sexism had made Sarah not only more conscious of how her own prospects were limited, but of ways in which she could help other women to overcome those obstacles.

Having given relatively greater thought to helping their communities and bringing about greater social equality, African American students had also spent considerably more time volunteering than their white peers. African Americans had a much higher rate of recurrent participation in community service and activism (i.e., protests, boycotts, campaigns, frequent donations, etc.) than their white counterparts (table 1).[5] Moreover, most African Americans volunteered to work in black communities, often as tutors or mentors. The tendency for African Americans to participate in more community or political activities than whites is indeed an established trait within the greater population. Prior research shows that holding socioeconomic status constant, African Americans have a higher rate of civic and political activism than whites (Ellison and London 1992). Similarly, African Americans from

Table 1 Participation rates of African American and white students and parents in community and social activism

Activities	Number of African Americans	Number of whites
Participate(d) in community service	14	2
Participate(d) in social activism	7	2
Parents Participate(d) in community service	10	3
Parents participate(d) in social activism	11	7

highly selective universities are considerably more engaged in community and social activism than their white counterparts (Bowen and Bok 1998).

In addition to their own activities, African American students were also more likely to be aware of close family members who had participated in civic or political activities. Many students' parents or extended family members were church or school volunteers and participants in local and national boycotts or protests, activities they discussed frequently with their children. In contrast, most white students were vague about the types of activities their family members may or may not have participated in and tended to speculate that their parents had participated in a demonstration in the 1960s or 1970s despite being unaware of any details.

Exposure to community service and political activism—either directly or indirectly—may be both a cause and an effect of black students' desire to aid black communities. The increased value that black students assign to community activism may have influenced them to think more concretely about how they could help disadvantaged communities. Thus, black students' exposure to underprivileged communities through philanthropic activities may have heightened the salience of race to them and thereby fueled a drive to continue these activities in a larger, long-term capacity.[6] On the other hand, having little exposure to community service or political activism and remaining unaware of their relative privilege, most white students had not yet developed a strong interest in social service and had limited personal contexts in which to do so.

Not only was community not a major part of white students' values, but many white men did not recognize the role others, even close family members, played in their achievements. In contrast to African American students and a number of white women, white men rarely mentioned any individuals when asked what they believed had influenced their career interests or what they felt might impact their ability to achieve their goals. Instead, most white men described themselves as being in complete control of their own destinies and seemed to believe they were solely responsible for their achievements and ambitions to date. Responses to my question, "What do you think are some of the top things that have influenced your career interests?" were often like the one provided by Rob, a white Stanford student who hoped to become a professor.

> It goes back, like back in elementary school and junior high, I was good at science and English and stuff. So in high school I took, I took physics, AP Physics and AP Chemistry. And I hated biology, so I never even thought about that. I mean, I think that the reason that I hated biology is just because of a bad teacher. But I really liked chemistry and I really liked physics, so I thought I would do one of them in addition to English when I went into college. And the problem was that I took physics my senior year, and so when I left, when I graduated high school I was like, "Oh, yeah, physics. I should do physics."

According to Rob, no individuals or experiences had played a role in his career interests except in a negative capacity, such as the bad biology teacher. Rather, his positive performance in chemistry and physics had fueled his interest in pursuing the latter as a career. He had not considered the benefit he had received from going to a well-funded high school or the positive experience in these fields his teachers had provided him. Instead, Rob was good at his courses and so he wished to pursue them.

Tom, a future physician at Berkeley whose mother and father were both doctors, also had nothing to say about influential persons in his life. Despite my repeated attempts to discuss the role his parents might have played in his life choices and to have him name at least one influential individual in his life, Tom did not acknowledge anyone but himself in his success. Instead, like Rob, his own talents and character were responsible for his academic performance and occupational aspirations.

Coupled with a limited sense of community and lack of exposure to underprivileged areas, the inability to see the contributions other people had made to their successes made the individualistic rationales for the occupational goals of Rob, Tom, and other white men understandable.

Translating Values into Careers: How Social Networks Matter

A greater racial consciousness and prior volunteer experience may well have induced black students to maintain stronger community values than their white peers. And most black students asserted that their careers would in some way contribute to reducing racial inequality. Yet not all African American students aspired to community-oriented, racialized occupations. Instead, students chose careers based on what they believed would benefit the black community and, as with several other issues dealt with in this book, their social group memberships were closely associated with these beliefs.

For some students, particularly ones in segregated networks, the commitment to helping the black community meant choosing racialized occupations. This may be because they feared selling out or not being able to succeed in "nonracialized" occupations—for themselves and the black community as a whole. As I pointed out in chapter 5, the nonracialized jobs that were referenced by these students in discussions of glass ceilings or discrimination were considered unproductive means toward black mobility. It may also be that the efficacy of careers that have helped black causes in the past such as politics, teaching, social work, and social activism (see chap. 2) were reified among students in segregated networks. Thus, not only was there something for students to push away from, but they also had a compelling set of careers to which they were simultaneously pulled.

Moreover, although the basic definition of selling out was unwavering among African Americans, for students in the Black Community, there was an addendum to the definition. Not only did it mean an unwillingness to contribute, but it meant rejecting your own race. This is seen clearly in Janelle's definition: "The way I've understood it to be is someone of a particular race that associates more with another race or another group. It's when you're not true to where you're from, or how people perceive where you should be from. And it's supposed to be that you don't know, you're not helping the community, you don't know your blackness."

According to this definition, selling out meant severing ties with blackness, something Janelle, a member of the Black Community whose friends were all black women believed she was obliged to avoid. She explained, "I think there's a lot of pressure [from other black students] to be involved in black volunteer service organizations and to be involved in the community." Similarly, Diedra, a future high school principal whose friends were all African American, described selling out as, "Just kind of like you don't use your position to help your race . . . Kind of like not acting like your race is supposed to act or not acknowledging your race or benefiting your race like you're supposed to."

In general, highly identified group members like Janelle and Diedra are more inclined to adapt to and follow the norms of their in-group than are those who are unaffiliated (Jetten, Spears, and Manstead 1996). Perhaps not surprisingly then, those students who chose nonracialized careers tended to feel less closeness with the Black Community or segregated social groups and frequently cited use of terms like sellout as antithetical to the pursuit of black equality.

Jason, who described feeling disliked by the Black Community, noted a distinction between the basic meaning of the term sellout among blacks and the one espoused by the Black Community.

> I'll give two definitions. I'll give the typical one and mine. The typical one is you—quote—you forget where you come from . . . The typical one is forgetting that you are a black person, which could mean not taking someone's traits, not giving money back to the community once you become successful, not trying to help other blacks once you become successful, it's pretty much trying to disassociate with the community.

While this first portion of his explanation demonstrates the lack of closeness Jason felt toward the Black Community on campus, the second portion illustrates his own sense of racial consciousness.

> My definition of sellout, however, is more direct. It's more, I think someone who does things that are just consciously against any kind of social improvement. If I were to pick one person, I'd pick Clarence Thomas . . . he does things that from a legal and a conscious point of view, I can't understand, in terms of decisions. How could you vote for Bush? And the Supreme Court case? I mean, come on, it's pretty obvious. At least write a decision or something to indicate some awareness of the legal problems with civil rights issues before you. At least take some kind of stand, anything. Use the law, even if you're not going to vote for it, but he does nothing but vote against civil rights. That's my definition of sellout. To me there has to be some kind of moral violation, not just, "Oh, well you don't give to the community." That's two different definitions.

He believed that rather than putting labels on other students as sellouts, the most important thing African Americans could do was to work toward being more inclusive.

> Include people who aren't part of the rubric. That, I think, is ripping the race apart. I think it is the most destructive thing ever. It's worse, I think it's worse than lynching, because at least lynching, one person dies . . . Change the mindset from being "You have to be a black person according to what we do"

to being like, "you're a black person on this campus. We want you in, please come in."

According to Jason, having the opportunity to pursue different interests—something he thought was hindered by both inter- and intra-racial antagonism—would strengthen black America. Having felt ostracized by the Black Community on campus and by childhood companions at home for his interests, Jason saw a real need for black people be receptive to achievement in a variety of realms. He asserted that those who played into the stereotypes simply "don't move forward; they're doing the same game."

Students like Jason who wanted to pursue nonracialized jobs, mostly ones with integrated social circles, did not perceive these jobs as antithetical to helping other African Americans. Instead, they spoke of the importance of infusing money back into black society or providing role models. Dave, a Stanford student with close African American and white friends, aspired to own a graphic arts studio. He felt a priority for black Americans should be, "CEO positions, money positions. Money." Similarly, Theresa, a future attorney whose membership on an athletic team had led her to make a racially diverse set of friends, saw money as the best way to affect black communities. She asserted, "I don't think the NAACP can help further the community if they're looking for help financially. I mean, I would say go for specific money things. I would say, be a doctor, be a lawyer; that will help your community get more rights." When Theresa saw other African Americans heading into these fields, she had a sense of pride.

> When I see them getting into Haas Business School [at Berkeley], my comment is like, good job, way to go. It's not very often that that happens; it makes me feel, I guess pride and happy for them that they're able to accomplish that. And in talking to other African Americans that are getting ready to apply for law school and are graduating the same time I am, it's kind of like, okay, let's work together.

John, another Stanford student who planned on entering the military as a pilot and engineer, had a different spin. To him the importance of less-traditional jobs was more about demonstrating African Americans' abilities to perform in any situation. Asked which careers would be particularly helpful to the black community, he responded: "All of them. Show, you know, show society, show the world that we're willing to do what it takes. We have the brains and intelligence to be the politicians and the lawyers, and at the same time we have the grit and the determination to be the cleaners." This belief may well have come from his mother who, as I cited in chapter 5, had instilled in John the need to maintain unrelenting confidence in the face of obstacles. It was this sort of conviction he felt would help decrease racial inequality and was perhaps also what kept him in a STEM major and led to his befriending a diverse group of close friends from his engineering classes— white, black, and Asian. As a particularly independent person, John saw his potential to contribute as "giving people the tools to succeed. Whether that's mentoring; whether that's tutoring; whether that's just sitting there and talking about my job with them."

In the end, the main issue in this study is not the exact mechanism by which students come to these different frames of understanding of how to help the community. The important thing is that students who recognize the significance of occupational diversity to decreasing inequality tend to have a more racially diverse set of friends and tend to choose careers in which there are fewer African Americans but greater financial rewards than the racially targeted, direct community work opted for by students in segregated circles.

Conclusion

This chapter underscores the strong orientation of African Americans toward community and social responsibility in their career interests. African American students have a salient target for their altruism, one that is closely related to their identity. Moreover, their perception of having been aided and encouraged along the way and the belief that they have been privileged and blessed by persons and influences beyond their own talents provide a significant impetus to give back to their communities.

How they choose to give back, however, is determined, in part, by another aspect of their racial identity. For those students who were deeply embedded in the Black Community, careers traditionally targeted at African Americans, racialized jobs, were considered the most direct route to handling the significant inequities faced by blacks. Those students who maintained a racially diverse set of friends, on the other hand, were more likely to believe that diversifying African American occupations was the best means to help the cause.

While working directly with black populations is of tremendous value, racialized jobs can be damaging if a disproportionate segment of the black population holds them. Concentration in these jobs keep African Americans out of other careers, many of which are more prestigious, and potentially more influential, and because such a significant portion of these opportunities are based within the public sector, their economic returns are relatively low and their stability relatively fragile (Collins 1997; Wilson 2007). Racialized jobs within nonminority companies and occupational categories can also be problematic. Not only are they subject to economic and political volatility, but they also provide little if any opportunity for vertical advancement, and therefore further marginalize the relatively small number of African Americans within mainstream careers (Collins 1997). They operate within peripheral segments of the private sector with little access to mainstream fields.

Effectively, racialized jobs equate to lower earnings and restricted career trajectories (Wilson 2007). Consider, for example, the difference in mean annual pay for three racialized occupations relative to three nonracialized occupations. Racialized fields, such as employment, recruitment, and placement specialists, high school teachers, and attorneys working in local government (e.g., public defenders), pay an average of $50,000, $54,000, and $89,000 annually. Those in mainstream and nonracialized occupations, such as financial managers, college professors, and in-house legal counsel for private companies, earn $101,000, $71,000, and $151,000 each year, based on 2006 estimates (US Bureau of Labor Statistics 2008).

While the value of black teachers, social workers, civil rights lawyers, and nonprofit staff and leaders is inarguable, workforce diversification is also essential to advancing African Americans. On one hand, diversification in the racial composition of the workforce, as in the stock market, minimizes the impact of economic downturns, especially in industries and occupations that are susceptible to political and economic shifts. The combination of residential and occupational segregation means that when these sectors encounter down cycles, the African American community faces economic devastation. Thus, diversification of the workforce is a way to protect black people from economic risks.

Further, because racism is endemic and built into the structure and institutions of American life, attacking inequalities in a minimal number of areas via a small number of channels is limiting. For example, handling educational inequalities as teachers and school administrators has finite efficacy unless paired with high-level politicians, academic researchers, and philanthropists who can direct funding to needy schools. Racialized occupations are neither ineffectual nor obsolete, but they are no longer sufficient to create the wide-ranging, long-term changes that are needed by the African American communities these students wish to serve. It is therefore imperative that black college students become better informed about the full spectrum of career opportunities that are compatible with their community service goals.

In broadening their perspectives, however, these young students will not only need guidance from university administrators and faculty, but also from the influential segments of their communities that shape their values, that is, black student organizations, churches, high schools, fraternities, and professional organizations, as well as highly visible advocacy groups like the NAACP, the Urban League, and other national organizations that have been promoting black interests for nearly a century. Ironically, these community elements themselves will also have to broaden their own perspectives in order to be able to provide career guidance to individual students that yields maximum benefits to their communities as a whole.

8

IT'S ALL ABOUT CONNECTIONS

Melanie, a white Berkeley student, had plans to become a criminal defense attorney. Raised in a suburb of Los Angeles, her parents' friends and friends' parents had exposed her to a variety of career options. Her mother, a fifth-grade teacher, and her father, an aerospace engineer, had included Melanie in meals and activities with their friends, all of whom were professionals. Over the years, she also spent evenings and weekends with her friends and their parents; the latter were mostly doctors and lawyers. Although Melanie's parents were not attorneys, their social networks and the ones she acquired during and prior to college made it possible for Melanie get a strong sense of her specific interest in a legal career and how to get there.

By networking, Melanie had received several internships at law firms and in courts over the past three summers. The first was at a law firm specializing in insurance owned by the father of one of her friends from Berkeley. Although she realized insurance law was not her calling, the internship, nonetheless, helped her learn "the ins and outs of the law firm a little bit." The second position, one she acquired through another friend at college, was at a women's legal center. Melanie felt the subject area was interesting and took a particular interest in the readings the attorney she worked for had assigned. Finally, in the summer before her junior year, Melanie found a job through contacts at one of her extracurricular activities at Berkeley. This one was at a courthouse where she was able to work on criminal cases. She was involved in interviewing alleged criminals, a point of her job about which she appeared to be extremely enthusiastic.

I did really interesting hands-on work, which was different than anything I'd done before in terms of the law. After I did the interviews, I would sit in the courtrooms and sometimes the judge would ask us questions about what we found out in the interviews. So they really cared about what you had to say sometimes. It was really great; you worked with the judge, you worked with the defense lawyers, and we did our work and so it was really interesting.

What helped Melanie solidify her desire to go into criminal law were the contacts she had with attorneys and the experiences she had during those three summers, all of which she had gathered from her social networks. As she made clear, "It's all about connections."

While Melanie's experience was relatively common among white students in this study, it was an unlikely one for African American participants. Black students are hampered by two basic aspects of their social networks. First, because of the endurance of residential segregation, the vestiges of occupational discrimination, and the persistence of occupational segregation, African Americans are not able to provide information to one another about the full scope of occupational options and pathways now available to well-educated black people. Second, the tendency to maintain segregated networks once in college hampers black students' access to information from peers of other races and mainstream campus channels.

Even African American students like Jason, an aspiring banker (and eventual CEO), was hindered by the limits of the social networks with which he had been brought up. He had no clear concept of how to break into that field. Although supportive, Jason's parents had little education and no understanding of what his options were, nor did anyone from the community in which he was raised. So Jason was left puzzled, wanting to go somewhere but unsure how. He acknowledged

I'm at a loss figuring out what to do or what's expected. There's no, it's almost like there's no way to define success if you're doing something that's just completely not expected.

According to Jason, there were simply no guidelines for him, and reassurance was not enough.

So when other people are like, "Oh you're doing well," I'm like, "But . . . Yeah, like what's the end goal? Why am I here?" Those are hard questions. So if I were to say there's anything missing, it's more like that. And I don't think there's any literature about this, but I don't think people would talk about it, absolutely not. It's the difficulty of being in this position of mine: being a black kid without any money going to Stanford.

Like other black students, Jason did not have a coherent strategy to reach his goals. However, detailed, educated strategies—ones that articulate intermediate educational and extracurricular activities—are crucial to occupational achievement (Schneider and Stevenson 1999). Hence, despite having aspirations for a less traditionally black field, Jason's ability to attain his goal was limited by his lack of exposure to or knowledge of individuals who could help him plan his career.

Janelle another African American student who aspired to own a public health nonprofit faced a slightly different obstacle relevant to her social networks. Although a variety of factors influenced Janelle's aspirations, including her values and her concerns about facing racial antagonism in her career, Janelle had a limited awareness of her options. Between her social networks at home and those at school, she had minimal exposure to occupational alternatives and few adults to provide her with concrete guidance.

As she was growing up, her mother's friends were frequent visitors to her home.

> One of her close friends is a nurse. Another one does something with computers, I'm not sure exactly. Some of her other friends have been in and out of different jobs, mostly clerical jobs. She has several friends that work in the hospital or have worked with her when she worked in a hospital. Some of them have continued to work in the hospital in various areas, either nurses, or administrators, or secretaries.

Like Janelle's mother, a licensed practical nurse, her friends worked primarily in health care and had not received college degrees. They may well have spurred some of Janelle's interest in public health, but their relatively low positions within the health care system meant their ability to give her advice on career options for college graduates was limited. And, though Janelle had attended a predominantly white boarding school, her peers' open use of the word "Niglet" to describe black children and the ambivalence of other students made Janelle feel extremely marginalized (chap. 5). Because of the racial animosity on her high school campus, Janelle had not formed close relationships with her schoolmates or their parents in high school.

Coming to Stanford from such an antagonistic environment, she had understandably made a conscious effort to maintain a racially segregated social network. Over the years at Stanford, Janelle had enjoyed an exclusively black, female circle of friends and increasingly prioritized having a career with visible black representation. Despite the comfort provided by this group of friends, however, it constrained the types of careers and related networks to which Janelle was exposed. Like Janelle, her friends, had very little awareness of the types of opportunities available to African Americans and sought out standard tracks. Among them, one wanted to be a pediatrician, another aspired to become a civil rights lawyer, a third expressed interest in nonprofit work with children, and all were clear that they wanted to work in black communities. Her summer jobs were with nonprofit agencies where she volunteered during the school year, and her friends spent their summers in much the same way.

Despite passage of civil rights legislation, African Americans like Jason and Janelle did not have easy access to the highly valuable sources of job information that white students like Melanie did. While some black students were able to overcome the deficits in their networks by seeking out adults outside of their communities or rigorously pursuing opportunities once in college, the fact remains that there is an inherent inequality in the social networks of African Americans and whites relative to careers that impedes black expansion into a variety of occupational fields.

Jason had no one from home to advise him in his pursuit of a job in a white-dominated industry, and Janelle had no one to show her all the available options to help other African Americans. Unfortunately, "black job seekers are primarily tied to social networks composed of other blacks who, on average, are not as well situated to know about as many desirable job openings as members of the social networks used by white job seekers" (Braddock and McPartland 1987, p. 8). This process, aptly termed "social network segregation," operates forcefully at various stages, not only at the job search stage referred to above. It functions when youth are learning about which jobs exist, which jobs are suitable for them, what those jobs entail, and how to obtain them. While the tides have changed enough racially that many companies are vying for qualified African Americans, at least in entry level positions, the networks of these students inhibit their awareness of any such shift.

The desire of the corporate sector in particular to maintain greater numbers of well-educated African Americans has been considerable. Fortune 500 companies have presented amicus briefs on behalf of institutions with affirmative action plans in the majority of prominent court cases over the past ten years. Most recently, in the cases of *Gratz v. Bollinger* and *Grutter v. Bollinger,* sixty-five leading American businesses, including General Electric,

Lockheed Martin, and Bank One (65 Leading American Businesses in Support of Respondents 2003, p. 5), testified that diversity in the workforce was essential to their ability to compete in a global marketplace. They stated,

> Because our population is diverse, and because of the increasingly global reach of American business, the skills and training needed to succeed in business today demand exposure to widely diverse people, cultures, ideas and viewpoints. Employees at every level of an organization must be able to work effectively with people who are different from themselves. [We] need the talent and creativity of a workforce that is as diverse as the world around it.

With the calls from Silicon Valley to produce more science, math, and engineering graduates, it is apparent that there is a disconnect between the opportunities available to talented black students and those of which black students are aware. Consider, for example, a study of professional job-seekers (Petersen, Saporta, and Seidel 2000). Initial findings show that whites were significantly more likely to have used prestigious job contacts within a company than their African American peers. Whereas 81 percent of whites had interviews within the company among upper management or in the placement department, only 21 percent of African Americans were interviewed at this level. The vast majority of African Americans interviewed on campus or with personnel in human resources. The upshot was that significantly fewer blacks were hired in the company. But when researchers held referral methods constant, being black actually had a positive and significant impact on the likelihood of being hired. Effectively, when blacks were not limited by what some refer to as the "wrong networks," they had greater success than their white counterparts.

What Limits the Flow of Information?

A critical piece of the "wrong network" puzzle comes down to understanding why minorities are underrepresented in networks that lead to jobs that are higher ranking and/or highly rewarded (Fernandez and Fernandez 2006). Ideally, individuals would have all the necessary information to make a fully informed, major life decision like occupational choice, but there are few conditions under which this occurs. Vestigial and ongoing racism makes it an exception in the case of African Americans.

A primary cause of the lack of information provided to African Americans today is segregation within residential and educational spheres, a phenomena growing rapidly on account of recent legislation. While the remainder of this chapter delves more deeply into the negative consequences of network segregation, the overarching point is that segregation restricts the flow of information essential to the formation of aspirations of African American youth. In essence, the saying cherished by parents over the years, "You can be anything you want to be" may well be applicable to white Americans (especially in their early careers). But if the exposure of black students to different professions continues to be as limited as it is today, then "anything" will be severely restricted and many occupations will remain racially segregated.

Residential Segregation and the New Black Middle Class

Community homogeneity is a principal mechanism restricting the occupational resources available to African American youth. The systematic discriminatory behavior of credit institutions, realtors, the Federal Housing Administration, and white neighbors, in addition to the lackadaisical enforcement of the 1968 Fair Housing Act (Massey and Denton 1993; Oliver and Shapiro 1997) have all resulted in the segregation of the black lower, working, and middle classes alike. The outcome is that while middle-class African Americans live in less segregated neighborhoods than low-income African Americans, their white neighbors tend to be considerably less affluent and educated than the neighbors of similarly situated whites (Alba, Logan, and Stults 2000). In other words, even middle-class African Americans in the suburbs live in communities that are less connected to a variety of occupations than their white counterparts.

The general differences between African American and white lower- and middle-class communities translate into significant differences in the backgrounds of college students, even those enrolled in highly prestigious universities. In a survey of more than 10,000 African American, white, Asian, and Latino college students from 28 selective universities across the country, African Americans had the lowest rate of neighborhood integration with whites. This was closely linked to the likelihood that blacks would report homelessness, prostitution, drug use, drug sales, and violence in their neighborhoods significantly more than any other racial group (Massey et al. 2003).

Class effects, however, reflect only a portion of the problems associated with black residential segregation. Consider the following scenario of the consequences of discrimination and segregation:

> [Imagine] that families are grouped together into communities and that lo-
> cal public goods like educational resources that are important for individual
> productivity are provided uniformly to children of the same community. In
> this setting, background influences achievement on two dimensions. First,
> less successful parents are not as able to provide important resources that
> augment human capital development—such as career information, job refer-
> ral networks and other forms of social and cultural capital. Second, children
> with less successful parents will tend to live in communities with inferior local
> public goods. [Fryer and Loury 2005, p. 155]

The legacy of divestiture that African Americans of all classes have faced
has left this population with limited access to pools of resources necessary for
achieving equality. While there is nothing inherently wrong with black neighborhoods, the systematic exclusion of African Americans from occupations
prior to the Civil Rights Act of 1964 means that even middle-class African
Americans with professional parents living among other black professionals
will see a smaller range of occupational options than their white counterparts.
Nevertheless, the reality is that African Americans are disproportionately
represented in blue-collar jobs, and African Americans in the middle class,
unlike their white counterparts, are clustered among lower-middle-class occupations (Patillo-McCoy 2000; Landry 1987). Hence, even middle-class
black communities look substantially different from white middle-class
neighborhoods in terms of the types of careers held by their residents.

Educational Segregation

Educational segregation, a direct consequence of residential segregation,
produces many of the same limitations. Specifically, it concentrates African
American students in institutions where the parents have lower average incomes and a smaller number and diversity of professionals than those of their
white peers. During the 2002/3 academic year, for example, over 60 percent
of African Americans attended high-poverty schools (where between 50
and 100 percent of students attending are poor) although only 18 percent of
whites attended high-poverty schools. Likewise, the racial composition of
extreme poverty schools (between 90 and 100 percent poor) was almost 39
and 41 percent black and Hispanic, respectively, but only 16 percent white
(Orfield and Lee 2006).

In the past fifteen years, the judicial system has effectively dismantled the
heightened integration yielded by the 1954 *Brown v. Board of Education* decision. Courts throughout the nation have ended desegregation policies, and

some states now prohibit the use of race-based student assignment plans (Frankenberg and Lee 2002). In the 1991 *Board of Education of Oklahoma v. Dowell* case, the Supreme Court sanctioned the resegregation of neighborhood schools. Between 1991 and 2004, the percent of black students attending predominantly nonwhite institutions rose throughout the country from 66 to 73 percent (Orfield and Lee 2006).

More recently, in the case of *Parents Involved in Community Schools v. Seattle School District No. 1,* the Supreme Court severely limited the tools available to school districts to achieve and maintain integration. The court struck down school-choice plans in Seattle, Washington, and Louisville, Kentucky, asserting that such plans were dependent on the unconstitutional use of racial criteria. The 5–4 vote led by conservative majority leader Chief Justice Roberts asserted that, "The way to stop discrimination on the basis of race is to stop discriminating on the basis of race." In a separate concurrence, Justice Thomas insisted that the purpose of the court was not to diminish inequalities:

> This Court does not sit to "create a society that includes all Americans" or to solve the problems of "troubled inner city schooling." We are not social engineers. The United States Constitution dictates that local governments cannot make decisions on the basis of race. Consequently, regardless of the perceived negative effects of racial imbalance, I will not defer to legislative majorities where the Constitution forbids it.

Thus, regardless of how compelling the need for desegregation might be, race can no longer be used as a factor to determine school assignments and African Americans increasingly attend highly segregated schools.

Networks Growing Up: Racial Differences in Who You Know

This research indicates that the outlook and aspirations of the social networks of white students were considerably different from those of both African American students who attended predominantly black secondary schools and African Americans who attended institutions with a higher proportion of whites. The great majority of white students I interviewed had exclusively college-bound friends while growing up, but African Americans had significantly more varied social networks. As shown in prior studies of students at selective institutions (Massey et al. 2003), black students' friends in high school were less concerned with academic achievement and performance than their white counterparts' friends, particularly those attending segregated schools. Black students maintained friendships not only with similarly upwardly mobile peers but also with students who did not go on to attend college and were currently employed in blue-collar positions or were unemployed. Accordingly, while white students frequently recited a series of elite colleges their friends were currently attending such as Harvard, Rice, Wellesley, Swarthmore, UCLA, and Princeton, African American students included many community colleges and smaller state schools.

What social ties offer, among other things, is encouragement to excel in life and exposure to its different facets. Bill, a white student at Stanford, articulated the value he had found in having friends from professional and well-educated families. Bill's stepfather was a policeman and his mother an elementary school teacher, but he lived within the school district of considerably more affluent whites in Southern California. He recalled that his school's standardized test scores were in the state's top ten and that it offered extensive AP classes: There "was a huge emphasis on getting kids into the University of California system. I'd say we had maybe over a hundred kids go to Berkeley, and more than that go to UCLA." He noted, as did many other white students, that much of the information he got about college was through his peers and adults unrelated to him:

> It was mostly through each other [friends] and teachers, I'd say. I don't think I would be at Stanford if I didn't go to that high school, just because growing up in middle school, elementary school, I didn't know anybody who went to any kind of Ivy League or any top tier university. And just being around my friends and people in my classes; they kind of opened my eyes to show me I could do this if I wanted to.

So Bill, whose parents had not attended exclusive universities or socialized regularly with those who had, attended a high school in which application to selective institutions was the norm. Indeed, for some of the white students, high academic achievement, as well as high educational and occupational aspirations, were requirements for membership in their social circles.

Greg explained that a college future was a "prerequisite" for his high school friends. He noted, "It was never a question whether or not we were going to go." More important, Greg attended a high school in which using such a condition for friendship was easy. He met friends through classes and extracurricular activities, the way most students meet friends, and had a large selection from which to choose. Not only were there numerically enough students to satisfy such conditions, but race did not have to consciously figure into his options.

Josh, a white student at Stanford who aspired to become an English professor, was one of the few white students who came from a situation in which he was not exposed to social networks with academically driven students or adults with professional careers. In large part this was due to the size of his hometown in the Northwest which had a population of approximately 5,000. His parents were, of course, very supportive of his educational achievement and had done their best to expose him to the joys of learning. But neither they, the students he attended school with, nor their parents had any concrete understanding of the value of college. According to Josh, "maybe 40 percent of the graduating class goes on to college, and most of that's to community college." Their aspirations were relatively low, and Josh estimated that 80 percent of graduating students would stay within a twenty-mile radius for their entire lives. Hence, Josh's exposure to social networks valuable to upward mobility looked more like those of his black counterparts than the rest of the white students. This type of social closure—in which the networks among friends, parents, coworkers, and the like are tightly linked to one another—can actually place considerable limitations on children. In particular, it restricts channels of opportunity that are available through access to the wider society (Morgan and Sorenson 1999). Like Josh, the friends mentioned by many African American students often had limited goals and accomplishments in large measure because of the considerable degree of social closure within their communities.

Although a significant portion of the black students in this study did attend schools in which their classes were primarily honors track, they often maintained a set of friends with lower ambitions and/or a more limited awareness of opportunities than white participants. The overall school curriculum of African American students who went to predominantly black or minority schools was most frequently geared toward a more basic or remedial level. Thus, in more segregated schools, a considerable number of students' classmates and friends who were themselves on a college track, were not from professional families or were not interested in professional careers.

Tamara, a graduate of a predominantly black southern public school, described the goals of the student body at her high school.

> They're just people who didn't have very, I'd say, big visions so to speak. Or
> at least some were more than happy to stay close to home, and weren't really
> interested in trying to see more of the world. It wasn't that people were stupid

or bad. They just didn't see how college or high school was really going to [help them] . . . People just didn't seem to think about anything beyond their immediate lives. Or they just didn't think that there was [anything] much bigger and better out there.

On the other hand, black students attending less segregated schools sometimes found themselves seeking out African Americans outside their academic track to befriend because of the lack of candidates within their own classes. The racial antagonism present in secondary schools sometimes catalyzed students' need to create refuges amongst black peers. Thus, for some of the same reasons African American students resolved to have all-black networks in college, as high school students, African American participants had sometimes made conscious decisions to socialize with other African Americans, sometimes exclusively. In fact, the only situation in which African American students were guaranteed to have a larger proportion of friends from professional, more affluent backgrounds (of any race) and who themselves held professional interests was at preparatory schools.

Hence, while white students like Bill and Greg came from social circles where college attendance was expected and where students exchanged goals and encouraged one another to excel (often doing so as if there were no alternative), many African Americans like Tamara came from social networks where only a fraction of their friends had the same educational ambitions and interests.

Friends' Parents and Parents' Friends

Though friends themselves sometimes transmitted information about careers and career tracks, information pertinent to occupations generally originated from adults—parents' friends or friends' parents. These adults often served as examples, role models, or simply as additional sources of exposure. Once again, white students had a greater range of exposure to professionals, regardless of their parents' backgrounds than did their black peers due in large measure to the interclass contact within predominantly white schools and neighborhoods.

Dianne, a white Stanford student planning to become a doctor, described what she knew about the careers of her high school friends' parents: "I know what all of them did. We talked about their jobs and how they enjoyed it. Some of them were doctors, some were investment bankers, and then some were businessmen." Through dinners at their homes, family outings, extracurricular activities, and sleepovers, Dianne had formed relationships with these adults. She was not necessarily close to all of them, but she interacted with them enough that they shared information with her that exposed her to a wide range of options for her future.

Another white student, Tim, who hoped to become a journalist or fiction writer, listed the occupations of his friends' parents whom he saw frequently as a journalist, a marketing executive, attorneys, a senior official in the Department of Defense, a neuro-psychopharmacologist, and an engineer at the Pentagon. After a number of indirect probes on the impact his friends' parents had on him, Tim asserted, "I guess a couple other of my friends' parents seemed to have a substantial interest in art, literature, and film, and I think that their influence was particularly important to me." Consequently, whether conscious of it at the time or not, contact with people who had a variety of professional careers and interests provided white students with exposure to a diversity of opportunities that few black students had.

Friends of their own parents—who were often also their friends' parents—served a similar role. Kelley, a white student, recalled that the majority of her parents' friends were professionals and credited her interest in psychology, her college major and future occupation, to her mother's friends who were mostly psychologists. She had sat through dinners, lunches, and other activities with these women and over time, developed an interest in the discipline. Kelley acknowledged, "I think my interest in psychology, since so many of my mom's friends are into psychology . . . It's just something that they discuss a lot, and it's just how I got interested in it." When she got to college she had sought out psychology classes and found that this truly was an appealing field with the potential for a future she might enjoy.

Although some African Americans also had friends who came from professional families or had family friends with professional backgrounds, this was considerably less common than it was for their white peers. African American students were likely to attend schools with a higher proportion of minorities and were exposed to fewer adults in professional fields. In general, African American children from middle-class families are likely to attend school with a sizeable number of children from lower-income or working-class backgrounds (Alba, Logan, and Stults 2000), making their encounters with those adults less valuable in terms of careers. For example, Sandra, one of my participants who came from a solidly middle-class family with a combined yearly income of approximately $80,000, had friends whose parents were mostly teachers but also included a factory worker and a baker. Similarly, Kyra, whose college-educated parents made over

$100,000 annually, had close friends from school whose parents included a janitor, a noontime aid at an elementary school, and a restaurant manager. Her friends, in turn, attended community colleges and third-tier California State institutions. This is in stark contrast to the investment bankers, doctors, attorneys, and engineers inhabiting the neighborhoods of middle-class whites. Like Kyra's and Sandra's parents, many middle-class African Americans are constrained to live in close proximity to lower-income neighborhoods and therefore cannot provide their children with as many opportunities to befriend other middle-class children or expose them to professionals unless they are able to live in predominantly white communities or manage to enroll their children in private institutions.

Private schools were, in fact, the primary source of black students who had grown up with integrated peer groups. Paul, who aspired to go into business and eventually land an upper-level management position in the government, had attended a private boarding school and befriended a relatively diverse group of students. One of his friends' fathers, an Iranian venture capitalist, had been particularly influential.

> He's a businessman; he just had the business attitude. And he showed me the respect you're supposed to have. He just taught me a lot of things. He treated me like a son a lot of the time, just as far as taking care of me. I was always invited over to their house; I've just stayed there when my friend wasn't there. He's just been there ever since I've been friends with his son. They've included me in their life and it's just, they have money. I think that's where I started to think, "It's possible, you know." Here are my best friend's parents; they're doing what I could be doing. So I think that's inspiring in itself.

By taking Paul into his home and his life, this man had encouraged him to pursue a career he would likely otherwise not have considered. He spoke with Paul about what his job entailed, made the field appealing, and encouraged Paul to think of this as a tangible possibility for himself.

What all these examples suggest is that the enrichment students need in order to aspire to a greater diversity of goals goes beyond basic differences in the education available to black and white students or disparities in class. Even African Americans who were themselves professionals, whose children performed exceptionally well in school, were unable to expose their children to the full range of occupational possibilities (chap. 3). Given that the cohort under consideration is part of the first generation that has been raised without de jure segregation (despite the very serious de facto segregation they still face), we cannot expect their parents, who did not have the same opportunities as their white counterparts, to have all of the information necessary to benefit their children.

Peer Networks in College

Because of deficits in their social and cultural capital relevant to occupations as they were growing up, many black participants entered college with considerably less information about and awareness of careers than did their white peers. Some based their aspirations on the limited number of occupations to which they had already been exposed while others with less traditionally black aspirations were unaware of how to achieve them. In contrast, most white students, even those with lower family incomes, entered college having attended school with significantly fewer low-income students than African Americans. Even white students who had attended less affluent schools had a high enough proportion of other students from professional families in their social networks to diminish the effects of their primary and secondary educations.

Despite their lack of exposure to occupational opportunities growing up, college does provide a chance for students to overcome some of the weaknesses in their social networks. Randy, an African American student at Stanford, saw his future without consistent direction. His hopes to attend law school and eventually become a movie producer were not encouraged by his mother, who worked as a high school career development counselor, or his estranged father, who had only a high school diploma. The majority of the other adults in his life worked blue-collar factory jobs and therefore had little advice to contribute to Randy toward attaining his goals. So at college, in his junior year, Randy was asking everyone he knew, about their plans for the future. "I just talk to people a lot about [it] . . . cause I'm very confused about my future so I like to talk to people about what they're doing and see what they're doing and see if I learn anything about what I can do."

Integration, one of the key factors to widening their options, is not, however, something all black students pursue. The problem with having a racially segregated peer network in college is that most African American students had a far more limited set of experiences and considerably less exposure to the possibilities available to them after college than their white counterparts. By isolating themselves, they stifled the flow of information imperative to making educated career decisions. One of the greatest legacies of de jure segregation is that it has left the black middle class generations behind the white middle class in terms of the social networks and cultural capital important to awareness of and success in all the opportunities that are today open to them. Because of this, African American students lose more than potential friendships when they retain segregated social networks in college. They lose exposure to fundamental information about occupational options.

Social capital is largely a matter of functional specificity (Kim and Schneider 2005). Although segregated social networks can be beneficial in comforting students and providing them with emotional support, they may be disadvantageous in terms of the opportunities to which they expose black students. Once in college, students with segregated networks remain insulated and often are not exposed to the opportunities available to them from the university, companies interested in hiring talented students from elite schools, and the social capital of many of their peers. In contrast, the black students with integrated circles of friends received many of the same types of network-related benefits as their white colleagues.

One of the ways in which the divide between white students, black students with integrated circles of friends, and black students with segregated networks becomes most obvious is in informal job networks used to find part-time work during the school year or summer jobs. On one extreme, African American students with segregated networks rarely considered summer positions outside of their hometown because their social networks lacked adequate connections to inform them of such opportunities. Instead they tended to take the same sorts of service-industry jobs during college that they had during high school—as waiters, daycare workers, or camp counselors. The handful of instances in which African Americans with segregated networks found work through social networks was mostly nonprofessional.

On the other end of the spectrum, African American students with integrated social networks and white students were far more likely to have involved themselves in career-related job activities during college than African Americans with segregated networks, and these same students were also far more likely to have found that employment through their social networks. For example, Sheryl, a white Stanford student, worked as a lab assistant over the summers at a geotechnical engineering firm owned by her father's friend. Likewise, Nancy, a white Berkeley student, got a job on the Human Genome Project from a neighbor: "We were just outside, and he's like, 'What are you doing for the summer?' And I was like, 'I don't have a job!' So he's like 'You should come work for me if you're interested.'" Nancy literally walked outside her door and got a job with a prestigious name and an interesting experience.

Josh, the white Stanford student planning to be an English professor, summed up the importance of these jobs: "Working for a research project has had a definite positive influence on my decision to be in academia." This job provided him with an opportunity to pursue the work of an academic before committing to a lengthy career in graduate school. Given Josh's hometown background, one with few professionals, this experience was especially beneficial. Such jobs provide all students with valuable information about specific careers and how to obtain them, as well as a beneficial addition to their resumes.

Edward, another white student at Berkeley who hoped to become an environmental lawyer, had received a summer job through one of his college connections. His friend Jim had helped him get a position at the recycling office at the university by "pulling some strings." According to Edward, Jim "basically got me the job at the recycling office. I didn't even think I wanted it, but he kept pressing me to take it and he convinced the . . . manager over there that I would be the best person for it. And so she got on my case about it. And you know, two years later, I'm still working there, and had all these successes working for him." Edward's job had clearly influenced his career interests in environmentalism.

> I'm working at the campus recycling office as a program coordinator, and basically get paid to do recycling education outreach for the whole campus. [I] developed a program in the residence halls, where I got one coordinator from each hall to be responsible for educating that hall about recycling, and what services are available, what can and can't be recycled. And I started that last semester, my second semester of my sophomore year. And it was a big hit, and the facility managers want them to be paid now and pulled into the actual infrastructure of the . . . whole system of running the residence halls.

The use of contacts by white students like Josh, Edward, Sheryl, and Nancy in finding career-oriented jobs is, in fact, the norm (Granovetter 1995), and the black students with integrated networks in this study appeared to be operating in a similar fashion. Jesse, for example, the Stanford student interested in product design, had taken a position as a research assistant in the Psychology Department the previous year. He explained that he found the job during a research fair he was encouraged to attend for a psychology course. Because he was specializing in product design within engineering, Jesse was required to take this class "in order to learn how consumers think and why they buy what they buy." A number of graduate students in the Psychology Department had presented their research during the fair and Jesse was especially drawn to one project for which he eventually became a research assistant.

Another African American student, Roger, was even more proactive. As a math major, he had directly approached his networks to obtain his summer jobs. In one case, he had been employed in an architectural firm by the CEO who was a "friend of the family" and in the other instance, he worked in the aerospace industry, also through friends and family. According to Roger, both jobs had been beneficial to his eventual career in computer programming and gaming. He had apparently come to the same conclusion as most white students: that part of getting through the door is knowing the right people. He noted, "Yeah, I like to think that I'm talented and I could just go out and apply for jobs and people would go 'oh, you know, let's hire this young man' but no, it's more like, 'hey, [Roger's] a great kid, let him in.'"

Although Roger had contempt for the system that necessitated using contacts in that way versus his "raw talent," he felt compelled to "take advantage of what [he could], because everyone else does."

Conclusion

In an ideal world, young people would use what social scientists have termed "rational choice." In its simplest form, individuals employ rational choice by performing a cost-benefit analysis of their options. Of course, the basis of rational choice is complete and accurate information, something severely lacking in the social networks of African Americans. While it would be convenient to pass this off as a strictly class-based problem, the persistence of residential and educational segregation in America makes it a racial problem as well. For lower- and middle-class African Americans alike, segregation— both while growing up and at college—presents a formidable barrier to the flow of information. The history of racial oppression in the United States has left a gap in the informational resources available to African Americans and whites of similar economic brackets that residential segregation perpetuates. Blacks in middle-income professions are, in many cases, the first generation of professionals in their families and therefore lag behind their white counterparts who have been privy for a longer time to the cultural and social capital necessary to make fully informed, rational decisions.

In college, the problem is much the same, but the opportunity for African American students to have racially diverse social networks is considerably greater than it was in their home communities. But, for a multitude of reasons, a substantial number of African Americans attending college prefer to maintain segregated social networks. This is more easily accomplished at schools with living situations designated for particular racial groups (chap. 4). While recognizing the impetus for such types of housing and the pressures often brought on school administrations to maintain this sort of accommodation, it is problematic. Black students are effectively ghettoized—isolated not only from students of other races but, more important, from the networks and information those students have.

For those African American students with the motivation to pursue nontraditional careers, there remains yet an additional obstacle: knowledge of how to attain their dreams. Segregation, whether educational or residential, inhibits the communication of information about next steps. Jason, the prospective investment banker, knew of no one at home who could explain to him what he should major in, how to spend his summers, or how to build his resume for his chosen career. He had family who loved and believed in him and was on his way to obtaining a degree from one of the top universities in the world, yet without information on how to do it, Jason, like other black students, was off to a difficult start. One of the benefits he and other black students enjoyed by befriending students of other races was access to the type of information previously unavailable to African Americans.

9

CONCLUSION

A saving remnant continually survives and persists, continually aspires, continually shows itself in thrift and ability and character. Exceptional it is to be sure, but this is its chiefest promise; it shows the capability of Negro blood, the promise of black men.
W. E. B. DUBOIS, "The Talented Tenth"

The elite black students in this study are exceptional—distinct from their white counterparts and distinct from other African American students. They are likely to play a pivotal role in the future welfare of blacks in America, having opportunities inaccessible to previous generations. Yet some are opting out of these newly available opportunities, choosing instead racialized positions that have proven valuable to black mobility in the past. In this study I have endeavored to provide a glimpse into their thoughts and decision-making processes with the hope of making them more understandable to those concerned with inequality and education.

Segregation Past and Present

An overarching theme of this book has been the effects of segregation—whether imposed by external forces or by self-selection. What binds these different forms of segregation is the role they play in constraining the boundaries of students' expectations for their future. While some black participants found themselves limited by inhibitions they had formed over a lifetime, others remained unexposed to the very opportunities disregarded by those students.

Social Networking

The most recent bout of court cases and legislation reversing affirmative action has reenergized arguments for racial diversity on America's campuses. Contemporary researchers argue that racial diversity breeds racial tolerance and greater learning opportunities for students—the benefits of which extend well beyond the college years (Bowen and Bok 1998; Chang, Astin, and Kim 2004; Gurin et al. 2002; Gurin and Biren 2006). I would argue, however, that racial integration also provides opportunities for minority students to network with individuals who have better connections with sources of job- and career-related information.

Although the civil rights movement eliminated many of the legal obstacles faced by African Americans, it did not provide compensation for the loss of cultural and social capital that African Americans had suffered for generations. The legal remedies of the 1960s could not undo the lack of exposure to opportunities, resources, and fundamental knowledge that previous generations of African Americans had endured. As a result, black students may be unaware of the enhanced occupational opportunities available to them today—opportunities which could be invaluable for decreasing black inequality—an issue all black students hoped to work toward in their lives.

College offers black students chances to do the same kinds of networking and to be exposed to the same information that most white students have had their entire lives. Yet many of the black students in this study established predominantly black social circles when they reached college. While black students may derive substantial value from these networks, there is also a considerable downside to their separation from the wider campus community. Racially integrated networks provide access to information otherwise unavailable to these students, including the existence of occupations they had never considered, the awareness of how to obtain training for them, and connections to professionals (white and nonwhite) who possess them. It is crucial, therefore, that university administrators consider the added value of diversity to black student success and provide the programming and structure to facilitate it.

Putting Values to Work

Regardless of the composition of their social networks, the African American students in this study placed great importance on helping the larger black community and had given careful consideration to the ways in which they could do so. Some believed that working directly with black communities would enable them to address racial inequities head on. Others thought that going into less traditional fields, making more money, gaining influence, and serving as role models would provide them with significant opportunities to contribute. Either way, the students' strong desire to support their communities is commendable.

Few would dispute that racialized careers are still essential—whether in teaching, civil rights law, community relations, or social work. Nevertheless, communities also need occupational diversity to minimize economic risks, promote tolerance, and provide multiple lines of attack against racial injustice. In other words, neither racialized nor mainstream occupations are sufficient; both are necessary. Unfortunately, occupational diversity did not seem to have been valued by the students in segregated networks. Universities therefore need to take proactive steps to ensure that segregated groups, like Stanford's Black Community, are made aware of the constructive roles that nonracialized careers can play in decreasing racial inequality—a goal to which all of the black students who participated in this study were committed.

Perceptions of Discrimination

Perhaps the greatest effect of segregation, one that goes unseen but governs the behaviors and desires of many otherwise successful African Americans, is fear. While social networks, cultural exposure, and values help determine what opportunities students are aware of and how they calculate the significance of such opportunities, fear influences whether those same students will consider what comes through those filters. Although the African American students in this study were sometimes able to overcome their backgrounds or extend their vision of how to better their communities, some of their fears seemed insurmountable. As Feagin and Sikes (1994, p. 76) assert,

> Encounters with white hostility and discrimination shape the lives and perspectives of middle-class African Americans. A black person's life perspective—the personal assumptions about the world—may be shaped by discrimination to include a sense of lack of control over one's life . . . Without it,

one feels a sense of powerlessness, creating a condition in which an individual may have difficulty in achieving desired goals.

While I have endeavored to present the case that the racism actually faced by African Americans of this generation is qualitatively different from that faced by older generations, it is still racism. Moreover, being only one generation removed from de jure discrimination, these students have been sensitized to expect discrimination of a sort faced by their parents and older generations. Thus, current discrimination may well not be as substantial as what existed in the past, but it still exists in the minds and choices of these students. Despite the small sample, what is striking is that fear was frequently a concern voiced by black students but never one for white men and for only a small number of white women.

The absence of a visible presence of blacks in different careers is a potentially inaccurate but routinely used measure of the racial climate in occupations. In this study black students formed part of their opinions about careers based on the number of black faces they expected or had seen in them. Their presumption is that the lower the presence of African Americans, the greater the likelihood that African Americans will face racial antagonism. Some students anticipated racism in the form of direct discrimination and weighed the threat of the glass ceiling heavily. Others anticipated racism in more subtle forms. Students wondered whether a white person would be capable of sympathizing with the experiences of African Americans or be capable of steering them from discrimination at the hands of others. Still others questioned the capacity of whites to refrain from racist remarks and maintain an amicable atmosphere. In most cases, these students believed the answer was no.

What appears to differentiate those African Americans who let fear affect their occupational interests from those who did not was, in part, their capacity to balance the role of race in their lives. Here again segregated racial ties, particularly those maintained in college, seem to be a contributor to the persistence and amplification of these fears. Racial diversity produces not only racial understanding, but a heightened sense of sameness and familiarity among persons of different racial groups. Although African Americans who maintained integrated social networks were concerned with the negative experiences related to being black in America, it seems that knowing people of other races not only breeds closeness, but decreases the suspicion with which some of these students perceive persons of other races and the occupational fields in which they are dominant.

Racial Diversity on Campus and Beyond

What is clear from this research and prior studies is that the degree and type of racial diversity on college campuses contributes to college students' personal and intellectual development as well as their ability to live in a global community (Gurin et al. 2002; Chang, Astin, and Kim 2004).[1] Positive interactions between diverse students and faculty lower anxiety about interracial interaction, increase students' sense of belonging, and have a variety of positive academic consequences (Locks, Hurtado, and Bowman 2008).

True diversity transcends numbers and requires an institutional commitment from the top down (*A Bridge for All* 2004). Administrators can communicate their priorities to students, staff, and faculty alike by increasing the proportion of faculty of color, designating some courses focused on marginalized groups as core requirements, requiring curricula within academic disciplines to reflect the experiences and opinions of minorities, and providing culturally diverse extracurricular programming targeted at students of all races. This approach informs faculty that their support for diverse course offerings is highly advantageous to their own careers (Maruyama and Moreno 2000; Stark and Lattuca 1997) and communicates to students that diversity is a core mission of the university.

Likewise, diversity must be viewed as a universitywide asset that is of value to students of all races. And it must be reinforced throughout the university in order to be fully effective (*A Bridge for All* 2004). Yet as it stands today, within the most elite institutions the most intensive diversity initiatives are implemented by admissions offices where the emphasis is on recruitment, admission, and enrollment — essential components but by no means sufficient to achieve true diversity.

Universities that profess an interest in racial diversity but concede to racially segregative practices, however, suffer, as Derek Bok, former president of Harvard, explains, "at least a partial defeat in the effort to reap the benefits of diversity. It also dilutes the message it sends to students about the importance of learning to live and work together harmoniously" (Bok 2006, pp. 209–10). Universities that express an interest in diversity should consider how consistent that message is, not only in admissions or dorm life, but in the types of courses offered and the interactions between faculty, administrators, and students. This means developing educational and extracurricular programs that call for the active participation of all students (Gurin and Biren 2006).

Throughout the 1990s, colleges across the nation were called to rethink their support and sponsorship of ethnic theme dorms. In the end, the dorms stayed, but questions remain about whether universities purporting to support diversity ought to sponsor programs that inevitably lead to some form of minority segregation. My intent here is not to question whether programs such as ethnic theme dorms should persist but to insist that university administrators acknowledge the consequences of their support for student requests to segregate themselves. While diversity has significant benefits for students of all races, the role it plays in black students' career aspirations cannot be overlooked. Reliable information about job markets is substantially less accessible to racial minorities. Although Silicon Valley executives have been trying to hire black talent, information about their desirability remained unknown to the black students in segregated social networks (chap. 6). It is incumbent upon universities to ensure that information about the existence, openness, and benefits of specific occupations are funneled to all their students, not only ones that are part of the mainstream campus environment.

STEM Fields

The loss of potential black scientists presents one of the greatest losses of human capital discussed in this book. As high-tech companies near Stanford and Berkeley were taking serious financial losses because of a lack of well-educated workers, some black students in this study were ruling out high-tech or scientific career categories because of their concerns about racial antagonism. African American students have indicated that there is a process at work during their college years that acts independently of their identification with a given discipline: stereotype threat. Black participants provided testimony that we are losing potential black scientists and engineers well before students are called on to make concrete career decisions. Stereotype threat is most influential on minority elites because it affects most severely those individuals with the ability and self-assurance to have identified with a field in which a negative stereotype about their group is salient (Steele 1997). Thus, increasing the number of African Americans in STEM fields may be as much an issue of retention in college as it is an issue of recruitment afterwards. As Bowen, Chingos and McPherson (2009, p. 7) point out, "Serious thought needs to be given to the incentives that influence choice of major among U.S. undergraduates and to the incentives used to encourage students to undertake—and complete—advanced degrees."

One thing is clear from evaluative research: money helps. The Gates

Millennium Scholars Program, for example, which provides funding for tuition, fees, books, and living expenses for up to five years of undergraduate study in STEM fields as well as library science and education has had a major impact on minority scholars' ability to attend more selective schools and to pursue disciplines in which they are less represented.[2] Free from financial responsibilities, Gates Scholars are better able to engage with their academic and extracurricular activities resulting in high GPAs and significant campus leadership positions (Erisman and McSwain 2006). Indeed, black Gates Scholars are more likely than those who are not Gates Scholars to study with other students outside of class, assist faculty research projects, and talk about academic problems with faculty members (Allen et al. 2008). Moreover, Gates Scholars are significantly more likely than similarly situated students of color to aspire to PhDs (Hurtado, Saenz, and Dar 2008), degrees of particular importance in STEM fields.[3]

However, while money may incentivize persistence in STEM fields, it cannot, on its own, curb the effects of stereotype threat. Research indicates that among Hispanics, Gates Scholars were more likely to agree that there were expectations of them to perform in certain, stereotypical ways than those in a control group who had not received the scholarship (Hurtado et al. 1999). Likewise, Gates scholarships did not lessen concerns students of color had concerning the discriminatory climate of their universities (Allen et al. 2008).

Some colleges and universities with a strong institutional commitment to increasing minorities in science, math, and engineering have developed special programs to improve the number of minorities who pursue graduate degrees in these fields. The Meyerhoff Scholars Program at the University of Maryland, Baltimore County (UMBC), has been particularly successful. This program provides students not only with full funding (tuition, room, and board) but also a variety of special supports geared toward students with a commitment to and proven ability in STEM fields.[4]

All incoming scholars attend an accelerated six-week program of credit and noncredit courses in science, math, and study skills in order to provide them with early exposure to the rigors of college life. Throughout their undergraduate careers, students meet with program advisors, attend seminars, take part in study groups, and participate in an array of research, internships, and conferences. The results of this special programming are impressive; between 1996 and 2001, 68 and 63 percent of African American and white students who participated went on to graduate studies in STEM or medical fields (Maton, Hrabowski, and Ozdemir 2007). And, although no one has yet pinpointed exactly which aspects of this particular program have contributed the most to the success of these students, it is evident that engaging African Americans in rigorous training, regardless of the racial composition of their classes or activities, has positive results. By providing ways to support students of color without priming an expectation of failure, programs like these may reinforce students' identification with STEM fields and help them overcome the anxiety they have about prevalent stereotypes. Unfortunately, while programs like Meyerhoff exist, they are largely absent from elite universities. It is worth noting that as of 2010, neither Stanford nor the University of California at Berkeley nor any schools in the Ivy League had implemented any comprehensive programs to increase the rate of minority student enrollment in or graduation from STEM fields though some had departmental initiatives.[5] Nevertheless, elite universities, public and private alike, must recognize the value of increasing the number of female and minority students graduating with STEM degrees.

At the least, administrators need the aid of faculty within STEM fields to do so. Regrettably, as it stands at present, faculty within those disciplines are significantly less likely than their colleagues in the humanities or social sciences to be advocates of diversity. This may be the result of at least two factors. First, although racial minorities are significantly more likely to advocate diversity than their white peers, there are fewer faculty of color within STEM fields (Park and Dennison 2009). Second, these disciplines focus far more on graduate students than undergraduate students since they rely heavily on the former to contribute to their research agendas. Therefore, these faculty members are largely unaware of the experiences of the minority undergraduate students they do teach or how to go about recruiting others (Buchanan 2008). Nonetheless, prior research indicates that African American students who have the opportunity to engage in research with faculty mentors of any race are more comfortable with their academic experiences than are those who do not participate in such projects (Strayhorn 2009). University administrators must therefore find ways to create rewards for STEM faculty to promote undergraduate research opportunities for African Americans and other underrepresented groups (Park and Denison 2009). Two clear incentives are tenure or promotion and pay.

Another key actor in the effort to increase minorities in STEM fields is the federal government. The private and public partnership of BEST (Building Engineering and Science Talent) recommends that federal agencies take the presence of diversity initiatives into account when giving out research awards to institutions of higher education. Likewise, the federal government should continue to provide funding for TRIO programs (originally three but now eight federally funded programs aimed at increasing access to higher education for disadvantaged students) such as the McNair Undergraduate Achievement Program, which provides grants to public and private colleges and universities to move more underrepresented students through the pipeline to PhDs by providing research opportunities, seminars, and tutoring. On average, the McNair project provides close to $9,000 to each student participating. Yet in 2010, only a small proportion of those institutions with McNair awards were elite or highly selective (*A Bridge for All* 2004).

Implications for Affirmative Action

Racial representation in a range of occupations and within universities has significant implications for public policy. The slow death of affirmative action comes at a time when our nation most needs it. In 1996, less than twenty years after the landmark 1978 decision in the *Bakke* case, the Court of Appeals for the Fifth Circuit, in the case of *Hopwood v. Texas* struck a staggering blow to affirmative action, holding nearly all forms of affirmative action unlawful, with the exception of those used to remedy discrimination practiced by a specific unit within a university. Similarly, in 1995, the Board of Regents of the University of California system voted to eliminate affirmative action in hiring and admissions, effective the following January. Such court decisions and legislation have had considerable consequences including a decrease in the enrollment of African Americans at selective universities. The most recent Supreme Court rulings (*Grutter v. Bollinger* and *Gratz v. Bollinger*), although painted in a relatively positive light by proponents of affirmative action, cannot undo the damage that the constant denigration of this policy has left.

Despite the court's holding that race was one of several factors that could be taken into account in admissions decisions and that attaining a critical mass of underrepresented minorities was not analogous to a quota system, many public schools, including Berkeley, have begun to discontinue recruitment programs targeting minorities. Although African Americans are arguably in a better position educationally than they were thirty years ago, there are simply not enough African Americans on predominantly white campuses to mollify their fears. That so many black students, regardless of affiliation with the Black Community at Stanford or Berkeley, cited concerns about racism on and off campus is indicative of lingering problems with minority underrepresentation and racial intolerance.

In addition to the loss of black students who might have been admitted under affirmative action and how these court decisions affect students' perspectives about racial antagonism, the loss of racially targeted retention programs in STEM may also be problematic. African American students' disproportionate movement away from technical and scientific fields suggests that losses in those areas will probably be greater than the general loss in other fields. Yet, this problem will likely remain unaddressed as university administrations like those at the University of California struggle to avoid being the next target of a lawsuit against what would inevitably be labeled "racial preferences." Unfortunately, racial representation is a cycle: the more African Americans there are in an occupation or academic field, the more there will be in the future.

Implications for the Future

Since the 1970s, class has created a notable divide in the life chances of African Americans (Wilson 1978), but race has played a predominant role in sustaining a division in the life chances of African Americans and whites, particularly those who are well-educated. The students I have profiled here—African American and white—are all intelligent, driven people. Yet race remains a key distinguisher in their futures. While the urban underclass is a significant problem within the African American population, the inattention that middle-class, well-educated African Americans receive trivializes the tremendous role race plays in the destiny of black people. My study focused on a segment of the black population that has not received much attention but is the one we expect to be making the greatest strides.

   As the political climate of this country remains conservative with regard to racially targeted programs, the chance that African Americas will attain occupational equality with whites dissolves (Brown et al. 2003). The very programs that could be instrumental in creating a self-perpetuating cycle of upward mobility for African Americans are relentlessly challenged as unfair to those who currently enjoy considerable structural and institutional advantages. Moreover, the consistency of these challenges leaves liberal educators and policymakers unwilling to review the efficacy of their programs, as they are too engrossed in maintaining the right to preserve them. The number of well-educated African Americans may still increase despite the discontinuation of affirmative action in admissions, but given the dynamics of occupational choices described here, racial differences in occupational attainment are likely to remain potent until increasing numbers of African Americans enter a greater diversity of occupations.

This lack of occupational diversity, while problematic for individual African Americans, contributes to a considerably larger community level problem. As Wilson (1978, 1987, 1996), Massey and Denton (1993) and others have aptly demonstrated, residential segregation coupled with economic inequalities can have profound impacts on the African American population. Yet the preference of black students for racialized, lower-paying jobs diminishes their financial impact on the communities in which they live or to which they hope to contribute, and lessens their potential influence on major social policies that impact African Americans.

I urge those who may be inclined to view this as a "black problem" to reconsider. This is an American problem. American companies have historically relied upon foreign human and intellectual capital (chap. 6). Not only does Europe dip from the same pool for talent as the United States, but the home countries of many of these highly-educated workers such as China and India are increasingly pushing to retain their nationals. In 1999 alone, the workforce gap cost the seven largest Silicon Valley industry clusters between $3 and $4 billion in incremental hiring and opportunity costs including salary premiums, human resources staff and managers, referral fees, time, search firms, orientation, relocation, and productivity losses (Joint Venture Silicon Valley Network 1999). This widening gap threatens the growth of our science- and technology-based industries and the economic vitality of the regions harboring them.

In March 2008, Bill Gates testified before the House of Representatives Committee on Science and Technology (Gates 2008). During his testimony, Gates repeatedly advanced the point that the United States is facing a grave deficit of scientists and engineers needed to develop new technology and maintain America's foothold in these fields. The two ways in which he proposed to alleviate this problem were changes in immigration law and making STEM education and occupations more appealing to youth, particularly minority youth.

Because African Americans receive 7 percent of American bachelor's degrees awarded, we must use this pool of talent as best we can. But to do so, we must also recognize what keeps them from pursuing a wider array of occupational fields and specialties. The problems facing this young generation are not the same as those confronted by their parents and grandparents. They are not constrained by de jure segregation or discrimination, yet its de facto cousin constricts the perimeters of their interests and perceived options. Although my explorations have identified a powerful set of obstacles facing these students, further work is needed to confirm the extent and applicability of my findings. But if the implications of my findings are correct, we are losing out on a pool of intellectual capital that could generate major benefits for the black community in particular and for our nation as a whole.

> Whether you like it or not the millions are here, and here they will remain. If you do not lift them up, they will pull you down . . . The Talented Tenth of the Negro race must be made leaders of thought and missionaries of culture among their people.
>
> W. E. B. DUBOIS, "The Talented Tenth"

NOTES

Chapter 1

1. In 1969, African Americans with at least a college degree earned 23.6% less than whites with at least a college degree. In 2000, African Americans with at least a college degree earned 22.1% less than their white counterparts.

2. Collins (p. 14) identifies racialized jobs as those with "a substantive or a symbolic connection to black communities, black issues, or civil rights agencies at any level of government" and mainstream jobs as those that have "neither explicit nor implicit connections to blacks." Racialized jobs include social services, both public and private, geared toward black communities, entrepreneurial work within black market niches, black specialties offered to mainstream institutions, such as attorneys specializing in federal or state contract compliance for private companies, as well as positions within mainstream corporations geared toward maintaining black community relations or implementing affirmative action.

3. It is possible that as the proportion of an occupation which is black increases, that occupation will become increasingly devalued just as women's work has been (Cohen and Huffman 2003; Gurin et al. 2002). That is, as an occupation becomes "blacker," its pay and prestige may diminish. This does not, however, negate the importance of diversifying occupations. Diversification lowers the impact of loss by distributing the proportion of African American professionals so that when one or another occupation becomes devalued, the black community is not as heavily impacted as if it had put all its proverbial eggs into one basket. Moreover, because African Americans would be a relatively small proportion of the workforce in any profession if it were truly diversified, it is unlikely those jobs would experience the devaluation that women's work does when it becomes predominantly female.

4. According to Melguizo's (2008) analyses of the National Education Longitudinal Study, the selectivity of schools is closely related to graduation rates. Specifically, black students at the most selective and at highly selective institutions

graduate at a rate of 92% within 8 years; white and Asian students at those same schools have graduation rates of 91 and 97%, respectively, in the same amount of time. But black students at very selective, selective, and nonselective schools graduate at rates of 69, 51, and 45%, respectively. Moreover, regression estimates indicate that when academic preparedness is controlled for, attending a highly selective institution is still significantly related to college graduation. Similarly, in a study of highly selective institutions, Espenshade and Radford (2009) found that attending the most selective tier of colleges significantly increased the likelihood of graduating within six years.

5. The interviews were conducted in the author's office at Stanford or at the Multicultural Center and Berkeley depending on students' affiliations.

6. Although I used convenience sampling to recruit participants, the respondents varied considerably from one another in many aspects of life. At both the University of California and Stanford, students came from a variety of departments, states, social networks, religions, political affiliations, interests, and socioeconomic backgrounds. Some African American students had attended private, predominantly white schools while others came from public schools whose largest populations were black or black and Hispanic. Most white students had attended predominantly white schools, although some went to public and others attended private schools. The point is these young people are diverse, representative of the diversity, racial and otherwise, at these schools.

7. I limited white participants to European Americans. All of the participants were American citizens and had been for the majority of their lives. Only a few of those who were naturalized citizens had spent the first few years of their childhood overseas.

8. Verbatim occupational categories identified by participants are available from the author by request and are cited throughout the paper.

9. I refer to an occupation as a racialized specialty in this book only if students specifically associated it with African Americans, for example, a nonprofit for black children, an African American news magazine, African American product marketing.

10. I use 9% to establish a threshold of difference between certain types of careers in which African Americans are more or less represented. African Americans comprise 7.2% of the professional, official, and management categories of workers (US Census Bureau 2000). Thus, 9% of an occupation represents a circumstance in which African Americans are overrepresented relative to their proportion of the professional and managerial/official workforce.

Chapter 2

1. *Pearson v. Murray.* 169 Md., 478 (1936); *McLaurin v. Oklahoma State Regents for Higher Ed.* 339 U.S. 637 (1950).

2. Soon after, Nixon issued Revised Order Number 4, which instituted a requirement for all federal contractors to have affirmative action plans with minority and female hiring goals (Sweet 2006).

3. Even prior to the Civil Rights Act of 1964, individual states began instituting programs similar to those of the federal government. As of 1964, almost half of the states had established laws against employment discrimination; these state

laws provided legal protections to 40% of African Americans and almost 100% of blacks living outside of the South (Stainback, Robinson, and Tomaskovic-Devey 2005). By the end of the 1980s, more than 200 state and local government programs existed although they were frequently limited to contracting (Sweet 2006).

4. The United States Supreme Court also decided several landmark cases in the 1970s that reinforced the efforts of the Equal Employment Opportunity Commission. These cases include *Albemarle Paper Co. v. Moody, Franks v. Bowman Transportation Co.,* and *International Brotherhood of Teamsters v. U.S.,* which respectively held that: retroactive seniority to the date of an individual's being denied a position was an appropriate relief for the victim of discrimination; back pay should be provided to victims of discrimination; and statistics are probative of discrimination (EEOC 2004).

5. In 1971, Executive Order 11625 authorized the Secretary of Commerce to implement federal policy to aid Minority Business Enterprises (MBE) usually covered under 8(a).

6. This was succeeded by the Small Business Investment Act amendments in 1978, which required bidders of government contracts for over $500,000 in goods and services or $1,000,000 for construction to submit plans with percentage goals for minority business enterprise subcontracting.

7. While some data may indicate that black prosperity increased through the 1970s and beyond, it is largely the result of distortions in the indicators of income (such as household income compared with per capita income). Instead, the relative density of black individuals with higher incomes had diminished since 1979.

8. Between 1979 and 1987, the proportion of whites receiving income under the poverty line increased by 20%, while the proportion earning three or more times the poverty level decreased only 9%. Over the same time, the proportion of African Americans earning below the poverty level also increased by 20% (to 40.6% of wage earners), while high-wage workers decreased by 22% (Harrison and Gorham 1992).

9. During a 1989 interview on CBS, Reagan stated that "One of the great things that I have suffered is this feeling that somehow I'm on the other side [of the civil rights movement]" (Rosenthal 1989).

10. With the exception of 1988, when Reagan requested $343 million but the Democratic Congress allocated only $319 million.

11. Complaints rose from 56,228 in 1981 to 87,942 in 1993. Between 1982 and 1992, the number of complaints received per year stayed almost consistently between 60,000 and 72,000.

12. This agency is charged with six primary tasks: "(1) conducting compliance reviews and investigating complaints; (2) negotiating conciliation agreements and letters of commitment from contractors and subcontractors who are in violation of regulatory requirements; (3) monitoring contractor compliance and compliance reports; (4) forming links between contractors and Department of Labor (DOL) job-training programs; (5) providing technical assistance to aid contractor understanding of and compliance with federal nondiscrimination requirements; and (6) recommending enforcement actions to the DOL Solicitor" (United States Commission on Civil Rights 1995).

13. The 1984 Supreme Court ruling in *Grove City College v. Bell* ruled that Title IX of the Education Amendments of 1972 which prohibits sexual discrimination in education, applied only to discrimination in a private institution's program or activity directly receiving Federal funding.

14. The lack of impact contract compliance has had on black professionals is directly related to the way in which nondiscrimination is measured by the government. Employers must file an EEO-1 form if they have government contracts of over $50,000 and 50 or more employees; or if they do not have a federal contract but have at least 100 employees. To avoid claims of discrimination by monitoring agencies such as the OFCCP or the EEOC, an employer must show that the proportion of minority employees in job groups or occupational strata within their organization is not significantly different from the proportion of available minorities within those job groups in the general vicinity and/or population. There is no hard and fast rule, however, for how the pools are measured within an organization or the general population; that is, how the contract compliance officer computes the available pool can vary drastically, especially when considering specific occupational categories at the professional level. It is, as the Equal Employment Opportunity Commission claims, "as much an art as a science" (OFCCP 2007). Therefore in monitoring discrimination against African Americans, it is considerably more difficult for the EEOC or the OFCCP to determine whether a firm is not in compliance for professionals since there is no strict measure of compliance with which to begin.

15. This is accomplished by the complainant providing evidence (1) that he or she is a member of a protected class; (2) was qualified for and/or satisfactorily performing the position in question; and (3) despite being qualified, suffered an adverse employment decision dissimilar to peers who are not members of a protected class.

16. This figure was arrived at by performing a Westlaw search every five years and in 2007 of keywords "employment discrimination," "race," and "black" and/or "African American" and subsequently reading through the case records to determine whether the case was (a) relevant and (b) whether the ruling was in favor of the plaintiff or defendant. Ultimately, decisions were in favor of defendants in 166 of the 237 cases, while an additional 33 cases had split decisions.

17. For explanations of the increase in the urban underclass, see Massey and Denton's *American Apartheid* or Wilson's *The Declining Significance of Race, When Work Disappears,* or *The Truly Disadvantaged.*

Chapter 3

1. High poverty schools are defined as schools in which at least 75% of students receive free or reduced-price lunches.

2. The black and white middle-classes in the greater population are relatively distinct. African Americans in the black middle class typically hold lower-middle-class jobs, but white middle-class workers are split evenly between lower-middle-class positions and upper-middle-class careers (Pattillo-McCoy 1999).

3. In this study I do not differentiate between the children of African or Caribbean immigrants and the children of long-time African American families; however, some might argue that this distinction is important; see, for example, Shaw-

Taylor and Tuch 2007 and Waters 1999. There were only two black students in my sample whose parents were African or Caribbean and I discuss their backgrounds, when applicable, in both cases.

4. The higher debt noted by students in this study is consistent with findings from the National Study of College Experience (Espenshade and Radford 2009). Both black and Hispanic students and the parents or relatives of black and Hispanic students were significantly more likely to have acquired debt from college than whites or the parents or relatives of white students.

5. Rothstein and Rouse (2007) found that debt has a positive effect on the choice of higher-salary careers and significantly decreases the probability that students will select lower-paid, public interest work. Using data garnered from the records of 8,641 students in cohorts entering between 1995 and 2002 at "Anonymous University," described as a "wealthy, highly selective university," the authors specified several models using debt as a primary independent variable. Their analyses show that the likelihood that a student will take a job in a nonprofit, government, or education decreases by 6 percentage points from the 17% baseline, with the addition of $10,000 of student debt. That is, the addition of $10,000 in debt decreases the likelihood of a student entering these fields to 11%. The authors also show that once college preparation is controlled for, debt has no significant impact on their graduating GPA, suggesting that the effects of debt on occupational choices reflect preferences rather than limitations based on academic performance.

6. This is similar to previous findings that, holding constant economic background, African Americans are significantly more likely to feel they owe a debt to their families for help and support than whites (Higginbotham and Weber 1992).

Chapter 4

1. Berkeley has a considerably smaller proportion of black and Hispanic students than Stanford due in part to Proposition 209, which eliminated the consideration of race in college admissions.

2. I defined segregated networks as those whose members had no close friendships with persons of other races. According to this definition, eleven of the thirty black participants in this sample (37%) had segregated networks. This is consistent with larger samples at similarly selective institutions. For example, 38% of black students in the National Study of College Experience reported that they had no close friendships with students of other races (Espenshade and Radford 2009). Likewise, Charles and others (2009) found that of their ten closest friends, African American students reported an average of 5.8 black friends and only 2.4 white friends.

3. Saenz, Hoi, and Hurtado (2007) found a significant positive relationship between the frequency with which black students studied with persons of other races before college and how positive their interracial interactions were in college. It is worth noting, however, that Espendshade and Radford's analyses (2009) showed no significant relationship between the degree of diversity at students' high schools and the diversity of college social networks.

4. Espenshade and Radford (2009) initially found a significant relationship be-

tween patterns of interracial interaction and social class in their descriptive statistics. However, logistic regressions controlling for additional factors such as the type of college, the percent of nonwhite students at an institution, and freshman year employment produced no statistically significant relationships between social class and a variety of interracial social interactions.

5. Their findings also indicate that students of color are more likely than whites to perceive classroom climates as unwelcoming to underrepresented minorities. Similarly, students of color are significantly more likely to see the campus racial climate as worsening while white students are apt to see the campus climate as improving.

6. One of the primary reasons I do not discuss the racial composition of white social networks often in this book is that few white students had more than one or two friends (or more than 20% of their friends) of another race and only one white student had a social network composed purely of nonwhite students. Because of this, any comparison of or between integrated and segregated white social networks would be very difficult and potentially erroneous.

7. Levin, van Laar, and Sidanius (2003) found that students who had more racial outgroup friends in their second and third years of college were less biased in favor of their own racial group and were less anxious about interracial interactions at the end of their fourth year, even once background characteristics and prior attitudes and friendships were controlled for. Ingroup friendships, however, had insignificant effects once outgroup relationships were taken into account.

8. Although it would be convenient to delineate black students with integrated and those with segregated social groups according to differences in previous experiences of racism or socioeconomic backgrounds, it simply is not possible here. African American students with segregated and integrated networks came from a similar range of socioeconomic circumstances. Both groups reported family incomes ranging from $20,000 to $120,000 and $14,000 to $300,000, respectively, and both had median incomes of $70,000. Moreover, there was considerable variation in the degree of racial antagonism previously faced by African American students with both types of social groups.

9. The difference in the types of interactions relative to the size of the black populations on these two campuses is consistent with Chang, Astin, and Kim's (2004) finding that certain informal student interactions such as dining and studying with students of other races is inversely related to the proportion of the student population that are minorities. This trend is the opposite of that of white students—specifically, as the proportion of minorities rises, white students' interracial interactions increase.

10. Fifty percent (approximately 66) of the seats are reserved for black students; these spaces equate to roughly 10% of the black undergraduate population.

11. Past research indicates that living arrangements have significant effects on students' subsequent behavior and achievement. For example, Espenshade and Radford (2009) found that living in race-focused housing can decrease the likelihood of students interacting with persons from other races. Similarly, living with a student of another race freshman year has a positive effect on the likelihood of socializing with and/or living with a person of another race in subsequent years.

12. "Incog" is short for "incog negro." In this context, it is used to describe black students who had gone "incognito" by not participating in the Black Community.

13. The report specifically cited Princeton's Minority Affairs Advisors, who provide social and academic guidance to minority students and develop race-related programming for the entire campus community.

14. Guiffrida (2003) observes that black student organizations serve as positive outlets for black students to openly discuss racial antagonism among persons they believe would offer support. The existence of such opportunities are directly associated with their degree of comfort on campus.

Chapter 5

1. Research on sensitivity to status-based rejection asserts that marginalized groups such as African Americans are prone to "develop expectations of rejection by those who do not share their stigma and by social institutions that have historically excluded or marginalized them" (Mendoza-Denton et al. 2002, p. 897) based on direct or vicarious experiences (Branscombe, Schmitt, and Harvey 1999).

2. McDermott and Samson (2005) point to a new area of research which explores variations in the meaning of whiteness.

3. Past research (Ellemers, Van Knippenberg, and Wilke 1990) has shown, under some conditions, in-group identity serves as a coping strategy, particularly when members of a disadvantaged group regard their position as discomfiting. That is, a strong attachment to a disadvantaged group can serve as a buffer of negative psychological effects (Branscombe and Ellemers 1998). The heightened perception of racism exhibited by students with segregated networks in this study is consistent with findings from several quantitative psychological and sociological studies. For example, Postmes and Branscombe (2002) found that African American college students living in segregated environments reported feeling more rejected by nonblacks than did African American students living in desegregated environments. Similarly, Kluegel and Bobo (2001) observed a weak negative relationship between having whites in a social network and perceptions of discrimination in the workplace. Other researchers have examined the impact on the size of students' in-group network. Levin and others (2006) found that African American students with more in-group friends at the end of their first year in college were significantly more likely to perceive discrimination during their second and third years.

Chapter 6

1. Quoted in "Jesse Jackson Blasted Out of the Sky," *American Enterprise* 10, no. 3 (1999): 12.

2. This figure includes outlays to health care services, health care research, and training, as well as general science, space, and technology outlays.

3. Over 60% of black women and 50% of black men who were originally interested in STEM moved to a non-STEM field.

4. Thus, there was no net change in the percent of white men in STEM majors in my sample; at all times 33% of white men intended to major in STEM.

5. Although small, this sample does report rates of attrition consistent with those observed in past quantitative analyses (McJamerson 1992; Elliott et al 1996).

6. According to findings from the National Study of College Experience, a longitudinal study of students at ten selective universities, 90% of black students reported that at least 50% of their professors were white (Espenshade and Radford 2009).

7. In 2000, African American women accounted for 61% of full-time black college enrollments (National Science Foundation 2007b). In this same year, African American women accounted for 65% of African American baccalaureate recipients.

8. It is also important to recognize that while some HBCUs like Morehouse, Spelman, Hampton, and Howard are themselves quite prestigious, these institutions receive considerably less funding for on-site research than equivalent predominantly white institutions and are, despite their stature, frequently considered less prestigious by nonblacks.

Chapter 7

1. In particular, African Americans express a significant commitment to social responsibility whereas whites display a strong adherence to individualistic principles. A series of meta-analyses confirm that African Americans (and Asian Americans) exhibit significantly higher degrees of collectivism than do whites (Coon and Kemmelmeier 2001; Cox, Lobel, and McLeod 1991).

2. One of the underlying differences in the definitions of collectivism and individualism that accounts for the differences in racial adherence to these principles is the belief in the fairness of the current distribution of goods. While individualism is premised on the notion that opportunities are openly accessible to those who avail themselves—free of constraints based on individual background characteristics—collectivism stresses egalitarianism and a duty to remedy unwarranted social inequalities. Those who benefit from a system of stratification are more likely to judge that system's inequalities as just, whereas those in disadvantaged situations will view such inequality as illegitimate (Robinson and Bell 1978; Ng and Allen 2005).

3. The only difference found between African American women and men in these ratings was that family-related activities rated higher among black women than men, but not considerably.

4. In a national sample 75% of African Americans concurred that what happens to African Americans in the country affects their lives at least "somewhat" while over 30% believed it affects their lives "a lot" or is "highly linked" (Dawson 1994).

5. The numbers in table 1 are based on students' estimation of their own participation in a variety of activities. It reflects the proportion of highly active students and parents. Many more students, both black and white, reported having participated in occasional events.

6. The importance of such activities in framing students' career choices is documented by McAdam (1988) in reference to Freedom Summer participants. Nearly fifteen years after their service in Mississippi, over 50% of volunteers reported being currently involved with one or more social movements. In con-

trast, only one-third of those who had applied to take part in Freedom Summer but did not participate made such claims.

Chapter 9

1. Specifically, informal interactions with diverse racial groups had a statistically significant effect on the intellectual engagement and self-assessed academic abilities of black, white, Latino, and Asian students (Gurin et al. 2002). Similarly, studying with persons of other races had a significant positive relationship on students' social abilities and civic interests; interracial dating had a positive influence on civic interests; and classroom diversity was positively related to intellectual abilities, social abilities, and civic interests (Chang, Astin, and Kim 2004).

2. Espenshade and Radford's (2009) analysis of the National Study of College Experience indicates that lower-class students are actually overrepresented at private colleges and working-class students are represented equally at in- and out-of-state public schools and private schools. Working- and lower-class students pay for selective private colleges by taking out loans, securing scholarships (such as the Gates Millennium Program), working, and receiving aid from family members. However, Avery and Hoxby's logit regressions (2004) indicate that while students whose parents have "high," "medium-high," or "medium-low" income are more likely to attend the most selective school into which they are accepted, the odds ratio for low-income students is insignificant. Instead, the amount of grant money promised from a given institution significantly impacts the likelihood of students from low-income backgrounds matriculating (as it did for students from low-medium, high-medium, and high-income backgrounds). Researchers conjecture that students selected as Gates Scholars are able to make school choices without considering the cost of more selective institutions and without burdening themselves with significant debt or work (Erisman and McSwain 2006).

3. Specifically, 33.6 percent of Gates Scholars aspired to PhDs relative to 22.3 percent of nonrecipients and 24.7 percent of students in the Cooperative Institutional Research Program survey 2002 cohort. The option of extending funding into graduate studies has resulted in a significantly higher rate of applications to and enrollment in graduate schools among Gates Scholars than among their nonrecipient counterparts (Erisman and McSwain 2006).

4. The Meyerhoff Scholars Program was developed in 1988 by Baltimore philanthropists Robert and Jane Meyerhoff. While it was originally available only to black male students, it opened its doors to black women in 1990 and to students of all races interested in increasing minority representation in STEM fields in 1996 as a result of increasing hostility toward race-specific programming.

5. By comprehensive I mean programs aimed specifically at the recruitment and retention of minority students in a range of STEM fields, not only in a specific department. Although Berkeley does not have any comprehensive programs, it does have a Biology Scholars Program that provides a variety of resources to student members including academic support, social activities, research opportunities, mentoring, and seminars on graduate degrees and careers in the biological sciences. Students of any race or gender are allowed to participate

and unlike the Meyerhoff Scholars Program, several components are remedial in nature. BSP students of all races are more likely to graduate with degrees in biology than nonparticipants who intended to major in the field. However, while Hispanic biology majors who participated in BSP have significantly higher GPAs than Hispanic biology majors who did not, African American, Asian American and white BSP students do not graduate with significantly higher GPAs than their non-BSP counterparts. See Matsui et al. 2003 for more information.

REFERENCES

Court Cases

Adarand Constructors, Inc. v. Federico Pena, Secretary of Transportation, et al., 515 U.S., 200 (1995).

Albemarle Paper Co. v. Moody, 422 U.S., 405 (1975).

Brown v. Board of Educ. of Topeka 347 U.S., 483 (1954).

Franks v. Bowman Transportation Co., 424 U.S. 747 (1976).

Gratz v. Bollinger, 539 U.S., 244 (2003).

Grove City College v. Bell, 465 U.S., 555 (1984).

Grutter v. Bollinger, 539 U.S., 306 (2003).

Hopwood v. State of Texas, 78 F. 3d, 932 (5th Cir. 1996).

Int'l Bhd. of Teamsters v. United States, 431 U.S., 324 (1977).

McLaurin v. Oklahoma State Regents for Higher Education, 339 U.S., 637 (1950).

Parents Involved in Community Schools v. Seattle School District No. 1, 515 U.S., 701 (2007).

Patterson v. McLean Credit Union, 491 U.S., 164 (1989).

Pearson v. Murray, 169 Md., 478 (1936).

Price Waterhouse v. Hopkins, No. 87-1167 U.S., 490, 228 (1989).

City of Richmond v. Croson, 488 U.S., 469 (1989).

The Board of Education of the Oklahoma City Public Schools v. Dowell, 498 U.S., 237 (1991).

Walton v. Cowin Equipment Co., Inc., 774 F.Supp., 1343 (N.D. Ala.1991).

Wards Cove Packing Company v. Antonio, 490 U.S., 642 (1989).

Publications

A Bridge for All: Higher Education Design Principles to Broaden Participation in Science, Technology, Engineering and Mathematics. 2004. San Diego: Building Engineering and Science Talent.

Adelman, Robert M. 2005. "The Roles of Race, Class, and Residential Preferences in the Neighborhood Racial Composition of Middle-Class Blacks and Whites." *Social Science Quarterly* 86 (1): 209–228.

Afshar-Mohajer, Ramin, and Evelyn Sung. 2002. *The Stigma of Inclusion: Racial Paternalism/Separatism in Higher Education.* New York: New York Civil Rights Coalition.

Alba, Richard D., John R. Logan, and Brian J. Stults. 2000. "How Segregated are Middle-Class African Americans?" *Social Problems* 47 (4): 543–558.

Alexander, Karl L., and Bruce K. Eckland. 1974. "Sex Differences in the Educational Attainment Process." *American Sociological Review* 39 (5): 668–682.

Alexander, Norman C., and Ernest Q. Campbell. 1964. "Peer Influences on Adolescent Educational Aspirations and Attainments." *American Sociological Review* 29 (4): 568–275.

Allen, Walter R. 1992. "The Color of Success: African-American College Student Outcomes at Predominantly White and Historically Black Public Colleges and Universities." *Harvard Educational Review* 62 (1): 26–44.

———.1978. "The Journal of Negro Education." *Race, Family Setting, and Adolescent Achievement Orientation* 47 (3): 230–243.

Allen, Walter R., Alexes Harris, Gniesha Dinwiddie, and Kimberly A. Griffin. 2008. "Saving Grace: A Comparative Analysis of African American Gates Millennium Scholars and Non-Recipients." In *Resources, Assets, and Strengths among Successful Diverse Students: Understanding the Contributions of the Gates Millennium Scholars Program,* edited by William T. Trent and Edward P. St. John, Readings on Equal Education, vol. 23, 17–48. New York: AMS Press.

Allport, Gordon W. 1979. *The Nature of Prejudice.* 25th Anniversary ed. Reading, MA: Addison-Wesley.

Alon, Sigal. 2007. "Overlapping Disadvantages and the Racial/Ethnic Graduation Gap among Students Attending Selective Institutions." *Social Science Research* 36 (4): 1475–1499.

Alon, Sigal, and Marta Tienda. 2005. "Assessing the 'Mismatch' Hypothesis: Differences in College Graduation Rates by Institutional Selectivity." *Sociology of Education* 78 (4): 294–315.

Amaker, Norman C. 1988. *Civil Rights and the Reagan Administration.* Washington, DC: Urban Institute Press.

Ancis, Julie R., William E. Sedlacek, and Jonathan J. Mohr. 2000. "Student Perceptions of Campus Cultural Climate by Race." *Journal of Counseling and Development* 78: 180–185.

Anderson, James D. 2001. "Race in American Higher Education: Historical Perspectives on Current Conditions." In *The Racial Crisis in American Higher Education: Continuing Challenges for the Twenty-First Century*, rev. ed., 3–22. Albany: State University of New York Press.

———. 1988. *The Education of Blacks in the South, 1860–1935*. Chapel Hill: University of North Carolina Press.

Arcidiacono, Peter, and Sean Nicholson. 2005. "Peer Effects in Medical School." *Journal of Public Economics* 89 (2–3): 327–350.

Aronson, Joshua, Diane M. Quinn, and Steven J. Spencer. 1998. "Stereotype Threat and the Academic Underperformance of Minorities and Women." In *Prejudice: The Target's Perspective*, edited by Janet K. Swim and Charles Stangor, 83–103. San Diego: Academic Press.

Aud, Susan, Mary A. Fox, and Angelina KewalRamani. 2010. *Status and Trends in the Education of Racial and Ethnic Minorities*. Washington, DC: US Government Printing Office.

Avery, Christopher, and Caroline Minter Hoxby. 2004. "Do and Should Financial Aid Packages Affect Students' College Choices?" In *College Choices: The Economics of Where to Go, When to Go, and How to Pay for It*, edited by Caroline Minter Hoxby, 239–302. Chicago: University of Chicago Press.

Avery, Derek R. 2003. "Reactions to Diversity in Recruitment Advertising—Are Differences Black and White?" *Journal of Applied Psychology* 88 (4): 672–679.

Babad, Elisha. 1995. "The 'Teacher's Pet' Phenomenon, Students' Perceptions of Teachers' Differential Behavior, and Students' Morale." *Journal of Educational Psychology* 87 (3): 361–374.

Barringer, Herbert, and Gene Kassebaum. 1989. "Asian Indians as a Minority in the United States." *Sociological Perspectives* 32 (4): 501–520.

Bates, Timothy. 2001. "Minority Business Access to Mainstream Markets." *Journal of Urban Affairs* 23 (1): 41–56.

Battle, Juan, and Deborah L. Coates. 2004. "Father-Only and Mother-Only, Single-Parent Family Status of Black Girls and Achievement in Grade Twelve and at Two-Years Post High School." *Journal of Negro Education* 73 (4): 392–407.

Bennett, Pamela R., and Amy Lutz. 2009. "How African American Is the Net Black Advantage? Differences in College Attendance among Immigrant Blacks, Native Blacks, and Whites." *Sociology of Education* 82 (1): 70–100.

Berg, Helen, and Marianne Ferber. 1983. "Men and Women Graduate Students: Who Succeeds and Why?" *Journal of Higher Education* 54 (6): 629–648.

Bergmann, Barbara R. 1996. *In Defense of Affirmative Action*. New York: Basic Books.

Blair, Sampson Lee, and Zhenchao Qian. 1998. "Family and Asian Students' Educational Performance: A Consideration of Diversity." *Journal of Family Issues* 19 (4): 355–374.

Blascovich, Jim, Steven J. Spencer, Diane Quinn, and Claude Steele. 2001. "African Americans and High Blood Pressure: The Role of Stereotype Threat." *Psychological Science* 12 (3): 225–229.

Blau, Peter Michael, and Otis Dudley Duncan. 1967. *The American Occupational Structure*. New York: John Wiley & Sons.

Bobo, Lawrence D. 2001. "Race, Interests, and Beliefs about Affirmative Action: Unanswered Questions and New Directions." In *Color Lines*, edited by John David Skrentny, 191–213. Chicago: University of Chicago Press.

———. 1998. "Race, Interests, and Beliefs about Affirmative Action." *American Behavioral Scientist* 41 (7): 985–1003.

———. 1991. "Social Responsibility, Individualism, and Redistributive Policies." *Sociological Forum* 6 (1): 71–92.

Bobo, Lawrence D., and Ryan A. Smith. 1998. "From Jim Crow Racism to Laissez-Faire Racism: The Transformation of Racial Attitudes." In *Beyond Pluralism*, edited by Wendy F. Katkin, Ned Landsman, and Andrea Tyree, 182–220. Urbana: University of Illinois Press.

Bok, Derek Curtis. 2006. *Our Underachieving Colleges: A Candid Look at How Much Students Learn and Why They Should Be Learning More*. Princeton: Princeton University Press.

Bonacich, Edna. 1973. "A Theory of Middleman Minorities." *American Sociological Review* 38 (5): 583–594.

Bonilla-Silva, Eduardo. 2004. "From Bi-Racial to Tri-Racial: Towards a New System of Racial Stratification in the USA." *Ethnic and Racial Studies* 27 (6): 931–950.

———. 2003. *Racism without Racists: Color-Blind Racism and the Persistence of Racial Inequality in the United States*. Lanham, MD: Rowman & Littlefield.

Bonilla-Silva, Eduardo, and Tyrone A. Forman. 2000. "'I Am Not a Racist but . . .': Mapping White College Students' Racial Ideology in the USA." *Discourse & Society* 11 (1): 50–85.

Bonilla-Silva, Eduardo, and Amanda Lewis. 1999. "The New Racism: Racial Structure in the United States, 1960s–1990s." In *Race, Ethnicity and*

Nationality in the USA: Toward the Twenty-First Century, edited by Paul Wong. Boulder, CO: Westview.

Bonilla-Silva, Eduardo, and Victor Ray. 2009. "When Whites Love a Black Leader: Race Matters in Obamerica." *Journal of African American Studies* 13 (2): 176–183.

Bositis, David. 2008. "Blacks and the 2008 Elections: A Preliminary Analysis." *Focus* 36: 12–16.

———. 2002. *Black Elected Officials A Statistical Summary 2001.* Washington, DC: Joint Center for Political and Economic Studies.

Bosson, Jennifer K., Ethan L. Haymovitz, and Elizabeth C. Pinel. 2004. "When Saying and Doing Diverge: The Effects of Stereotype Threat on Self-Reported Versus Non-Verbal Anxiety." *Journal of Experimental Social Psychology* 40 (2): 247–255.

Bourdieu, Pierre, and Jean-Claude Passeron. 1977. *Reproduction in Education, Society, and Culture.* Translated by Richard Nice. Sage Studies in Social and Educational Change, vol. 5. London, Beverly Hills: Sage Publications.

Bowen, William G., and Derek Curtis Bok. 1998. *The Shape of the River: Long-Term Consequences of Considering Race in College and University Admissions.* Princeton: Princeton University Press.

Bowen, William G., Matthew Chingos, and Michael S. McPherson. 2009. *Crossing the Finish Line: Completing College at America's Public Universities.* Princeton: Princeton University Press.

Braddock, Jomills Henry, and James M. McPartland. 1989. "Social-Psychological Processes That Perpetuate Racial Segregation: The Relationship between School and Employment Desegregation." *Journal of Black Studies* 19 (3): 267–289.

———. 1987. "How Minorities Continue to be Excluded from Equal Employment Opportunities: Research on Labor Market and Industrial Barriers." *Journal of Social Issues* 43 (1): 34–5.

Branscombe, Nyla R., and Naomi Ellemers. 1998. "Coping with Group-Based Discrimination: Individualistic Versus Group-Level Strategies." In *Prejudice: The Target's Perspective,* edited by Janet K. Swim and Charles Stangor, 243–266. San Diego: Academic Press.

Branscombe, Nyla R., Michael T. Schmitt, and Richard D. Harvey. 1999. "Perceiving Pervasive Discrimination among African Americans: Implications for Group Identification and Well-Being." *Journal of Personality and Social Psychology* 77 (1): 135–149.

Brekhus, Wayne. 1998. "A Sociology of the Unmarked: Redirecting Our Focus." *Sociological Theory* 16 (1): 34–51.

Brint, Steven G., and Jerome Karabel. 1989. *The Diverted Dream: Community Colleges and the Promise of Educational Opportunity in America, 1900–1985.* New York: Oxford University Press.

Brodkin, Karen. 1998. *How Jews Became White Folks and What That Says about Race in America.* New Brunswick, NJ: Rutgers University Press.

Brower, Aaron M., and Annemarie Ketterhagen. 2004. "Is There an Inherent Mismatch between How Black and White Students Expect to Succeed in College and What Their Colleges Expect from Them?" *Journal of Social Issues* 60 (1): 95–116.

Brown, Michael K., Martin Carnoy, Elliott Currie, Troy Duster, and David B. Oppenheimer. 2003. *Whitewashing Race: The Myth of a Color-Blind Society.* Berkeley: University of California Press.

Brown, Lisa M., and Heather Dobbins. 2004. "Students of Color and European American Students' Stigma-Relevant Perceptions of University Instructors." *Journal of Social Issues* 60 (1): 157–174.

Brown, Ryan P., and Robert A. Josephs. 1999. "A Burden of Proof: Stereotype Relevance and Gender Differences in Math Performance." *Journal of Personality and Social Psychology* 76 (2): 246–257.

Bruce, Marino A., and Michael C. Thornton. 2004. "It's My World? Exploring Black and White Perceptions of Personal Control." *Sociological Quarterly* 45 (3): 597–612.

Buchanan, Donna M. 2008. "How Is an Undergraduate Engineering Program Uniquely Positioned to Create a Diverse Workforce through the Recruitment of African American Students? A Faculty Perspective." EdD diss, Rossier School of Education, University of Southern California.

Budget of the United States Government: Historical Tables Fiscal Year 2005. Washington, DC: Government Printing Office.

Burke, Peter J. 1988. "Identity and Sex—Race Differences in Educational and Occupational Aspirations Formation." *Social Science Research* 17: 29–47.

Burstein, Paul. 1989. "Attacking Sex Discrimination in the Labor Market: A Study in Law and Politics." *Social Forces* 67 (3): 641–665.

Caldwell, Christopher. 1999. "Bill Gates, Minority Leader: A Billion Dollars Is a Terrible Thing to Waste." *Weekly Standard*, October 4, 1999, 11.

Cancio, A. Silvia, T. David Evans, and David J. Maume, Jr. 1996. "Reconsidering the Declining Significance of Race: Racial Differences in Early Career Wages." *American Sociological Review* 61 (4): 541–556.

Carnevale, Anthony P., and Steven J. Rose. 2003. *Socioeconomic Status, Race/Ethnicity, and Selective College Admissions.* The Century Foundation.

Carter-Black, Jan. 2001. "The Myth of 'The Tangle of Pathology': Resilience

Strategies Employed by Middle-Class African American Families." *Journal of Family Social Work* 6 (4): 75–100.

Cartwright, Lillian K. 1972. "Conscious Factors Entering into Decisions of Women to Study Medicine." *Journal of Social Issues* 28 (2): 201–215.

Casteel, Clifton A. 1998. "Teacher Student Interactions and Race in Integrated Classrooms." *Journal of Educational Research* 92 (2): 115.

Catsambis, Sophia. 1994. "The Path to Math: Gender and Racial-Ethnic Differences in Mathematics Participation from Middle School to High School." *Sociology of Education* 67 (3): 199–215.

Chambliss, Elizabeth. 2000. *Miles to Go 2000: Progress of Minorities in the Legal Profession.* Chicago: American Bar Association Commission on Racial and Ethnic Diversity in the Profession, 2000.

Chang, Mitchell J., Alexander W. Astin, and Dongbin Kim. 2004. "Cross-Racial Interaction among Undergraduates: Some Consequences, Causes, and Patterns." *Research in Higher Education* 45 (5): 529–553.

Charles, Camille Z., Vincent J. Roscigno, and Kimberly C. Torres. 2007. "Racial Inequality and College Attendance: The Mediating Role of Parental Investments." *Social Science Research* 36 (1): 329–352.

Charles, Camille Zubrinsky, Mary J. Fischer, Margarita A. Mooney, and Douglas S. Massey. 2009. *Taming the River: Negotiating the Academic, Financial, and Social Currents in Selective Colleges and Universities.* Princeton: Princeton University Press.

Chavous, Tabbye M., Angel Harris, Deborah Rivas, Lumas Helaire, and Laurette Green. 2004. "Racial Stereotypes and Gender in Context: African Americans at Predominantly Black and Predominantly White Colleges." *Sex Roles* 51 (1–2): 1–16.

Choi, Namkee G. 1999. "Racial Differences in the Contribution of Wife's Earnings to Family Income Distribution." *Journal of Poverty* 3 (3): 33–51.

Clegg, Roger. 2000. "Why I'm Sick of the Praise for Diversity on Campuses." *Chronicle of Higher Education* 46 (July 14): B8.

Clinton, William J. 1995. *Memorandum for Heads of Executive Departments and Agencies.* Washington, DC: Office of the Press Secretary.

Cohen, Philip N., and Matt L. Huffman. 2003. "Individuals, Jobs, and Labor Markets: The Devaluation of Women's Work." *American Sociological Review* 68 (3): 443–463.

Cohen, Steven Martin, and Robert E. Kapsis. 1978. "Participation of Blacks, Puerto Ricans, and Whites in Voluntary Associations: A Test of Current Theories." *Social Forces* 56 (4): 1053–1071.

Cole, Stephen, and Elinor G. Barber. 2003. *Increasing Faculty Diversity: The*

Occupational Choices of High-Achieving Minority Students. Cambridge, MA.: Harvard University Press.

Collins, Sharon M. 1997. *Black Corporate Executives: The Making and Breaking of a Black Middle Class.* Labor and Social Change. Philadelphia: Temple University Press.

——. 1993. "Blacks on the Bubble: The Vulnerability of Black Executives in White Corporations." *Sociological Quarterly* 34 (3): 429–447.

Coon, Heather M., and Markus Kemmelmeier. 2001. "Cultural Orientations in the United States: (Re)Examining Differences among Ethnic Groups." *Journal of Cross-Cultural Psychology* 32 (3): 348–364.

Corcoran, Mary. 1995. "Rags to Rags: Poverty and Mobility in the United States." *Annual Review of Sociology* 21: 237–267.

Cose, Ellis. 2009. "Revisiting 'The Rage of a Privileged Class': Obama's Presidency Renders Absurd the Argument That Blacks Are Barred from Playing at the Highest Levels; but Do Isolated Victories Add Up to Systemic Change?" *Newsweek*, February 2, 2009, 42.

——. 1993. *The Rage of a Privileged Class.* 1st ed. New York: HarperCollins.

Cox, Taylor H., Sharon A. Lobel, and Poppy Lauretta McLeod. 1991. "Effects of Ethnic Group Cultural Differences on Cooperative and Competitive Behavior on a Group Task." *Academy of Management Journal* 34 (4): 827–847.

Crocker, Jennifer, and Brenda Major. 1989. "Social Stigma and Self Esteem: The Self-Protective Properties of Stigma." *Psychological Review* 96 (4): 608–630.

Cunnigen, Donald. 2006. "Black Leadership in the Twenty-First Century." *Society* 43 (5): 25–29.

Darling-Hammond, Linda. 2004. "The Color Line in American Education: Race, Resources, and Student Achievement." *Du Bois Review: Social Science Research on Race* 1 (2): 213–246.

——. 1995. "Cracks in the Bell Curve: How Education Matters." *Journal of Negro Education* 64 (3): 340–353.

Davidson, Martin, and Raymond A. Friedman. 1998. "When Excuses Don't Work: The Persistent Injustice Effect among Black Managers." *Administrative Science Quarterly* 43 (1): 154–183.

Davies, Paul G., Steven J. Spencer, and Claude M. Steele. 2005. "Clearing the Air: Identity Safety Moderates the Effects of Stereotype Threat on Women's Leadership Aspirations." *Journal of Personality and Social Psychology* 88 (2): 276–287.

Davis, James Earl. 1994. "College in Black and White: Campus Environment and Academic Achievement of African American Males." *Journal of Negro Education* 63 (4): 620–633.

Dawson, Michael C. 1994. *Behind the Mule: Race and Class in African-American Politics.* Princeton: Princeton University Press.

De Graaf, Nan Dirk, and Hendrik Derk Flap. 1988. "'With a Little Help from My Friends': Social Resources as an Explanation of Occupational Status and Income in West Germany, the Netherlands, and the United States." *Social Forces* 67 (2): 452–472.

Devasher, Madhavi. 2002. "Stanford Defends Its Ethnic Theme Houses." *Stanford Daily,* November 19, 2002.

DiMaggio, Paul. 1982. "Cultural Capital and School Success: The Impact of Status Culture Participation on the Grades of U.S. High School Students." *American Sociological Review* 47 (2): 189–201.

DiMaggio, Paul, and John Mohr. 1985. "Cultural Capital, Educational Attainment, and Marital Selection." *American Journal of Sociology* 90 (6): 1231–1261.

DiTomaso, Nancy, Rochelle Parks-Yancy, and Corrine Post. 2003. "White Views on Civil Rights: Color Blindness and Equal Opportunity." In *White Out: The Continuing Significance of Race,* edited by Ashley W. Doane and Eduardo Bonilla-Silva, 189–198. New York: Routledge.

DiTomaso, Nancy, and Donna E. Thompson. 1988. "The Advancement of Minorities into Corporate Management: An Overview." *Research in the Sociology of Organizations* 6: 281–312.

Donnelly, Denise A., and Stacy Kenyon. 1996. "'Honey, We Don't Do Men': Gender Stereotypes and the Provision of Services to Sexually Assaulted Males." *Journal of Interpersonal Violence* 11 (3): 441–448.

Doverspike, Dennis, Mary Anne Taylor, Kenneth S. Shultz, and Patrick F. McKay. 2000. "Responding to the Challenge of a Changing Workforce: Recruiting Nontraditional Demographic Groups." *Public Personnel Management* 29 (4): 445.

Dovidio, John F., Kerry Kawakami, and Samuel L. Gaertner. 2000. "Reducing Contemporary Prejudice: Combating Explicit and Implicit Bias at the Individual and Intergroup Level." In *Reducing Prejudice and Discrimination,* edited by Stuart Oskamp, 137–163. Mahwah, NJ: Lawrence Erlbaum Associates.

Downey, Douglas, and Shana Pribesh. 2004. "When Race Matters: Teachers' Evaluations of Students' Classroom Behavior." *Sociology of Education* 77: 15–267.

Dreeben, Robert, and Adam Gamoran. 1986. "Race, Instruction and Learning." *American Sociological Review* 51 (5): 660–669.

D'Souza, Dinesh. 1991. *Illiberal Education: The Politics of Race and Sex on Campus.* Toronto: Collier Macmillan Canada.

DuBois, W. E. B. 1903. "The Talented Tenth." In *The Negro Problem.* New York: Arno Press, 1969.

Dugger, Ronnie. 1983. *On Reagan: The Man and His Presidency.* New York: McGraw-Hill.

Duncan, Otis D. 1968. "Peer Influences on Aspirations: A Reinterpretation." *American Journal of Sociology* 74 (2): 119–137.

Durr, Marlese, and John R. Logan. 1997. "Racial Submarkets in Government Employment: African American Managers in New York State." *Sociological Forum* 12 (3): 353–370.

Durrant, Thomas, and Kathleen H. Sparrow. 1997. "Race and Class Consciousness among Lower- and Middle-Class Blacks." *Journal of Black Studies* 27 (3): 317–334.

Ellemers, Naomi, ed. 1993. *The Influence of Socio-Structural Variables on Identity Management Strategies.* European Review of Social Psychology. Edited by W. Strobe and M. Hewstone. Vol. 4. New York: Wiley and Sons.

Ellemers, Naomi, Ad Van Knippenberg, and Henk Wilke. 1990. "The Influence of Permeability of Group Boundaries and Stability of Group Status on Strategies of Individual Mobility and Social Change." *British Journal of Social Psychology* 29 (3): 233–246.

Elliott, Rogers, Christopher Strenta, Russell Adair, Michael Matier, and Jannah Scott. 1996. "The Role of Ethnicity in Choosing and Leaving Science in Highly Selective Institutions." *Research in Higher Education* 37 (6): 681–709.

Elliott, James R., and Ryan A. Smith. 2004. "Race, Gender, and Workplace Power." *American Sociological Review* 69 (3): 365–386.

Elliott, Marta. 1998. "School Finance and Opportunities to Learn." *Sociology of Education* 71 (3): 223–245.

Ellison, Christopher G., and Bruce London. 1992. "The Social and Political Participation of Black Americans: Compensatory and Ethnic Community Perspectives Revisited." *Social Forces* 70 (3): 681–701.

Equal Employment Opportunity Commission, 2004. *The 1970's: The "Toothless Tiger" Gets Its Teeth—Focusing Enforcement Efforts on Systemic Discrimination.* http://www.eeoc.gov/eeoc/history/35th/1970s/.

Erisman, Wendy, and Courtney McSwain, 2006. *Expanding Access and Op-*

portunity: The Impact of the Gates Millennium Scholars Program. Washington, DC: Institute for Higher Education Policy.

Erwin, Loma, and Paula Maurutto. 1998. "Beyond Access: Considering Gender Deficits in Science Education." *Gender and Education* 10 (1): 51–69.

Espenshade, Thomas J., and Alexandra Walton Radford. 2009. *No Longer Separate, Not Yet Equal: Race and Class in Elite College Admission and Campus Life.* Princeton: Princeton University Press.

Ethington, Corinna A., and Lee M. Wolfle. 1988. "Women's Selection of Quantitative Undergraduate Fields of Study: Direct and Indirect Influences." *American Educational Research Journal* 25: 157–175.

Evangelista, Benny. 1999. "High-Tech Workforce Gap in the Valley." *San Francisco Chronicle,* May 18, 1999, D1.

Farkas, George, Christy Lleras, and Steve Maczuga. 2002. "Does Oppositional Culture Exist in Minority and Poverty Peer Groups?" *American Sociological Review* 67 (1): 148–155.

Farley, Reynolds. 1985. "Three Steps Forward and Two Back? Recent Changes in the Social and Economic Status of Blacks." *Ethnic and Racial Studies* 8 (1): 4–28.

Feagin, Joe R. 2006. *Systemic Racism: A Theory of Oppression.* New York: Routledge.

———. 1992. "The Continuing Significance of Racism: Discrimination against Black Students in White Colleges." *Journal of Black Studies* 22 (4): 546–578.

Feagin, Joe R., and Melvin P. Sikes. 1994. *Living with Racism: The Black Middle-Class Experience.* Boston: Beacon Press.

Feagin, Joe R., and Hernan Vera. 1995. *White Racism: The Basics.* New York: Routledge.

Feagin, Joe R., Hernan Vera, and Nikitah Imani. 1996. *The Agony of Education: Black Students at White Colleges and Universities.* New York: Routledge.

Ferguson, Robert F. 1998. "Can Schools Narrow the Black-White Test Score Gap?" In *The Black-White Test Score Gap,* edited by Christopher Jencks and Meredith Phillips. Washington, DC: Brookings Institution Press.

Fernandez, Roberto M., and Isabel Fernandez-Mateo. 2006. "Networks, Race, and Hiring." *American Sociological Review* 71 (1): 42–71.

Fisher, Bradley J., and David J. Hartmann. 1995. "The Impact of Race on the Social Experience of College Students at a Predominantly White University." *Journal of Black Studies* 26 (2): 117–133.

Fisher, Celia B., Scyatta A. Wallace, and Rose E. Fenton. 2000. "Discrimination Distress during Adolescence." *Journal of Youth and Adolescence* 29 (6): 679–695.

Flagg, Barbara J. 1995. "Fashioning A Title VII Remedy for Transparently White Subjective Decision Making." *Yale Law Journal* 104 (1009).

Flowers, Lamont, and Ernest T. Pascarella. 1999. "Cognitive Effects of College Racial Composition on African American Students After 3 Years of College." *Journal of College Student Development* 40 (6): 669–677.

Fordham, Signithia, and John U. Ogbu. 1986. "Black Students' School Success: Coping with the "Burden of 'Acting White.'" *Urban Review* 18 (3): 176–206.

Frankenberg, Ruth. 2001. "The Mirage of an Unmarked Whiteness." In *The Making and Unmaking of Whiteness,* edited by Birgit Brander Rasmussen, Eric Klinenberg, Irene J. Nexica, and Matt Wray. Durham, NC: Duke University Press.

———. 1993. *White Women, Race Matters: The Social Construction of Whiteness.* Minneapolis: University of Minnesota Press.

Frankenberg, Erica, and Chungmei Lee. 2002. *Race in American Public Schools: Rapidly Resegregating School Districts.* Cambridge, MA: Harvard Civil Rights Project.

Fryer, Roland G., and Glenn C. Loury. 2005. "Affirmative Action and Its Mythology." *Journal of Economic Perspectives* 19 (3): 147–162.

Fu, Vincent Kang. 2007. "How Many Melting Pots? Intermarriage, Pan Ethnicity, and the Black/Non-Black Divide in the United States." *Journal of Comparative Family Studies* 38 (2): 215–232.

Gallagher, Charles A. 2003. "Color-Blind Privilege: The Social and Political Functions of Erasing the Color Line in Post-Race America." *Race, Class, and Gender* 10 (4): 22–37.

———. 2003. "Miscounting Race: Explaining Whites' Misperceptions of Racial Group Size." *Sociological Perspectives* 46 (3): 381–396.

Gallup. 2005. "Race, Ideology, and Support for Affirmative Action." http://www.gallup.com.

Garland, David. 2001. *The Culture of Control: Crime and Social Order in Contemporary Society.* Chicago: University of Chicago Press.

Gates Millennium Scholars Program. "About GMS." accessed 08/10, http://www.gmsp.org/publicweb/aboutus.aspx.

Gates, William H. 2008. Written Testimony of William H. Gates, Chairman, Microsoft Corporation, Co-Chair, Bill and Melinda Gates Foundation. Committee on Science and Technology, U.S. House of Representatives, March 12, 2008.

Gill, Sukhdeep, and Arthur Reynolds. 1999. "Educational Expectations and

School Achievement of Urban African American Children." *Journal of School Psychology* 37 (4): 403–424.

Granovetter, Mark. 1995. *Getting a Job: A Study of Contacts and Careers.* 2nd ed. Chicago: University of Chicago Press.

Grant, G. Kathleen, and Jeffrey R. Breese. 1997. "Marginality Theory and the African American Student." *Sociology of Education* 70 (3): 192–205.

Greenhaus, Jeffrey H., Saroj Parasuraman, and Wayne M. Wormley. 1990. "Effects of Race on Organizational Experiences, Job Performance Evaluations, and Career Outcomes." *Academy of Management Journal* 33 (1): 64–86.

Guiffrida, Douglas A. 2003. "African American Student Organizations as Agents of Social Integration." *Journal of College Student Development* 44 (3): 304–319.

Guinier, Lani. 1994. *The Tyranny of the Majority: Fundamental Fairness in Representative Democracy.* New York: Free Press.

Gurin, Patricia, Eric L. Dey, Sylvia Hurtado, and Gerald Gurin. 2002. "Diversity and Higher Education: Theory and Impact on Educational Outcomes." *Harvard Educational Review* 72 (3): 330–366.

Gurin, Patricia, and Edgar G. Epps. 1975. *Black Consciousness, Identity, and Achievement: A Study of Students in Historically Black Colleges.* New York: Wiley.

Gurin, Patricia, and Biren A. Nagda. 2006. "Getting to the 'What,' 'How,' and 'Why' of Diversity on Campus." *Educational Researcher* 35 (1): 20–24.

Hagen, Janet W., and Willis W. Hagen II. 1995. "What Employment Counselors Need to Know about Employment Discrimination and the Civil Rights Act of 1991." *Journal of Employment Counseling* 32 (1): 2–10.

Hall, Marcia, Arlene F. Mays, and Walter Allen. 1984. "Dreams Deferred: Black Student Career Goals and Fields of Study in Graduate/Professional Schools." *Phylon* 45 (4): 271–283.

Haller, Archibald O., and Alejandro Portes. 1973. "Status Attainment Processes." *Sociology of Education* 46 (1): 51–91.

Hanson, Sandra L. 2009. *Swimming against the Tide: African American Girls and Science Education.* Philadelphia: Temple University Press.

Harrison, Bennett, and Lucy Gorham. 1992. "Growing Inequality in Black Wages in the 1980s and the Emergence of an African-American Middle Class." *Journal of Policy Analysis and Management* 11 (2): 235–253.

Herndon, Michael K., and Joan B. Hirt. 2004. "Black Students and Their Families: What Leads to Success in College." *Journal of Black Studies* 34 (4): 489–513.

Herring, Cedric, and Sharon M. Collins. 1995. "Retreat from Equal Opportunity: The Case of Affirmative Action." In *The Bubbling Cauldron : Race, Ethnicity, and the Urban Crisis,* edited by Michael P. Smith and Joe R. Feagin, 163–181. Minneapolis: University of Minnesota Press.

Higginbotham, Elizabeth, and Lynn Weber. 1992. "Moving Up with Kin and Community: Upward Social Mobility for Black and White Women." *Gender & Society* 6 (3): 416–440.

Hill, Shirley A., and Joey Sprague. 1999. "Parenting in Black and White Families: The Interaction of Gender with Race and Class." *Gender & Society* 13 (4): 480–502.

Hill Collins, Patricia. 1990. *Black Feminist Thought: Knowledge, Consciousness, and the Politics of Empowerment.* Perspectives on Gender, vol. 2. Boston: Unwin Hyman.

Hines, Revathi I. 2002. "The Silent Voices: 2000 Presidential Election and the Minority Vote in Florida." *Western Journal of Black Studies* 26 (2): 71.

Hirsch, Barton J., Maureen Mickus, and Rebecca Boerger. 2002. "Ties to Influential Adults among Black and White Adolescents: Culture, Social Class, and Family Networks." *American Journal of Community Psychology* 30 (2): 289–303.

Hirsh, Elizabeth. 2008. "Settling for Less? Organizational Determinants of Discrimination-Charge Outcomes." *Law and Society Review* 42 (2): 239–274.

Hollinger, C. L. 1983. "Self-Perception and the Career Aspirations of Mathematically Talented Female Adolescents." *Journal of Vocational Behavior* 22: 49–62.

Holzer, Harry, and David Neumark. 2000. "Assessing Affirmative Action." *Journal of Economic Literature* 38 (3): 483–568.

Huber, Joan and William Humbert Form. 1973. *Income and Ideology: An Analysis of the American Political Formula.* New York: Free Press.

Hunt, Matthew O., and David C. Wilson. 2009. "Race/Ethnicity, Perceived Discrimination, and Beliefs about the Meaning of an Obama Presidency." *Du Bois Review* 6 (1): 173–191.

Hurtado, Sylvia, Jeffrey Milem, Alma Clayton-Pedersen, and Walter R. Allen. 1999. *Enacting Diverse Learning Environments: Improving the Climate for Racial/Ethnic Diversity in Higher Education.* Association for the Study of Higher Education, Higher Education ERIC Clearinghouse. Higher Education Report, vol. 26, no. 8. Washington, DC: George Washington University Graduate School of Education and Human Development.

Hurtado, Sylvia, Victor B. Saenz, and Luciana Dar. 2008. "Low-Income Students of Color in Higher Education and the Gates Millennium Scholars Program." In *Resources, Assets, and Strengths among Successful Diverse*

Students: Understanding the Contributions of the Gates Millennium Scholars Program, edited by William T. Trent and Edward P. St. John, Readings on Equal Education, vol. 23, 229–252. New York: AMS Press.

Jackson, Pamela Braboy, and Qunicy Thomas Stewart. 2003. "A Research Agenda for the Black Middle Class: Work Stress, Survival Strategies, and Mental Health." *Journal of Health and Social Behavior* 44 (3): 442–455.

Jacobs, Jerry A., David Karen, and Katherine McClelland. 1991. "The Dynamics of Young Men's Career Aspirations." *Sociological Forum* 6 (4): 609–639.

Jacoby, Tamar. 1999. "Color Blind: The African American Absence in High Tech." *New Republic*, March 29, 1999, 28.

Jenkins, Adelbert H., Ernest Harburg, Norman C. Weissberg, and Thomas Donnelly. 2004. "The Influence of Minority Group Cultural Models on Persistence in College." *Journal of Negro Education* 73 (1): 69–80.

"Jesse Jackson Blasted Out of the Sky." 1999. *American Enterprise* 10 (3): 12.

Jetten, Jolanda, Russell Spears, and Anthony S. R. Manstead. 1996. "Intergroup Norms and Intergroup Discrimination: Distinctive Self-Categorization and Social Identity Effects." *Journal of Personality and Social Psychology* 71 (6): 1222–1233.

Johns, Michael, Toni Schmader, and Andy Martens. 2005. "Knowing Is Half the Battle." *Psychological Science* 16 (3): 175–179.

Johnson, James H., Jr., Walter C. Farrell, Jr., and Jennifer A. Stoloff. 2000. "An Empirical Assessment of Four Perspectives on the Declining Fortunes of the African-American Male." *Urban Affairs Review* 35 (5): 695–716.

Joint Venture Silicon Valley Network, 1999. *Workforce Study: An Analysis of the Workforce Gap in Silicon Valley*. San Jose, CA: Joint Venture: Silicon Valley Network.

Josephs, R., R. Larrick, Claude M. Steele, and R. Nisbett. 1992. "Protecting the Self from the Negative Consequences of Risky Decisions." *Journal of Personality and Social Psychology* 62 (1): 26–37.

Jussim, Lee. 1989. "Teacher Expectations: Self-Fulfilling Prophecies, Perceptual Biases, and Accuracy." *Journal of Personality and Social Psychology* 57 (3): 469–480.

Jussim, Lee, Jacquelynne S. Eccles, and Stephanie Madon, eds. 1996. *Social Perception, Social Stereotypes, and Teacher Expectations: Accuracy and the Quest for the Powerful Self-Fulfilling Prophecy*. Advances in Experimental Social Psychology, vol. 28. San Diego: Academic Press.

Jussim, Lee, and Kent D. Harber. 2005. "Teacher Expectations and Self-Fulfilling Prophecies: Knowns and Unknowns, Resolved and Unresolved Controversies." *Personality and Social Psychology Review* 9 (2): 131–155.

Kao, Grace. 2002. "Ethnic Differences in Parents' Educational Aspirations." *Research in Sociology of Education* 13: 85–103.

Kao, Grace, Marta Tienda, and Barbara Schneider. 1996. "Racial and Ethnic Variation in Academic Performance." *Research in Sociology of Education and Socialization* 11: 263–297.

Kaufman, Julie E., and James E. Rosenbaum. 1992. "The Education and Employment of Low-Income Black Youth in White Suburbs." *Educational Evaluation and Policy Analysis* 14 (3): 229–240.

Keith, Timothy, and Mark J. Benson. 1992. "Effects of Manipulable Influences on High School Grades." *Journal of Educational Research* 86 (2): 85–93.

Kellner, Douglas. 2007. "The Katrina Hurricane Spectacle and Crisis of the Bush Presidency." *Cultural Studies—Critical Methodologies* 7 (2): 222–234.

Kennedy, Randall. 1986. "Persuasion and Distrust: A Comment on the Affirmative Action Debate." *Harvard Law Review* 99 (6): 1327–1346.

Kerckhoff, Alan C., and Richard T. Campbell. 1977. "Black-White Differences in the Educational Attainment Process." *Sociology of Education* 50 (1): 15–27.

Kiefer, Amy K., and Denise Sekaquaptewa. 2007. "Implicit Stereotypes and Women's Math Performance: How Implicit Gender-Math Stereotypes Influence Women's Susceptibility to Stereotype Threat." *Journal of Experimental Social Psychology* 43 (5): 825–832.

Kim, Doo Hwan, and Barbara L. Schneider. 2005. "Social Capital in Action: Alignment of Parental Support in Adolescents' Transition to Postsecondary Education." *Social Forces* 84 (2): 1181–1206.

Kim, Eun-Young. 1993. "Career Choice among Second-Generation Korean-Americans: Reflections of a Cultural Model of Success." *Anthropology and Education Quarterly* 24 (3): 224–248.

Kluegel, James R., and Lawrence D. Bobo. 2001. "Perceived Group Discrimination and Policy Attitudes: The Sources and Consequences of the Race and Gender Gaps." In *Urban Inequality*, 163–213. New York: Russell Sage.

Kluegel, James R., and Eliot R. Smith. 1986. *Beliefs about Inequality: Americans' Views of What Is and What Ought to Be.* Social Institutions and Social Change. New York: A. de Gruyter.

Kossek, Ellen Ernst, and Susan C. Zonia. 1993. "Assessing Diversity Climate: A Field Study of Reactions to Employer Efforts to Promote Diversity." *Journal of Organizational Behavior* 14 (1): 61–81.

Kraiger, Kurt, and Kevin J. Ford. 1985. "A Meta-Analysis of Ratee Race Effects in Performance Ratings." *Journal of Applied Psychology* 70 (1): 56–65.

Kram, Kathy E. 1985. *Mentoring at Work: Developmental Relationships in Organizational Life.* Glenview, IL: Scott Foresman.

Kraus, Neil, and Todd Swanstrom. 2005. "The Continuing Significance of Race: African American and Hispanic Mayors, 1968–2003." *National Political Science Review* 10: 54–70.

Krenn, Michael L. 1999. *Black Diplomacy: African Americans and the State Department, 1945–1969.* Armonk, NY: M. E. Sharpe.

Lacy, Karyn R. 2004. "Black Spaces, Black Places: Strategic Assimilation and Identity Construction in Middle-Class Suburbia." *Ethnic and Racial Studies* 27 (6): 908–930.

Landry, Bart. 1987. *The New Black Middle Class.* Berkeley: University of California Press.

LaNoue, George. 1994. "Standards for the Second Generation of Croson Inspired Disparity Studies." *Urban Lawyer* 26: 485–485–540.

Lareau, Annette. 2003. *Unequal Childhoods: Class, Race, and Family Life.* Berkeley: University of California Press.

———. 2002. "Invisible Inequality: Social Class and Childrearing in Black Families and White Families." *American Sociological Review* 67 (5): 747–776.

———. 2000. *Home Advantage: Social Class and Parental Intervention in Elementary Education.* 2nd ed. Lanham, MD: Rowman & Littlefield Publishers.

Leaper, Campbell, and Christia Spears Brown. 2008. "Perceived Experiences with Sexism among Adolescent Girls." *Child Development* 79 (3): 685–704.

Lee, James Daniel. 1998. "Which Kids Can 'Become' Scientists? Effects of Gender, Self-Concepts and Perceptions of Scientists." *Social Psychology Quarterly* 61 (3): 199–219.

Leonard, Jonathan S. 1990. "The Impact of Affirmative Action Regulation and Equal Employment Opportunity Law on Black Employment." *Journal of Economic Perspectives* 4: 47–63.

———. 1984. "Employment and Occupational Advance Under Affirmative Action." *Review of Economics and Statistics* 66 (3): 377–385.

Leong, Frederick T. L., and Elayne L. Chou. 1994. "The Role of Ethnic Identity and Acculturation in the Vocational Behavior of Asian Americans: An Integrative Review." *Journal of Vocational Behavior* 44: 155–172.

Leong, Frederick T. L., and Thomas J. Hayes. 1990. "Occupational Stereotyping of Asian Americans." *Career Development Quarterly* 39 (2): 143–154.

Levin, Shana, Colette Van Laar, and Winona Foote. 2006. "Ethnic Segregation and Perceived Discrimination in College: Mutual Influences and Effects on Social and Academic Life." *Journal of Applied Social Psychology* 36 (6): 1471–1501.

Levin, Shana, Colette van Laar, and Jim Sidanius. 2003. "The Effects of Ingroup and Outgroup Friendships on Ethnic Attitudes in College: A Longitudinal Study." *Group Processes & Intergroup Relations* 6 (1): 76–92.

Lin, Nan. 2001. "Building a Network Theory of Social Capital." In *Social Capital: Theory and Research,* edited by Nan Lin, Karen S. Cook, and Ronald S. Burt, 3–29. Hawthorne, NY: Aldine de Gruyter.

———. 1999. "Social Networks and Status Attainment." *Annual Review of Sociology* 25: 467–487.

Lipsitz, George. 1998. *The Possessive Investment in Whiteness: How White People Profit from Identity Politics.* Philadelphia: Temple University Press.

Locks, Angela M., Sylvia Hurtado, and Nicholas A. Bowman. 2008. "Extending Notions of Campus Climate and Diversity to Students' Transition to College." *Review of Higher Education* 31 (3): 257–285.

Loewen, James W. 1988. *Mississippi Chinese: Between Black and White.* 2nd ed. Waveland Press.

Longres, John F., and Gary B. Seltzer. 1994. "Racism: Its Implications for the Education of Minority Social Work Students." *Journal of Multicultural Social Work* 3 (1): 59–75.

Looker, Dianne, and Peter Pineo. 1983. "Social Psychological Variables and Their Relevance to the Status Attainment of Teenagers." *American Journal of Sociology* 38 (6): 1195–1219.

Major, Brenda, and Toni Schmader. 1998. "Coping with Stigma through Psychological Disengagement." In *Prejudice: The Target's Perspective,* edited by Janet K. Swim and Charles Stangor, 219–241. San Diego: Academic Press.

Markowitz, Harry M. 1991. "Foundations of Portfolio Theory." *Journal of Finance* 46 (2): 469–477.

———. 1952. "Portfolio Selection." *Journal of Finance* 7 (1): 77–91.

Maruyama, Geoffrey, and José F. Moreno. 2000. "University Faculty Views about the Value of Diversity on Campus and in the Classroom." In *Does Diversity Make a Difference? Three Research Studies on Diversity in College Classrooms,* 9–36. Washington, DC: American Council on Education and American Association of University Professors.

Massey, Douglas S., Camille Z. Charles, Garvey F. Lundy, and Mary J. Fischer. 2003. *The Source of the River: The Social Origins of Freshmen at America's Selective Colleges and Universities.* Princeton: Princeton University Press.

Massey, Douglas S., and Nancy A. Denton. 1993. *American Apartheid: Segregation and the Making of the Underclass.* Cambridge, MA: Harvard University Press.

Maton, Kenneth I., Freeman Hrabowski III, and Metin Ozdemir. 2007. "Opening an African American STEM Program to Talented Students of All Races: Evaluation of the Meyerhoff Scholars Program, 1991–2005." In *Charting the Future of College Affirmative Action: Legal Victories, Continuing Attacks, and New Research,* edited by Gary Orfield, Patricia Marin, Stella M. Flores, and Liliana M. Garces, 125–156. Los Angeles: Civil Rights Project at UCLA.

Mattis, Jacqueline S., William Pierce Beckham, Benjamin A. Saunders, Jarvis E. Williams, D'Yal McAllister, Valerie Myers, Damon Knight, Donald Rencher, and Charles Dixon. 2004. "Who Will Volunteer? Religiosity, Everyday Racism, and Social Participation among African American Men." *Journal of Adult Development* 11 (4): 261–272.

Maume, David J., Jr. 2004. "Is the Glass Ceiling a Unique Form of Inequality? Evidence from a Random-Effects Model of Managerial Attainment." *Work and Occupations* 31 (2): 250–274.

McAdam, Doug. 1988. *Freedom Summer.* New York: Oxford University Press.

———. 1982. *Political Process and the Development of Black Insurgency, 1930–1970.* Chicago: University of Chicago Press.

McAdoo, Harriette Pipes. 1978. "Factors Related to Stability in Upwardly Mobile Black Families." *Journal of Marriage and the Family* 40 (4): 761–776.

McDermott, Monica. 2002. "Trends in the Race and Ethnicity of Eminent Americans." *Sociological Forum* 17 (1): 133–160.

McDermott, Monica, and Frank L. Samson. 2005. "White Racial and Ethnic Identity in the United States." *Annual Review of Sociology* 31: 245–261.

McDill, Edward, Gary Natriello, and Pallas Aaron. 1986. "A Population at Risk: Potential Consequences of Tougher School Standards for Student Dropouts." *American Journal of Education* 94 (2): 135–181.

McIntosh, Peggy. 1993. "White Privilege and Male Privilege: A Personal Account of Coming to See Correspondence through Work in Women's Studies." In *Gender Basics: Feminist Perspectives on Women and Men,* edited by Anne Minas, 30–38. Belmont, CA: Wadsworth Publishing.

McJamerson, Evangeline McConnell. 1992. "Undergraduate Academic Major and Minority Student Persistence: Individual Choices, National Consequences." *Equity and Excellence* 25 (2–4): 35–48.

McNeal, Ralph B., 1999. "Parental Involvement as Social Capital: Differential Effectiveness on Science Achievement, Truancy, and Dropping Out." *Social Forces* 78 (1): 117–144.

———. 1997. "High School Dropouts: A Closer Examination of School Effects." *Social Science Quarterly* 78 (1): 209–222.

McWhorter, John H. 2000. *Losing the Race: Self-Sabotage in Black America.* New York: Free Press.

Melguizo, Tatiana. 2008. "Quality Matters: Assessing the Impact of Attending More Selective Institutions on College Completion Rates of Minorities." *Research in Higher Education* 49 (3): 214–236.

Mendoza-Denton, Rodolfo, Geraldine Downey, Valerie J. Purdie, Angelina Davis, and Janina Pietrzak. 2002. "Sensitivity to Status-Based Rejection: Implications for African American Students' College Experience." *Journal of Personality and Social Psychology* 83 (4): 896–918.

Merton, Robert K. 1948. "The Self-Fulfilling Prophecy." *Antioch Review* 8 (2): 193–210.

Milem, Jeffrey. 2003. "The Educational Benefits of Diversity: Evidence from Multiple Sectors." In *Compelling Interest: Examining the Evidence on Racial Dynamics in Colleges and Universities,* edited by Mitchell J. Chang et al., 126–169. Palo Alto: Stanford University Press.

Miller, Dale T., and William Turnbull. 1986. "Expectancies and Interpersonal Processes." *Annual Review of Psychology* 37 (1): 233–256.

Morgan, Stephen, and Aage Sorensen. 1999. "Parental Networks, Social Closure, and Mathematics Learning: A Test of Coleman's Social Capital Explanation of School Effects." *American Sociological Review* 64 (5): 661–681.

Mouw, Ted. 2003. "Social Capital and Finding a Job: Do Contacts Matter?" *American Sociological Review* 68 (6): 868–898.

Murray, Carolyn B. 1996. "Estimating Achievement Performance: A Confirmation Bias." *Journal of Black Psychology* 22 (1): 67–85.

Nakao, Keiko. 1992. "Occupations and Stratification: Issues of Measurement." *Contemporary Sociology* 21: 658–662.

Nakao, Keiko, and Judith Treas. 1994. "Updating Occupational Prestige and Socioeconomic Scores: How the New Measures Measure Up." *Sociological Methodology* 24: 1–72.

National Science Foundation, Division of Science Resources Statistics.

2007a. *S&E Degrees, by Race/Ethnicity of Recipients: 1995–2004*. Arlington, VA.

National Science Foundation, Division of Science Resources Statistics. 2007b. *Women, Minorities, and Persons with Disabilities in Science and Engineering: 2007*. Arlington, VA.

The Negro Problem. 1903. New York: Arno Press, 1969

Nelson, Viscount. 2003. *The Rise and Fall of Modern Black Leadership: Chronicle of a Twentieth Century Tragedy*. Lanham, MD: University Press of America.

Neuman, William Lawrence. 2006. *Social Research Methods: Qualitative and Quantitative Approaches*. 6th ed. Boston: Pearson/Allyn and Bacon.

Newman, Barbara M. 1999. "What Does It Take to Have a Positive Impact on Minority Students' College Retention?" *Adolescence* 34 (135): 483–492.

Newport, Frank. 2009. *Little "Obama Effect" on Views about Race Relations*. Gallup.

Ng, Sik Hung, and Michael W. Allen. 2005. "Perception of Economic Distributive Justice: Exploring Leading Theories." *Social Behavior and Personality* 33 (5): 435–454.

Nora, Amaury, Libby Barlow, and Gloria Crisp. 2006. "Examining the Tangible and Psychosocial Benefits of Financial Aid with Student Access, Engagement, and Degree Attainment." *American Behavioral Scientist* 49 (12): 1636–1651.

O'Brien, Laurie T., and Christian S. Crandall. 2003. "Stereotype Threat and Arousal: Effects on Women's Math Performance." *Personality and Social Psychology Bulletin* 29 (6): 782–789.

Office of Federal Contract Compliance, 2007. *Federal Contract Compliance Manual (FCCM)*: Washington, DC: Office of Federal Contract Compliance.

Ogbu, John. 1995. "Cultural Problems in Minority Education: Their Interpretations and Consequences—Part Two: Case Studies." *Urban Review* 27 (4): 271–297.

———. 1992. "Adaptation to Minority Status and Impact on School Success." *Theory into Practice* 31 (4): 287–295.

———. 1991. "Minority Coping Responses and School Experience." *Journal of Psychohistory* 18 (4): 433–456.

———. 1990. "Minority Education in Comparative Perspective." *Journal of Negro Education* 59 (1): 45–57.

———. 1987. "Variability in Minority School Performance: A Problem in

Search of an Explanation." *Anthropology and Education Quarterly* 18 (4): 312–334.

Ogbu, John, and Signithia Fordham. 1986. "Black Students' School Success: Coping with the Burden of 'Acting White.'" *Urban Review* 18 (3): 176–206.

Oliver, Melvin L., and Thomas M. Shapiro. 1997. *Black Wealth White Wealth: A New Perspective on Racial Inequality.* New York: Routledge.

Olsen, Marvin E. 1970. "Social and Political Participation of Blacks." *American Sociological Review* 35 (4): 682–697.

Omi, Michael, and Howard Winant. 1994. *Racial Formation in the United States: From the 1960s to the 1990s.* 2nd ed. New York: Routledge.

Orfield, Gary, and Chungmei Lee, 2007. *Historic Reversals, Accelerating Resegregation, and the Need for New Integration Strategies.* Los Angeles: Civil Rights Project, UCLA.

———. 2006. *Racial Transformation and the Changing Nature of Segregation.* Los Angeles: Civil Rights Project, UCLA.

———. 2005. *Why Segregation Matters: Poverty and Educational Inequality.* Cambridge, MA: Harvard Civil Rights Project.

Park, Julie J., and Nida Denson. 2009. "Attitudes and Advocacy: Understanding Faculty Views on Racial/Ethnic Diversity." *Journal of Higher Education* 80 (4): 415–438.

Pascarella, Ernest T., Marcia Edison, Amaury Nora, Linda Serra Hagedorn, and Patrick T. Terenzini. 1996. "Influences on Students' Openness to Diversity and Challenge in the First Year of College." *Journal of Higher Education* 67 (2): 174–195.

Pascarella, Ernest T., and Patrick T. Terenzini. 1991. *How College Affects Students: Findings and Insights from Twenty Years of Research.* San Francisco: Jossey-Bass.

Pattillo-McCoy, Mary. 2000. "The Limits of Out-Migration for the Black Middle Class." *Journal of Urban Affairs* 22 (3): 225–241.

———. 1999. *Black Picket Fences: Privilege and Peril among the Black Middle Class.* Chicago: University of Chicago Press.

Peng, S., and D. Wright. 1994. "Explanation of Academic Achievement of Asian American Students." *Journal of Educational Research* 87: 346–352.

Perlman, Merrill. 1989. "The Crimes and Punishments of Wedtech." *New York Times,* October 22.

Persell, Caroline Hodges, Sophia Castimbis, and Peter W. Cookson. 1992. "Differential Asset Conversion: Class and Gendered Pathways to Selective Colleges." *Sociology of Education* 65 (3): 208–225.

Petersen, Trond, Ishak Saporta, and Marc-David L. Seidel. 2000. "Offering a Job: Meritocracy and Social Networks." *American Journal of Sociology* 106 (3): 763–816.

Pettigrew, Thomas F., and Joanne Martin. 1987. "Black Employment Opportunities: Macro and Micro Perspectives." *Journal of Social Issues* 43 (1): 37–41.

Phillips, Kyra. 2001. "Congressional Black Caucus Objects to Florida's 25 Electors." *CNN*, January 6, 2001.

Pinel, Elizabeth C. 1999, "Personality Processes and Individual Differences—Stigma Consciousness: The Psychological Legacy of Social Stereotypes." *Journal of Personality and Social Psychology* 76 (1): 114–128.

Pitts, Byron. 2001. "The 'Re-Segregation of America': In Atlanta Suburbs, Blacks Choose to Live in Mostly Black Areas." *CBS Eye on America*, August 14, 2001.

Piven, Frances Fox, and Richard A. Cloward. 1979. *Poor People's Movements: Why They Succeed, How They Fail*. New York: Vintage books.

Porter, James N. 1976. "Socialization and Mobility in Educational and Early Occupational Attainment." *Sociology of Education* 49 (1): 23–33.

Postmes, Tom, and Nyla R. Branscombe. 2002. "Influence of Long-Term Racial Environmental Composition on Subjective Well-Being in African Americans." *Journal of Personality and Social Psychology* 83 (3): 735–751.

Powers, Michael. 2006. "U.S. DOT Is Cracking Down on DBE Contracting Fraud." *ENR: Engineering News-Record* 256, no. 18.

Putnam, Robert D. 1995. "Tuning in, Tuning Out: The Strange Disappearance of Social Capital in America." *Political Science and Politics* 28 (4): 664–683.

Qian, Zhenchao, and Daniel T. Lichter. 2007. "Social Boundaries and Marital Assimilation: Interpreting Trends in Racial and Ethnic Intermarriage." *American Sociological Review* 72 (1): 68–94.

Ragins, Belle Rose. 1997. "Diversified Mentoring Relationships in Organizations: A Power Perspective." *Academy of Management Review* 22 (2): 482–521.

Rankin, Susan R., and Robert D. Reason. 2005. "Differing Perceptions: How Students of Color and White Students Perceive Campus Climate for Underrepresented Groups." *Journal of College Student Development* 46 (1): 43–61.

Rayman, Paula, and Belle Brett. 1995. "Women Science Majors: What Makes a Difference in Persistence after Graduation?" *Journal of Higher Education* 66 (4): 388–414.

Reed, Deborah. 2005. *Educational Resources and Outcomes in California by Race and Ethnicity*. San Francisco: Public Policy Institute of California.

Robinson, Robert, and Wendell Bell. 1978. "Equality, Success, and Social Justice in England and the United States." *American Sociological Review* 43 (2): 125–143.

Roscigno, Vincent J., and James W. Ainsworth-Darnell. 1999. "Race, Cultural Capital, and Educational Resources: Persistent Inequalities and Achievement Returns." *Sociology of Education* 72 (3): 158–178.

Rosen, Bernard. 1959. "Race, Ethnicity and the Achievement Syndrome." *American Sociological Review* 24: 47–60.

Rosenbaum, Emily, and Samantha Friedman. 2003. "Generational Patterns of Neighborhood Conditions in New York City, 1999." Color Lines Conference, Harvard University, Cambridge, MA.

Rosenthal, Jonathan. 1989. "Reagan Hints Rights Leaders Exaggerate Racism to Preserve Cause." *New York Times,* January 14, 1989.

Roth, Louise Marie. 2004. "Bringing Clients Back in: Homophily Preferences and Inequality on Wall Street." *Sociological Quarterly* 45 (4): 613–635.

Rothstein, Jesse M., and Cecilia Elena Rouse, 2007. *Constrained after College: Student Loans and Early Career Occupational Choices.* Cambridge, MA: National Bureau of Economic Research.

Rowser, Jacqueline F. 1997. "Do African American Students' Perceptions of Their Needs Have Implications for Retention?" *Journal of Black Studies* 27 (5): 718–726.

Rubie-Davies, Christine M. 2006. "Teacher Expectations and Student Self-Perceptions: Exploring Relationships." *Psychology in the Schools* 43 (5): 537–552.

Rutledge, Dennis M. 1995. "Introduction: The Black Middle Class as Racial Class." *Research in Race and Ethnic Relations* 8: 1–17.

Saenz, Victor B., Hoi Ning Ngai, and Sylvia Hurtado. 2007. "Factors Influencing Positive Interactions across Race for African American, Asian American, Latino, and White College Students." *Research in Higher Education* 48 (1): 1–38.

Sanchez, Juan I., and Petra Brock. 1996. "Outcomes of Perceived Discrimination among Hispanic Employees: Is Diversity Management a Luxury or a Necessity." *Academy of Management Journal* 39 (3): 704–719.

Schaeffer, Peter. 2005. "Human Capital, Migration Strategy, and Brain Drain." *Journal of International Trade and Economic Development* 14 (3): 319–335.

Schlesinger, Arthur M. 1992. *The Disuniting of America: Reflections on a Multicultural Society.* 1st ed. New York: WW Norton and Co.

Schmader, Toni. 2002. "Gender Identification Moderates Stereotype Threat

Effects on Women's Math Performance." *Journal of Experimental Social Psychology* 38 (2): 194–201.

Schmader, Toni, and Michael Johns. 2003. "Converging Evidence That Stereotype Threat Reduces Working Memory Capacity." *Journal of Personality and Social Psychology* 85 (3): 440–452.

Schmader, Toni, Brenda Major, and Richard H. Gramzow. 2001. "Coping with Ethnic Stereotypes in the Academic Domain: Perceived Injustice and Psychological Disengagement." *Journal of Social Issues* 57 (1): 93–111.

Schneider, Barbara L., and David Stevenson. 1999. *The Ambitious Generation: America's Teenagers, Motivated but Directionless.* New Haven: Yale University Press.

Schoon, Ingrid. 2001. "Teenage Job Aspirations and Career Attainment in Adulthood: A 17-Year Follow-Up Study of Teenagers Who Aspired to Become Scientists, Health Professionals, or Engineers." *International Journal of Behavioral Development* 25 (2): 124–132.

Schumacker, Randall E., and Richard G. Lomax. 1996. *A Beginner's Guide to Structural Equation Modeling.* Mahwah, NJ: Lawrence Erlbaum Associates.

Seifert, Tricia A., Jerri Drummond, and Ernest T. Pascarella. 2006. "African-American Students' Experiences of Good Practices: A Comparison of Institutional Type." *Journal of College Student Development* 47 (2): 185–205.

Sellers, Robert M., and J. Nicole Shelton. 2003. "The Role of Racial Identity in Perceived Racial Discrimination." *Journal of Personality and Social Psychology* 84 (5): 1079–1092.

Shaw-Taylor, Yoku, and Steven A. Tuch. 2007. *The Other African Americans: Contemporary African and Caribbean Immigrants in the United States.* Lanham, MD: Rowman & Littlefield Publishers.

Shepelak, Norma J. 1989. "Ideological Stratification: American Beliefs about Economic Justice." *Social Justice Research* 3 (3): 217–231; 217.

———. 1987. "The Role of Self-Explanations and Self-Evaluations in Legitimating Inequality." *American Sociological Review* 52 (4): 495–503.

Sidanius, Jim, Colette Van Laar, Shana Levin, and Stacey Sinclair. 2004. "Ethnic Enclaves and the Dynamics of Social Identity on the College Campus: The Good, the Bad, and the Ugly." *Journal of Personality and Social Psychology* 87 (1): 96–110.

Sigelman, Lee, and Steven A. Tuch. 1997. "Metastereotypes: Blacks' Perceptions of Whites' Stereotypes of Blacks." *Public Opinion Quarterly* 61 (1): 87–101.

Singh, Gopal K., and Augustine J. Kposowa. 1996. "Occupation-Specific Earnings Attainment of Asian Indians and Whites in the United States: Gender and Nativity." *Applied Behavioral Science Review* 4 (2): 137–175.

Slaughter, Jerel E., Evan F. Sinar, and Peter D. Bachiochi. 2002. "Black Applicants' Reactions to Affirmative Action Plans: Effects of Plan Content and Previous Experience with Discrimination." *Journal of Applied Psychology* 87 (2): 333–344.

Smith, Jessi L., and Paul H. White. 2002. "An Examination of Implicitly Activated, Explicitly Activated, and Nullified Stereotypes on Mathematical Performance: It's Not just a Woman's Issue." *Sex Roles* 47 (3): 179–191.

Smith, Sandra S., and Mignon R. Moore. 2000. "Intraracial Diversity and Relations among African-Americans: Closeness among Black Students at a Predominantly White University." *American Journal of Sociology* 106 (1): 1–39.

Sniderman, Paul M., and Thomas Leonard Piazza. 2002. *Black Pride and Black Prejudice*. Princeton: Princeton University Press.

Snyder, Thomas D., and Charlene M. Hoffman, 1992. *Digest of Education Statistics*. Washington, DC: US Government Printing Office, Superintendent of Documents.

Solorzano, Daniel, Miguel Ceja, and Tara Yosso. 2000. "Critical Race Theory, Racial Microaggressions, and Campus Racial Climate: The Experiences of African American College Students." *Journal of Negro Education* 69 (1–2): 60–73.

South, Scott J., and Kyle D. Crowder. 1997. "Residential Mobility between Cities and Suburbs: Race, Suburbanization, and Back-to-the-City Moves." *Demography* 34 (4): 525–538.

Spaights, Ernest, and Ann Whitaker. 1995. "Black Women in the Workforce: A New Look at an Old Problem." *Journal of Black Studies* 25 (3): 23–296.

Spencer, Steven J., Claude M. Steele, and Diane M. Quinn. 1999. "Stereotype Threat and Women's Math Performance." *Journal of Experimental Social Psychology* 35 (1): 4–28.

St. John, Edward P., Sandra Andrieu, Jeffrey Oescher, and Johnny B. Starkey. 1994. "The Influence of Student Aid on within-Year Persistence by Traditional College-Age Students in Four-Year Colleges." *Research in Higher Education* 35 (4): 455–480.

St. John, Edward P., and Shouping Hu. 2001. "The Impact of Aid Packages on Educational Choices: High Tuition-High Loan and Educational Opportunity." *Journal of Student Financial Aid* 31 (2): 35–54.

Stainback, Kevin, Corre L. Robinson, and Donald Tomaskovic-Devey.

2005. "Race and Workplace Integration: A Politically Mediated Process?" *American Behavioral Scientist* 48 (9): 1200–1228.

Stanford University. 2009. "Undergraduate Housing Draw Statistics."

———. 2002/3. *Common Data Set: 2002–2003*. Vol. 2003. Stanford University.

Stangor, Charles, and Gretchen Sechrist. 1998. "Conceptualizing the Determinants of Academic Choice and Task Performance across Social Groups." In *Prejudice: The Target's Perspective,* edited by Janet K. Swim and Charles Stangor, 105–124. San Diego: Academic Press.

Stark, Joan S., and Lisa R. Lattuca. 1997. *Shaping the College Curriculum: Academic Plans in Action*. Boston: Allyn and Bacon.

Steele, Claude M. 1997. "A Threat in the Air: How Stereotypes Shape Intellectual Identity and Performance." *American Psychologist* 52 (6): 613–629.

Steele, Claude M., and Joshua Aronson. 1995. "Stereotype Threat and the Intellectual Test Performance of African Americans." *Journal of Personality and Social Psychology* 69 (5): 797–811.

Steele, Claude M., Steven J. Spencer, and Joshua Aronson. 2002. "Contending with Group Image: The Psychology of Stereotype and Social Identity Threat." In *Advances in Experimental Social Psychology,* vol. 34, edited by Mark P. Zanna, 379–440. San Diego: Academic Press.

Steck, Laura West, Druann Maria Heckert, and D. Alex Heckert. 2003. "The Salience of Racial Identity among African-American and White Students." *Race and Society* 6 (1): 57–73.

Strayhorn, Terrell. 2009. "Gender Differences in the Influence of Faculty-Student Mentoring Relationships on Satisfaction with College among African Americans." *Journal of African American Studies* 13 (4): 476–493.

Strouse, Jean. 2000. "How to Give Away $21.8 Billion." *New York Times,* April 16, 2000.

Sweet, Martin J. 2006. "Minority Business Enterprise Programmes in the United States of America: An Empirical Investigation." *Journal of Law and Society* 33 (1): 160–180.

Tang, Mei, Nadya Fouad, and Phillip Smith. 1999. "Asian Americans' Career Choices: A Path Model to Examine Factors Influencing Their Career Choices." *Journal of Vocational Behavior* 54 (1): 142–157.

Tatum, Beverly Daniel. 1997. "Why Are All the Black Kids Sitting Together in the Cafeteria?": And Other Conversations about Race. New York: Basic Books.

Thernstrom, Stephan, and Abigail Thernstrom. 1997. *America in Black and White: One Nation Indivisible*. New York: Simon and Schuster.

Thomas, David A., and John J. Gabarro. 1999. *Breaking Through: The Making of Minority Executives in Corporate America*. Boston: Harvard Business School Press.

Thomas, Kecia M. 2000. *Diversity Dynamics in the Workplace*. San Francisco: Wadsworth Publishing.

Tidball, M. Elizabeth. 1986. "Baccalaureate Origins of Recent Natural Science Doctorates." *Journal of Higher Education* 57: 606–620.

Toliver, Susan Diane. 1998. *Black Families in Corporate America*. Thousand Oaks, CA: Sage Publications.

Tomaskovic-Devey, Donald. 1993. "The Gender and Race Composition of Jobs and the Male/Female, White/Black Pay Gaps." *Social Forces* 72 (1): 45–76.

Torres, Kimberly C., and Camille Z. Charles. 2004. "Metastereotypes and the Black-White Divide: A Qualitative View of Race on an Elite College Campus." *Du Bois Review* 1 (1): 115–149.

Trouilloud, David O., Philippe G. Sarrazin, Thomas J. Martinek, and Emma Guillet. 2002. "The Influence of Teacher Expectations on Student Achievement in Physical Education Classes: Pygmalion Revisited." *European Journal of Social Psychology* 32 (5): 591–607.

US Bureau of Labor Statistics. 2008. *Occupational Employment and Wages, May 2006*. Washington, DC: Government Printing Office.

US Census Bureau. 1983–. *Statistical Abstract of the United States*. Washington, DC.

———. 2008. "Current Population Survey Historical Tables." http://www.census.gov/population/www/socdemo/educ-attn.html.

———. "Table F-3. Mean Income Received by each Fifth and Top 5 Percent of White Families: 1966 to 2006." http://www.census.gov/hhes/www/income/data/historical/families/index.html.

———. 2001. *Money Income in the United States*. Washington, DC.

———. "Census 2000 EEO Data Tool." http://www.census.gov/eeo2000/index.html.

———. 1973. *1970 Census of Population: Earnings by Occupation and Education*. Washington, DC.

US Commission on Civil Rights. 2005. *Federal Procurement after Adarand*. Washington, DC.

———. 1995. *Funding Federal Civil Rights Enforcement: A Report of the United States Commission of Civil Rights*.

US Government Accountability Office. 2005. *Higher Education: Federal Science, Technology, Engineering and Mathematical Programs and Related Trends*. Washington, DC.

University of California Office of the President. 2007. *Student/Workforce Data.*

University of Texas at Austin. 2007. Implementation and Results of the Texas Automatic Admissions Law at the University of Texas at Austin.

Useem, Elizabeth L. 1992. "Middle Schools and Math Groups: Parents' Involvement in Children's Placement." *Sociology of Education* 65 (4): 263–279.

Wadhwa, Vivek, Guillermina Jasso, Ben Rissing, Gary Gereffi, and Richard B. Freeman. 2007. *Intellectual Property, the Immigration Backlog, and a Reverse Brain-Drain: America's New Immigrant Entrepreneurs,* Part III. Available at Social Science Research Network.

Wallace, Mike. 2002. "Going Home to the South: The Migration Back to the South." *60 Minutes,* October 27, 2002.

Walsh, Edward, and Juliet Eilperin. 2001. "Gore Presides as Congress Tallies Votes Electing Bush." *Washington Post,* Sunday, January 7, 2001.

Wand, Jonathan N., Kenneth W. Shotts, Jasjeet S. Sekhon, Walter R. Mebane Jr., Michael C. Herron, and Henry E. Brady. 2001. "The Butterfly Did It: The Aberrant Vote for Buchanan in Palm Beach County, Florida." *American Political Science Review* 95 (4): 793–810.

Waters, Mary C. 1999. *Black Identities: West Indian Immigrant Dreams and American Realities.* Cambridge, MA: Harvard University Press.

———. 1990. *Ethnic Options: Choosing Identities in America.* Berkeley: University of California Press.

Weinstein, Rhona S. 2002. *Reaching Higher: The Power of Expectations in Schooling.* Cambridge, MA: Harvard University Press.

———. 1993. "Children's Knowledge of Differential Treatment in Schooling: Implications for Motivation." In *Motivating Students to Learn: Overcoming Barriers to High Achievement.,* edited by Tommy M. Tomlinson. Berkeley, CA: McCutchan.

Werts, Charles E. 1968. "A Comparison of Male vs Female College Attendance Probabilities." *Sociology of Education* 41 (1): 103–110.

Western, Bruce, and Becky Pettit. 2010. "Incarceration and Social Inequality." *Daedalus* Summer: 1–19.

Wheeler, S. Christian, and Richard E. Petty. 2001. "The Effects of Stereotype Activation on Behavior: A Review of Possible Mechanisms." *Psychological Bulletin* 127 (6): 797–826.

Wiley, Ed III. 1989. "Mentor Programs Successful in Minority Retention." *Black Issues in Higher Education* 5 (22): 8.

Wilie, Charles. 1989. *Caste and Class Controversy on Race and Poverty.* Dix Hills, NY: General Hall.

Willie, Sarah Susannah. 2003. *Acting Black: College, Identity, and the Performance of Race.* New York: Routledge.

Wilson, George. 2007. "Racialized Life-Chance Opportunities across the Class Structure: The Case of African Americans." *Annals of the American Academy of Political and Social Science* 609: 215–232.

Wilson, Karen R., and Walter R. Allen. 1987. "Explaining the Educational Attainment of Young Black Adults: Critical Familial and Extra-Familial Influences." *Journal of Negro Education* 56 (1): 64–76.

Wilson, William J. 1996. *When Work Disappears: The World of the New Urban Poor.* New York: Knopf.

———. 1987. *The Truly Disadvantaged: The Inner City, the Underclass, and Public Policy.* Chicago: University of Chicago Press.

———. 1978. *The Declining Significance of Race: Blacks and Changing American Institutions.* Chicago: University of Chicago Press.

Witkin, Gordon. 1995. "Trying to Beat the System." *U.S. News & World Report*, February 13, 1995, 42.

Woldemikael, Tekle. 1989. "A Case Study of Race Consciousness among Haitian Immigrants." *Journal of Black Studies* 20 (2): 224–239.

Wu, Dane W. 2002. "Regression Analyses on the Butterfly Ballot Effect: A Statistical Perspective of the US 2000 Election." *International Journal of Mathematical Education in Science and Technology* 33 (2): 309–317.

Xu, Wu, and Ann Leffler. 1992. "Gender and Race Effects on Occupational Prestige, Segregation, and Earnings." *Gender and Society* 6 (2): 376–392.

Zweig, David. 2006. "Competing for Talent: China's Strategies to Reverse the Brain Drain." *International Labour Review* 145 (1–2): 65–89.

INDEX

Page numbers in italics refer to illustrations.